MARCUS AURELIUS

In this new study, John Sellars offers a fresh examination of Marcus Aurelius' *Meditations* as a work of philosophy by placing it against the background of the tradition of Stoic philosophy to which Marcus was committed.

The *Meditations* of Marcus Aurelius is a perennial bestseller, attracting countless readers drawn to its unique mix of philosophical reflection and practical advice. The emperor is usually placed alongside Seneca and Epictetus as one of three great Roman Stoic authors, but he wears his philosophy lightly, not feeling the need to state explicitly the ideas standing behind the reflections that he was writing for himself. As a consequence, his standing as a philosopher has often been questioned. Challenging claims that Marcus Aurelius was merely an eclectic thinker, that the *Meditations* do not fit the model of a work of philosophy, that there are no arguments in the work, and that it only contains superficial moral advice, Sellars shows that he was in constant dialogue with his Stoic predecessors, engaging with themes drawn from all three parts of Stoicism: logic, physics, and ethics. The image of Marcus Aurelius that emerges is of a committed Stoic, engaging with a wide range of philosophical topics, motivated by the desire to live a good life.

This volume will be of interest to scholars and students of both Classics and Philosophy.

John Sellars is Lecturer in Philosophy at Royal Holloway, University of London, a Visiting Research Fellow at King's College London, and a member of Wolfson College, Oxford. His previous books include *The Art of Living*, *Stoicism*, *Hellenistic Philosophy*, and *Lessons in Stoicism*. He is also the editor of *The Routledge Handbook of the Stoic Tradition*.

PHILOSOPHY IN THE ROMAN WORLD

Cicero
The Philosophy of a Roman Sceptic
Raphael Woolf

Marcus Aurelius
John Sellars

https://www.routledge.com/Philosophy-in-the-Roman-World/book-series/PHILROM

MARCUS AURELIUS

John Sellars

Routledge
Taylor & Francis Group
LONDON AND NEW YORK

First published 2021
by Routledge
2 Park Square, Milton Park, Abingdon, Oxon OX14 4RN

and by Routledge
52 Vanderbilt Avenue, New York, NY 10017

Routledge is an imprint of the Taylor & Francis Group, an informa business

© 2021 John Sellars

The right of John Sellars to be identified as author of this work has been asserted by him in accordance with sections 77 and 78 of the Copyright, Designs and Patents Act 1988.

All rights reserved. No part of this book may be reprinted or reproduced or utilised in any form or by any electronic, mechanical, or other means, now known or hereafter invented, including photocopying and recording, or in any information storage or retrieval system, without permission in writing from the publishers.

Trademark notice: Product or corporate names may be trademarks or registered trademarks, and are used only for identification and explanation without intent to infringe.

British Library Cataloguing-in-Publication Data
A catalogue record for this book is available from the British Library

Library of Congress Cataloging-in-Publication Data
Names: Sellars, John, 1971– author.
Title: Marcus Aurelius / John Sellars.
Identifiers: LCCN 2020006226 (print) | LCCN 2020006227 (ebook)
Subjects: LCSH: Marcus Aurelius, Emperor of Rome, 121–180. Meditations.
Classification: LCC B583.S455 2020 (print) |
LCC B583 (ebook) | DDC 188–dc23
LC record available at https://lccn.loc.gov/2020006226
LC ebook record available at https://lccn.loc.gov/2020006227

ISBN: 978-0-367-14606-1 (hbk)
ISBN: 978-0-367-14607-8 (pbk)
ISBN: 978-0-429-05265-1 (ebk)

Typeset in Bembo
by Newgen Publishing UK

CONTENTS

Preface   *vii*
References and abbreviations   *ix*

Introduction   1

PART I
Marcus and his *Meditations*   5

1   Marcus the Stoic philosopher   7

2   The *Meditations*, a philosophical text   20

PART II
Logic   37

3   Impressions and judgements   39

PART III
Physics   55

4   Nature and change   57

5   Fate and providence   68

| 6 | Soul and emotion | 81 |
| 7 | Time and death | 90 |

PART IV
Ethics — 105

| 8 | Virtue and justice | 107 |
| 9 | The cosmic city | 117 |

Conclusion — 127

Appendix — *128*
Bibliography — *130*
Index of passages — *138*
Subject index — *145*

PREFACE

This book is a study of the philosophy of Marcus Aurelius, as presented in his work widely known as the *Meditations*. Its aim is to present Marcus as a serious philosopher. It tries to do this in a number of ways. First, it tries to show that Marcus was a committed Stoic philosopher and not, as some have suggested, a confused eclectic thinker. Second, it reflects on how Marcus understood what it meant to do philosophy, rather than anachronistically judging him by present-day standards. Third, it examines the unique literary form of the *Meditations* and asks what sort of philosophical text this might be. Fourth – and most important of all – it examines the philosophical content in the *Meditations*, placing it within the wider context of previous Stoic philosophy. As we shall see, Marcus is engaged with a wide range of material spanning the three traditional parts of Stoic philosophy – logic, physics, and ethics – and bringing this out will hopefully also challenge the claim that Marcus was merely interested in what is sometimes called "practical ethics".

I was first invited to write this book some years ago by Steven Gerrard, founder and editor of Acumen Publishing. I was happy to accept the commission but at the time found myself unsure about how best to proceed. As a consequence, other projects jumped the queue. Marcus was not forgotten, however, and a series of smaller commissions gave me a number of opportunities to write about him in the interim. For these opportunities I should thank Diskin Clay, Marcel van Ackeren, Will Shearin, Christopher Moore, and Matthew Dennis. The acquisition of Acumen by Routledge reinvigorated the project, but the final impetus to completing it came in 2018–19 when I had the opportunity to teach Marcus's *Meditations* at Royal Holloway, University of London, as part of a course entitled "The Good Life in Ancient Philosophy". I thank all the students who participated in that course and embraced Marcus as a philosopher who had valuable things to say. I should also particularly like to acknowledge Christopher Gill, my PhD examiner many years ago and more recently collaborator on a number of projects. I have learned much about Marcus from Chris over the years, both in conversation and through his publications.

Chapter 2 draws on material published in Sellars (2012a, 2018b), and a chapter due to be published in *The Oxford Handbook of Roman Philosophy* (a version of the latter appeared in German in 2016, in a volume entitled *Philosophie als Lebenskunst*). Part of Chapter 3 was read to seminars in Paris and London in 2017 and 2018, and an earlier draft of Chapter 8 was presented at the Gesellschaft für antike Philosophie conference in Frankfurt in September 2019; I thank all these audiences for their helpful comments. Robin Waterfield read more or less the final version, catching some minor errors and making some helpful suggestions, for which I am very grateful.

REFERENCES AND ABBREVIATIONS

I have consulted a variety of editions of the *Meditations*. The most recent complete critical edition is Dalfen (1987). I have often used Farquharson (1944), which includes a translation and the only substantial modern commentary on the entire text. I have also had to hand Haines (1916), which offers a convenient portable parallel Greek–English text, even if the translation is now somewhat dated.

I refer to the *Meditations* by book and section number. All otherwise unattributed references are to the *Meditations*. Some of the longer sections have been subdivided by editors and the three editions noted above all do this in slightly different ways. Because of this, I generally avoid citing those further subdivisions, although where on occasion it seemed helpful I have followed the system used by Dalfen, which is the most finely grained, putting these in square brackets.

I have read and re-read the *Meditations* in multiple translations over the years, including Staniforth (1964), Hammond (2006), and Hard (2011), as well as those by Farquharson and Haines in the editions mentioned above. In general, I quote from Farquharson's translation, often modifying it, but occasionally from the others too. In a few instances I have translated a passage afresh myself. I have not attempted to keep track of all this, which would have generated a cumbersome and not especially interesting apparatus.

Other ancient authors and texts are cited by fairly standard abbreviations, often those used in the *Oxford Classical Dictionary* (for Galen, see the list in Singer 2013: 429–42); further information is given in the Index of passages. Note also the following abbreviations:

DK H. Diels and W. Kranz, *Die Fragmente der Vorsokratiker*, 3 vols (Berlin: Weidmann, 1964)

DPhA *Dictionnaire des Philosophes Antique*, ed. R. Goulet, 7 vols and suppl. (Paris: CNRS, 1989–2018)

EK L. Edelstein and I. G. Kidd, *Posidonius I: The Fragments* (Cambridge: Cambridge University Press, 1972)

Kühn C. G. Kühn, *Claudii Galeni Opera Omnia*, 20 vols in 22 (Leipzig: Knobloch, 1821–33)

LCL	Loeb Classical Library
LM	A. Laks and G. W. Most, *Early Greek Philosophy*, 9 vols, LCL (Cambridge, MA: Harvard University Press, 2016)
LS	A. A. Long and D. N. Sedley, *The Hellenistic Philosophers*, 2 vols (Cambridge: Cambridge University Press, 1987)
LSJ	H. G. Liddell, and R. Scott, *A Greek-English Lexicon*, rev. H. S. Jones (Oxford: Clarendon Press, 1940)
SVF	*Stoicorum Veterum Fragmenta*, ed. H. von Arnim, 4 vols (Leipzig: Teubner, 1903–24)

INTRODUCTION

Marcus Aurelius is primarily remembered for two things: he was Roman Emperor and he wrote a work of philosophy, the *Meditations*. His role as Emperor is uncontroversial and a matter of historical record.[1] He took up the role in AD 161, at the age of forty, and stayed in it until his death in 180. His status as a philosopher, however, is far more complex and contested. Although he has consistently attracted a large number of general readers who unproblematically regard him as a philosopher, professional philosophers have by and large ignored him. Whatever it was that Marcus was doing when writing the *Meditations*, it was certainly not what professional philosophers do today. Even among specialists in ancient philosophy, few would be prepared to rank the *Meditations* alongside the dialogues of Plato or the treatises of Aristotle. Indeed, some have denied that Marcus was a philosopher at all. Although he is widely presented as a Stoic philosopher, a number of influential sceptical voices have either dismissed him as an unsophisticated eclectic or charged him with reducing Stoic philosophy to an unthinking religious faith.[2]

He was not always judged so harshly by philosophers. In the nineteenth century John Stuart Mill described Marcus as "the best and most enlightened among his contemporaries" and the *Meditations* as "the highest ethical product of the ancient mind".[3] In the century before, the Scottish Enlightenment philosopher Francis Hutcheson translated the *Meditations* in collaboration with James Moor, writing in their introduction that Marcus's book presents "a great soul, adorned with the soundest understanding, the most amiable sweetness and kindness of affection, the most invincible meekness, steady justice, humility, and simplicity".[4] Earlier in the same century the moral philosopher Anthony Ashley Cooper, the Third Earl of Shaftesbury, drew extensively from the *Meditations* in his own notebook reflections,[5] while in the seventeenth century the Cambridge Platonist Henry More made great use of the *Meditations* in his own handbook of ethics, praising the clarity and quality of his ethical guidance.[6]

Indeed, many people have found Marcus's ethical guidance compelling and the *Meditations* continues to attract new readers drawn to his thoughtful reflections on how to live. In previous generations Marcus was often presented as a kind pagan saint, either closely aligned with Christian teaching or offering a "gospel" for those "who have no faith in the supernatural".[7] These days he is more often presented as a writer of psychological therapy, offering practical tips on how to cope with the stresses and strains of daily life.[8] There is certainly much in the *Meditations* that people can and have found useful when reflecting on their own lives.

The aim of this book is to approach the *Meditations* as a work of philosophy and to defend Marcus's standing as a philosopher. It will try to do this in a number of different ways. The opening chapter argues that Marcus was a committed Stoic philosopher, well versed in the literature of the Stoic tradition, and not, as some have suggested, a confused eclectic thinker. It will do this by considering the biographical evidence for his interest in philosophy and his own education in philosophy under a series of Stoic teachers, including Apollonius of Chalcedon, Sextus of Chaeronea, and Junius Rusticus. It also considers his relationship with Cornelius Fronto and the evidence in Marcus's correspondence with Fronto that sheds light on Marcus's interest in philosophy. It then examines Marcus's debts to previous Stoic philosophers, including Chrysippus, Aristo, Cleanthes, Seneca, and Epictetus. It also considers Galen, whom Marcus knew personally. Although their interactions may have been minimal, Galen's own therapeutic works add valuable context to the *Meditations*. The chapter concludes by asking what it meant to be a Stoic in the second century AD.

The second chapter examines the unique literary form of the *Meditations*, asking what sort of philosophical text this might be and how Marcus understood what it meant to do philosophy. It presents the *Meditations* as a private notebook, never intended for publication, in which Marcus engaged in a series of written exercises aimed at self-examination. In particular, these exercises were aimed at assimilating and digesting key philosophical principles. Central to this process was the practice of paying close attention to principles at all times. This activity is then placed within the wider context of the Stoic conception of philosophy as an art of living, understood in analogy with medicine as involving two distinct stages: first, a grasp of theoretical principles, followed by training aimed at digesting those principles. It is argued that the *Meditations* ought to be read as text focused on the second stage of such an education. In this context, the notion of a spiritual exercise is introduced and its use by Musonius Rufus and Seneca is examined; then some specific spiritual exercises in the *Meditations* are discussed.

The subsequent chapters turn to the philosophical content in the *Meditations*. For the sake of presentation, I have divided themes under the traditional Stoic headings of logic, physics, and ethics. As we shall see, many themes central in the *Meditations* cut across these divisions, involving more than one part of philosophy at once. Yet this division is, I hope, helpful in that it helps to show that it would be a mistake to approach the *Meditations* as merely a work of practical ethical advice. It has often been claimed that Marcus was not interested in logic or physics, but instead with "shaping the life of the individual".[9] That seems like a false dichotomy, and the claim of this book will be that Marcus's concern with self-transformation presupposes Stoic logic and physics as much as it does ethics. Although there is of course much practical advice in the work, it is built upon foundations found in all three traditional parts of Stoic philosophy.

With that claim in mind, Chapter 3 considers the presence of logical themes in the *Meditations*. It begins by outlining the way in which logic was understood in antiquity, in particular the Stoic account of logic, encompassing rhetoric and dialectic. Within the context of this broad conception of logic, the chapter examines the notions of impressions and judgements as they appear in the *Meditations*. It looks at the way in which Marcus sees some impressions as reliable and some as deceptive and compares this with the earlier Chrysippean account. The role of judgements in the *Meditations* is placed against the background of early

Stoic epistemology and the ways in which Roman Stoics such as Epictetus and Marcus shift attention to value judgements. The chapter concludes by showing the close connection between the notions of impressions and judgements.

Chapters 4–7 examine a range of themes in Stoic physics. This is the largest part of the book, reflecting the fact that physical themes are by far the most common in the *Meditations*. Chapter 4 begins by considering the place of reflections on physics and Nature in Marcus's thought, along with central themes such as the unity of Nature and the presence of two basic causal and material principles. These themes are then discussed in the light of early Stoic physics. It then moves on to consider Marcus's reflections on perpetual change, relating this to Heraclitus's doctrine of flux. The question of Heraclitus's influence on Marcus is discussed. Finally, it asks why Marcus might have thought it useful to reflect on change in Nature, and how such reflections fit within his wider philosophical project.

Next, Chapter 5 examines the concepts of fate and providence as they appear in the *Meditations*, placing both concepts against the background of early Stoic accounts of both, and discussing their relationship. After looking at how Marcus uses these two concepts, the chapter considers those passages where Marcus draws the contrast "providence or atoms" and appears not to commit to either view. It argues that this ought not to be taken as deviation from a Stoic commitment to providence. The chapter concludes by summarizing the variety of ways in which Marcus characterizes the cosmos in these passages and identifies his own view from among the options.

In Chapter 6, a range of issues broadly connected to the theme of the self are discussed. Central to Marcus's thinking on this topic is the concept of *hêgemonikon*. This is considered within the wider context of Stoic psychology, as the ruling part of the Stoic soul. It argues that Marcus adopted the Stoic psychological model, notwithstanding a few passages that appear to express heterodox views. It also examines Marcus's thoughts about emotions, which take place in the ruling part of the soul, along with the idea that the ruling part ought to be treated as an inner citadel. It concludes by considering a way in which Marcus might be seen to expand the traditional Stoic scale of nature.

One of the central themes in the *Meditations* is reflection on the shortness of human life. Chapter 7 examines this theme via an analysis of Marcus's reflections about time and about death. It has been argued that Marcus developed a distinctive theory of time in response to early Stoic ideas, drawing a distinction between time and eternity. This chapter argues against that interpretation, suggesting that Marcus's principal aim was simply to highlight the brevity of human life. Marcus's reflections on death are also examined, and an echo of Epicurus's famous argument concerning death is noted. It asks why Marcus was so concerned with death as a topic and considers how it relates to his equally common reflections about living in the present moment.

The final two chapters turn to ethical and political themes. Chapter 8 considers ethical themes in the *Meditations* against the wider context of early Stoic ethics. It examines his references to living consistently with Nature against the backdrop of early Stoic debates about the *telos* formula. It also considers Marcus's many references to the traditional virtues, again against the backdrop of the early Stoic focus on four cardinal virtues of wisdom, moderation, courage, and justice. Among all the virtues he mentions, Marcus reflects on justice more than any other. Potential Platonic influences are considered, but discounted, and his concern with justice is connected back to his commitment to the Stoic *telos* of living consistently with Nature. Finally, it considers passages that advocate spontaneous ethical action.

The last chapter looks at broadly political themes in the *Meditations*. It begins by placing these against the background of the Stoic theory of *oikeiôsis*, as expressed by the Roman Stoic Hierocles, and early Stoic cosmopolitanism. These set the scene for an examination of Marcus's comments presenting Nature as a cosmic city. Connected to this are his claims that individuals ought to put the concerns of this city ahead of narrowly conceived individualistic needs. This leads to reflection about different part–whole relationships and the claim that individuals ought to see themselves as organic parts or limbs of an integrated whole.

As in the *Meditations* itself, there is a certain amount of repetition in what follows, with some key passages discussed more than once. Marcus has a particular skill in compressing almost all the key themes running through his thought into a single brief paragraph and he does this on many occasions. There are consequently a handful of passages that will appear in multiple chapters below, each time discussed from a different angle. The compressed way in which Marcus writes his thoughts to himself makes this almost inevitable, and certainly difficult to avoid. Yet, as we shall also see, the repetition in the *Meditations* – and perhaps also here too – serves a deliberate purpose in helping readers to digest the key ideas through repeated exposure.

Notes

1 For modern biographies, see Birley (2000) and McLynn (2009).
2 See, for example, Rist (1982: 43) (an "unphilosophical religion") and Cooper (2004: 368) ("a sort of religious faith"). In Cooper (2012: 217), Marcus is presented as engaged in a rhetorical practice aimed at resignation and avoidance of emotion, based on imagination rather than reason. In this sense, according to Cooper, Marcus does not rationally comprehend Stoic first principles and so fails to live Stoicism as a philosophical way of life. For a survey of the some of the most common objections see Gill (2012: 382–3).
3 These come from Mill's *On Liberty*, in Mill (1859: 48–9).
4 See the introduction in Hutcheson and Moor ([1742] 2008: 4). (I have slightly updated their text here.) For the wider context see Maurer (2016).
5 See the recent critical edition of his notebooks in Ashley Cooper (2011). His interest in Marcus Aurelius is discussed in Sellars (2016) and Collis (2016).
6 See More's *Enchiridion Ethicum*, first printed in 1668, for example, 2.8.16, translated in More (1690: 143). See further Sellars (2017: 923).
7 On Marcus's sanctification see Richlin (2012). The quotation comes from Renan (1904: 134), who is discussed in Sellars (2012b).
8 For an early presentation of Marcus in these terms, see Rutherford (1989: 13). For a more recent account, focused on extracting useful therapeutic material from the *Meditations*, see Robertson (2019).
9 This comment, just one representative example among many, is from Edelstein (1966: 46).

PART I
Marcus and his *Meditations*

1

MARCUS THE STOIC PHILOSOPHER

Marcus the philosopher

One popular and quite common image of Marcus Aurelius is as a wise old man writing his *Meditations* late in life while on campaign.[1] At the end of Book 1 (or the beginning of Book 2) of the *Meditations* there is a note that reads "Written among the Quadi on the river Gran", a tributary of the Danube.[2] At the end of Book 2 (or the beginning of Book 3) there is a similar note that says "Written in Carnuntum", which was close to the border between Germany and the Roman Empire.[3] These notes seem to confirm this image, for Marcus was on campaign in this area during the 170s, the last decade of his life. Marcus was born in 121, so he was probably in his 50s when writing the *Meditations*. A less flattering image would present him not as an accomplished sage but instead a world-weary man in late middle age, half-remembering a few scraps of philosophy he had studied as an adolescent.[4]

Marcus did indeed study philosophy in his youth. The biography of Marcus in the *Historia Augusta* opens with the statement that Marcus was "devoted to philosophy as long as he lived" (*HA* 4.1.1).[5] It goes on to say that Marcus's education in philosophy began at an early age (*HA* 4.2.1). He was, we are told, committed to philosophy as a youth and "when he was twelve years old he adopted the dress and, a little later, the hardiness of a philosopher, pursuing his studies clad in a rough Greek cloak and sleeping on the ground" (*HA* 4.2.6). We have a list of his philosophy teachers, to whom we shall turn shortly, but it is worth noting that all this predated his adoption into the Imperial family. Although Marcus was born into the upper echelons of Roman society, he was by no means destined to become Emperor. It is difficult to know to what extent, if any, he may have anticipated his later role during his early years. Marcus's natural father was an important person – prefect of the city of Rome – and the family were intimates of the then Emperor Hadrian. Hadrian had a reputation as an intellectual, interested in Greek culture, and a passing interest in philosophy. We are told that he was an admirer of Epictetus (*HA* 1.16.10), and there survives a generic question-and-answer dialogue between Hadrian and Epictetus.[6] Hadrian was childless and, after looking around for a potential heir, decided to adopt Antoninus Pius as his successor. Antoninus, Marcus's uncle, was himself without heir, so at the same time Hadrian arranged that Antoninus should adopt two sons himself as potential successors, Commodus and Marcus. The historian Dio Cassius reports that Hadrian chose Marcus "because he was already giving indication of exceptional strength of character" (Dio Cassius 69.21.2). In short, Marcus's interest in philosophy began during his childhood, predated his elevation into the Imperial family, and may have even contributed to him being chosen for the role.

Marcus's philosophy teachers

Marcus was taught philosophy by Apollonius of Chalcedon, the Stoic (*HA* 4.2.7), and the *Historia Augusta* makes a point of saying that he continued to seek instruction from Apollonius even after joining the Imperial family (*HA* 4.3.1–2), which might be taken to imply that Apollonius was one of his childhood instructors in philosophy.[7] Marcus acknowledges Apollonius in Book 1 of the *Meditations*, writing that from him he learned what we would now think of as archetypal Stoic lessons: to remain firm in the face of fortune and "to look to nothing else, even for a little while, except to reason" (1.8). Elsewhere, in a letter to Fronto, Marcus called Apollonius "my master in philosophy" (*Ad M. Caes.* 51).[8]

As well as studying with Apollonius, the *Historia Augusta* tells us that Marcus "attended the lectures of Sextus of Chaeronea, the nephew of Plutarch, and of Junius Rusticus, Claudius Maximus, and Cinna Catulus, all Stoics" (*HA* 4.3.2). He also attended the lectures of Claudius Severus, a Peripatetic (*HA* 4.3.3). Of all these teachers, the *Historia Augusta* reports that Junius Rusticus was the most important influence on Marcus, a man "exceedingly well acquainted with the Stoic system" (*HA* 4.3.4).[9] Marcus himself acknowledges his debt to Rusticus in Book 1 of the *Meditations*, noting that it was from him that he learned the need "for reform and treatment of character" (1.7),[10] as well as an attitude of suspicion towards rhetoric and towards speculative writing or the production of commentaries on texts. At the same time, Marcus tells us that Rusticus encouraged him to read books carefully and deeply, and that he lent Marcus his own copy of the *Discourses* of Epictetus.

Marcus also acknowledges his teacher Sextus of Chaeronea in the *Meditations*, from whom he says he learned what we would now think of as core Stoic doctrines: "the notion of life according to Nature" and "to be at once entirely passionless and yet full of natural affection" (1.9). The *Historia Augusta* describes Sextus as a Stoic while also noting his more famous uncle, Plutarch, who of course wrote a number of extended polemics against the Stoics (*HA* 4.3.2).[11] Dio Cassius reports that Marcus took on Sextus as a teacher *after* he had become Emperor, as evidence for his lifelong commitment to philosophy (Dio Cassius 71.1.2). By that point, it is likely that Marcus was already committed to the philosophy of the Stoa. Philostratus, in his *Lives of the Sophists*, reports an anecdote from one Lucius, who visited Marcus in Rome when he was Emperor. When Lucius found Marcus going out one day, he asked where the Emperor was going, to which Marcus is reported to have replied, "It is a good thing even for one who is growing old to acquire knowledge. I am going to Sextus the philosopher to learn what I do not yet know" (*VS* 2.11.1). The impression we begin to get, then, is of someone with a lifelong interest in philosophy, stretching from early childhood to old age. The other noteworthy feature of this anecdote is that, as Emperor, Marcus did not summon Sextus to visit him, but made the trip to visit Sextus himself. This tells us something about both Marcus's character and the nature of his relationship with his teacher.

The remaining teachers mentioned in the *Historia Augusta* are also all acknowledged in Book 1 of the *Meditations*. Claudius Maximus, another Stoic, held a number of important governmental posts, including consul sometime around 142. Marcus's description of him lists a whole series of positive character traits that feature throughout the *Meditations* – self-mastery, coping with adversity, dignity, generosity, and so on (1.15) – that suggest that he was an important influence on Marcus's own outlook on life. Indeed, at 1.17 he mentions Maximus alongside Apollonius and Rusticus as a formative influence. We do not know that much about Maximus but, if the identification is correct, he appears in the *Apology* of the Platonist Apuleius. This text, written as a defence speech in response to charges of using magic, is addressed to one Claudius Maximus who, as proconsul of Africa, presided over the court proceedings.[12] Here he is presented as a Stoic (*Apol.* 19) who had read widely in the works of ancient philosophers (*Apol.* 38). Although, in a text like this, it should come as no surprise to see Apuleius praise Maximus, he describes him as a most honourable (*sanctissimus*) man (*Apol.* 85).

Cinna Catulus is mentioned only briefly by Marcus (1.13), and we do not know anything else about him beyond the comment in the *Historia Augusta* that he was a Stoic.[13] When we turn to the last of these teachers, Claudius Severus, we meet the only one not described as a Stoic. As we have seen, the *Historia Augusta* describes him as a Peripatetic. He too, like a number of Marcus's other teachers, was a high-ranking Roman active in politics. Marcus's description of him presents an image of a close friend rather than a formal teacher and this is perhaps borne out by the fact that Severus's son married Marcus's daughter.[14] Beyond that we do not know very much. But one thing that comes through very clearly from this brief survey of Marcus's teachers in philosophy is that the dominant influence during his education was Stoicism.

Marcus and Fronto

Alongside philosophy Marcus also studied rhetoric in his youth. The *Historia Augusta* names a number of teachers – Aninius Macer, Caninius Celer, Herodes Atticus, and Cornelius Fronto (*HA* 4.2.4) – the most important of whom, we are told, was Fronto.[15] Marcus's relationship with Fronto gained even greater significance when, in the early nineteenth century, Angelo Mai discovered in Milan fragments of a correspondence between Fronto and Marcus as a palimpsest, on manuscript leaves partly erased and reused for another text. A few years later, in Rome, Mai found further leaves from the same original manuscript of Fronto and Marcus, reused for another text. The combined discoveries were first published together in 1823.[16]

Many of the letters that were recovered date from Marcus's youth, but some are from later, when Marcus was Emperor. The correspondence was, however, over before the *Meditations* were written. Fronto was around 25 years older than Marcus, so when Marcus was a pupil of 15, his teacher was around 40 years old. Fronto was originally from Africa and in the correspondence describes himself as "a Libyan of the Libyan nomads" (*Ad M. Caes.* 2.3).[17] Their relationship, then, was one of master and pupil, even if the pupil was of high social rank. The letters are often personal, with regular references to each other's physical ailments, and very affectionate in places, leading some to see them as evidence for a homosexual relationship.[18] The younger Marcus we find in the letters is quite different from the popular image of the austere sage: he often alludes to Latin comedy and can be, in the words of Fleury, "light-hearted and emotional" (2012: 74).

It has been commented that, given the close relationship often in evidence in the letters, the brevity of Marcus's note on Fronto in Book 1 of the *Meditations* is somewhat surprising.[19]

An explanation might be found in the fact that the portraits Marcus paints in Book 1 are primarily of moral *exempla* embodying traits that he admires. Although Fronto may have been an important teacher of rhetoric, by the time Marcus was writing the *Meditations* that was not uppermost in his mind. There his concern is not with how to write well, but how to live well. As Rutherford has commented, the overarching theme in Book 1 is Marcus's "awakening to philosophic self-awareness", which explains his only brief comment on Fronto, not to mention the "damning omission" of his other teachers of rhetoric (1989: 103). By contrast, the fuller descriptions that Marcus gives of his Stoic teachers itself tells us something about his focus of attention at the time he was writing.[20]

Although the correspondence with Fronto is a valuable window into the earlier part of Marcus's life, that is not our main concern here. It is, however, also an important source of information about Marcus's philosophical interests at various points in time. Consequently, we shall return to it often in the following sections focused on Marcus's relationship with Stoicism.

Marcus and the early Stoics

Marcus makes few references to the early Stoics in the *Meditations*. In fact, he only mentions Chrysippus and he does so just twice. In one passage (7.19), Chrysippus is named alongside Socrates and Epictetus as an example of an admirable person long since dead. In the other (6.42), Marcus refers to a play mentioned by Chrysippus – a mere passing reference, although one that implies that Marcus had been reading his works. There are, however, further references to early Stoics in the correspondence with Fronto.

In a letter that Fronto wrote to Marcus around 162, he refers to "your Chrysippus" (*Fer. Als.* 3.6),[21] while in another letter from around the same time he discusses the tensions between Marcus's devotion to philosophy and his newly acquired duties as Emperor. Fronto writes, "Suppose that you, Caesar, succeed in attaining to the wisdom of Cleanthes or Zeno, yet against your will you must put on the purple cloak, not the philosopher's cloak of coarse wool" (*De eloqu.* 2.11).[22] Here Fronto, the master of rhetoric, carefully chooses examples that Marcus takes to be the very height of wisdom, namely the two earliest heads of the Stoa. In the same letter Fronto continues by noting – perhaps against most modern expectations – that Marcus was more fascinated by the sorts of logical paradoxes that occupied Chrysippus than he was with practically oriented oratory that has a real impact on the world (*De eloqu.* 2.13).[23] In order to win Marcus round from the dry logical treatises of Chrysippus to the eloquence of a Plato or Xenophon, Fronto appeals to examples where Chrysippus acknowledges the value of rhetorical techniques. He says, "if Chrysippus himself has shown that these should be used, what more do I ask, unless it be that you should not employ the verbiage of the dialecticians but rather the eloquence of Plato?" (*De eloqu.* 2.14).[24] The important point in the present context is that Fronto clearly regarded Marcus to be a devoted admirer of the early Stoics and, in particular, Chrysippus.[25]

To put this into context, Chrysippus had by this time become *the* canonical Stoic. Authors roughly contemporary with Marcus such as Plutarch, Galen, and Aulus Gellius all engaged with Chrysippus, quoting his works sometimes at length, indicating that they were still readily available.[26] A little earlier, Epictetus made plain that studying the works of Chrysippus was a standard part of his classroom practice in Nicopolis.[27] Slightly earlier still, we hear of members of the circle around Seneca signalling their ownership of a complete set of Chrysippus's works.[28]

Equally noteworthy is that critics of Stoicism, such as Plutarch and Galen, paid relatively little attention to contemporary Stoics, instead directing their arguments against Chrysippus. He had clearly become the authoritative point of reference for Stoics in the second century AD.[29] Indeed, much of our evidence for the thought of Chrysippus comes from authors active in this period, indicating that he was being widely read and studied. It is a commonplace to present Marcus as the last of the Stoics and so, implicitly, to see the second century as a period of decline and fall for Stoicism. While in some respects – and with hindsight – that seems to be true, it is also worth noting that there was intense study of Chrysippus's works at this time. This was in some respects a vibrant period in the history of Stoicism. Fronto's remarks indicate that Chrysippus was also an authority for Marcus.

We also hear from Marcus himself, this time some 20 years earlier when he would have been in his mid-20s. In a letter written in the 140s, Marcus reports to Fronto that he has been reading the work of the Stoic Aristo of Chios. Despite his reputation as a heterodox Stoic, Aristo appears to have remained popular among Roman Stoics such as Seneca.[30] Marcus was clearly impressed by what he read, commenting that it made him feel uneasy because "they truly show me how far my character is left behind by these better ideas" (*Ad M. Caes.* 4.13).[31] By way of context, Fronto had asked Marcus to write *pro* and *contra* a topic as an exercise in rhetoric. Marcus responded by saying that he can write for one side or the other, but not both, because Aristo would not approve of him arguing for opposed views in the manner of a sophist.[32]

Some commentators have taken this letter as evidence for a sudden conversion of Marcus from the study of rhetoric to philosophy, although others have suggested that this would be overstating it.[33] Marcus was already interested in philosophy, and his interests in rhetoric did not disappear completely. The identity of Aristo has also been questioned, with some claiming that Marcus is referring to a legal expert of the same name.[34] Yet that seems unlikely: Marcus is explicit that the Aristo that he is reading is outlining ideas about having an ideal character, which is what one would expect from a philosopher noted for concentrating on ethics. Indeed, a number of aspects of Aristo's thought resonate with what we find in both Marcus and Epictetus, such as a relative neglect of the distinction between preferred and non-preferred indifferents, the comparison between a sage and an actor playing a role, and limited interest in the technical aspects of logic and physics (Diog. Laert. 7.160).[35] The first two of these are especially striking in Epictetus; the third is true to a point although, as we shall see in later chapters, there are a number of logical and physical themes running through the *Meditations*. Where a potential Aristonian influence stands out is in Marcus's relative disinterest in the distinction between preferred and non-preferred indifferents. For Marcus, everything that happens is in harmony with Nature, even non-preferred indifferents such as disease and death (e.g. 5.8, 9.3, 12.23), while at 11.16 he exhorts himself to live "indifferent to indifferent things (*ta adiaphora*)", seemingly unconcerned by any finer grained distinction. On this point Aristo may well have been *an* influence on Marcus, but he was not *the* defining influence on his thought.[36]

A third early Stoic worth mentioning here is Cleanthes. He also appears to have remained popular among Roman Stoics. Musonius Rufus draws on him and Seneca and Epictetus both quote his otherwise lost *Prayer to Zeus*.[37] Marcus does not mention him in the *Meditations*, but he does appear in the correspondence with Fronto, where Fronto mentions him as an exemplar of Stoic wisdom admired by Marcus (*De eloqu.* 2.11).[38] There are a number of themes in Cleanthes' thought that resonate with what we find in Marcus, such as a belief in the providential ordering of Nature and the use of parallels between the microcosm and macrocosm.[39]

More intriguingly, Cleanthes is remembered for his interest in Heraclitus and he is reported to have written a four-volume commentary on Heraclitus.[40] Marcus too appears to have been interested in Heraclitus: he mentions him as an eminent philosopher in a number of places alongside Socrates, Diogenes, and Pythagoras (6.47, 8.3) and he preserves a number of lines from him not otherwise known (at 4.46, 6.42).[41] Marcus was evidently reading something, now lost, that contained texts by Heraclitus. It is conceivable that it could have been a work by Cleanthes, although there is no firm evidence for this.

One other feature of the Roman Stoic reception of Cleanthes is repeated note of the way in which he managed to combine his commitment to philosophy with a need to work. Epictetus holds him up as a role model to his students in this regard (*Diss.* 3.26.23), while Seneca uses it in an argument to show that anyone can study philosophy, no matter what their personal circumstances (*Ep.* 44.3). In both cases they allude to the biographical tradition that reports that Cleanthes studied with Zeno during the day while supporting himself by drawing water in gardens at night (Diog. Laert. 7.168). Although Marcus makes no mention of this himself, one can see a certain parallel with his own situation.

Marcus and Seneca

Moving significantly closer to Marcus's own time, although still a full century earlier, we might also consider the potential influence of Seneca. At first glance this might seem minimal to say the least, given that there are no references to Seneca in the *Meditations*. While, on the one hand, this might not come as much of a surprise, given that Seneca wrote in Latin and the *Meditations* was composed in Greek, on the other, Seneca was without doubt the preeminent Stoic in Rome from the previous century. Surely Marcus was aware of his works. We do find references to Seneca in the correspondence with Fronto. They are in general not very complimentary, but it is Fronto, not Marcus, who is critical of Seneca and it is worth adding that he is primarily critical of Seneca's literary style rather than his philosophy.[42] Fronto the rhetorician disliked Seneca's style of Latin prose.[43] Yet the sense we get is that Fronto is warning Marcus about Seneca's style precisely because Marcus was reading his works. Indeed, in one letter Fronto describes Seneca to Marcus as "your Annaeus", implying that Seneca was already one of Marcus's favourites (*De orat.* 3).[44] This should come as no surprise given what we have already seen regarding Marcus's interest and education in Stoicism. What it does do is confirm that Marcus was familiar with at least some of Seneca's works. There are numerous passages in the *Meditations* that repeat or echo ideas that can already be found in Seneca, and a number of these will be discussed in subsequent chapters. In general, commentators have tended to put these down to their shared Stoic commitments, but it is at least possible that in some cases Marcus may have been drawing directly on Seneca.

Marcus and Epictetus

We are on much firmer ground when it comes to Epictetus. As we saw earlier, Marcus borrowed a copy of the *Discourses* of Epictetus from Rusticus (1.7). Presumably this was a copy of the full eight books compiled by Arrian and not just the four that survive today, given that Marcus quotes passages from Epictetus that are not in the extant books (at 4.41, 11.37, 11.38, 11.39).[45] An alternative is that these were Rusticus's own notes taken at Epictetus's lectures, rather than Arrian's notes by which we know Epictetus today. A further, intermediate, possibility is that this was Rusticus's personal copy of Arrian's *Discourses*, with his own annotations. Marcus refers to the *hupomnêmata* of Epictetus, "notes", a term that also appears in Arrian's prefatory letter attached to the surviving four books (*Diss.* Praef. 2).[46] Whichever it was, it is widely assumed that Epictetus was an important – and perhaps the decisive – influence on Marcus's philosophical development. Indeed, Marcus quotes from Epictetus more often than he does any other author.[47]

Epictetus's reputation was already firmly established during this period. A number of ancient sources comment on his fame. Marcus's contemporary Lucian ridiculed an admirer of Epictetus who paid a large sum of money for the philosopher's clay lamp (*Ind.* 13). Origen, writing some decades after Marcus, commented that while Plato was read by the learned, "Epictetus is admired even by common folk, who have an inclination to receive benefit because they perceive the improvement which his words effect in their lives" (*C. Cels.* 6.2).[48] Yet, as we have already seen, many discussions of Stoicism during this period tended to refer back to the canonical early Stoics, and in particular Chrysippus, as the main points of reference. Marcus's explicit mention of Epictetus in the *Meditations*, combined with a sparsity of references to other Stoics, has led some to present Epictetus as the defining influence on the *Meditations*.[49] While he was no doubt one important influence, it may be overstating things to claim that, for instance, the *Meditations* were consciously shaped by certain features of Epictetus's thought.[50] A number of central themes in Epictetus, such as his focus on *prohairesis*, barely feature in the *Meditations*. Nor does Marcus take up Epictetus's tendency to use personalist language when referring to the Stoic God. The influence is clearly there, but it does not seem overbearing. For someone just reading the *Meditations*, the reference to Marcus having borrowed a copy of Epictetus's *Discourses* stands out, but if one takes into account the correspondence with Fronto, one finds a much wider range of Stoic influences on Marcus, including Aristo, Chrysippus, and Seneca.

Marcus and Galen

Perhaps the most significant philosopher with whom we know Marcus directly interacted is Galen.[51] There is frustratingly little information about the nature of their relationship, beyond the fact that Marcus requested Galen to be his personal physician.[52] In one of his works, Galen recounts his successful diagnosis and treatment of Marcus with some pride (*Praen.* 11.1-8),[53] reporting at the end that Marcus respected him as both a physician and a philosopher, calling him "unique among philosophers" (*monon tôn philosophôn*). However, a passing comment by Galen suggests that he found his imperial commitments to be an unwanted burden (*Ind.* 49-50), and rather than welcome the opportunity to attend Marcus on campaign, he managed to make his excuses and remain in Rome, where he focused on his writing (*Praen.* 9.5-8).[54] There is certainly no evidence for any influence between the two of them either way. Even so, some of Galen's philosophical concerns shed light on the immediate philosophical context in which Marcus wrote his *Meditations*, and so are worth mentioning here.

Galen was well versed in the ideas of all the major philosophical schools. He was schooled in philosophy from an early age and he tells us that as a teenager he attended lectures in Pergamum – "mostly those of a Stoic, a pupil of Philopator" (*Aff. Pecc. Dig.* 1.8.3).[55] Later, Galen would write works on Epictetus and Chrysippus, although his works on Chrysippus were certainly critical.[56] He also wrote on Plato, Aristotle, and Epicurus. In his major work on the nature of the soul, *On the Doctrines of Hippocrates and Plato*, he argued for an agreement between Plato and Hippocrates on the physical location of parts of the soul and, along the way, launched into a major polemic against the Stoic psychology of Chrysippus.[57] In a later work, *The Soul's Dependence on the Body*, he appears to shift towards a more Peripatetic view (*QAM* 3), while elsewhere he doubts the veracity of the views of all the major philosophical schools (*Foet. Form.* 6.31), leading him to adopt what one commentator has called a position of "principled agnosticism".[58] On questions of psychological theory, Galen was certainly interested in Stoic and other accounts of the soul, without being fully committed to any one of them.

More relevant in the present context is his contribution to psychological therapeutics. In various works, Galen offered advice for people dealing with anger and grief.[59] But he also reflected on the techniques involved in therapeutic practices. We see this in his *The Affections and Errors of the Soul*.[60] Here he explicitly says that he will be drawing on the therapeutic works of Chrysippus, even though he distances himself from the Stoic account of emotions and the underpinning psychology (*Aff. Pecc. Dig.* 1.1.4). He goes on to stress the importance of self-examination and training for the soul. In a passage reminiscent of Marcus or Epictetus, he writes:

> In the first place, you should not trust your judgement, however carefully it has been arrived at, if it tells you that the criticism is insulting, false, or ignorant, and that you have done no wrong. This is the first rudiment of philosophy, to put up with unfair criticism.
>
> *Aff. Pecc. Dig. 1.3.10*

He goes on to characterize the task of taking care of one's soul as a discipline that must continue throughout one's life. His insistence on the need for "constant training (*askêsis*)" (*Aff. Pecc. Dig.* 1.4.4) parallels Marcus's own many reminders to himself to maintain a state of continual vigilance (e.g. 4.36, 4.40, 4.46, 4.48).[61] Galen comments on the value of repetition in the practice of this training – "if a proposition is of great importance, there is no harm in repeating it twice or even three times" (*Aff. Pecc. Dig.* 1.5.1) – which is something Marcus practices throughout the *Meditations*. Galen continues with further advice that could easily come from the *Meditations*:

> First, on rising in the morning one should pose oneself this question, before embarking on the day's tasks: is it better to live a constant slave to the affections, or to employ reason on every occasion? [...] One must, further, keep constantly in mind, every day and every hour of the day, the desirability of counting oneself amongst the good and the upright.
>
> *Aff. Pecc. Dig. 1.5.6*

Similarly,

> One should remind oneself of this, preferably many times a day, or, failing that, at least at dawn before beginning one's daily activities and in the evening when one is about to take one's rest.
>
> *Aff. Pecc. Dig. 1.6.10*

There is much more in Galen's discussion that echoes what we find in Marcus's *Meditations*, no doubt because they were both drawing on the same works that formed the ancient tradition of philosophical therapeutics, running from Pythagoras and Socrates down to Epictetus and into their own day. The most significant difference, of course, is that Galen's treatise is offering advice, while Marcus's notebook is an attempt to enact such advice. Even so, it is striking how close these two works come to one another at certain points. Here is just one more passage from Galen:

> All we must do is keep the doctrines regarding insatiability and self-sufficiency constantly to hand (*procheiros*) and commit ourselves to the daily cultivation of the particular actions which follow from these doctrines.
>
> *Aff. Pecc. Dig. 1.9.20*

There is no firm evidence about when Galen wrote this treatise, and certainly none to indicate that Marcus ever read it, but putting that question to one side it is clear that Marcus's practice of philosophical reflection in the *Meditations* did not come out of nowhere; it was part of a wider interest in this period for this kind of therapeutic attention to the disturbances and errors of the soul. Indeed, one of the most interesting works dealing with this topic is also by Galen. In a short text entitled *Avoiding Distress*, Galen recounts to an old friend how he coped with the loss of many of his possessions – and not least his library, containing copies of his own works – that perished in a fire that engulfed the centre of Rome in 192.[62] What is distinctive about this text is that Galen does not merely impart advice; he reports that he has used these techniques himself and that they worked. In particular, he recommends the technique usually referred to as the premeditation of future evils: "I schooled my imagination to prepare for the total loss of everything that I had" (*Ind.* 54), adding "I advise you to train your soul's imagination to cope with almost any turn of events" (*Ind.* 56). Although he lost a lot of important things in the fire, he did not suffer any great distress, he reports, because although he lost much, what he had left was still sufficient for his needs (*Ind.* 46). Galen puts this down in part to his upbringing, during which he was never encouraged to place excessive value on external goods (*Ind.* 65). But it is the philosophical technique of reflecting on how much worse it could have been that he insists has enabled him not to be distressed by the loss. Although this text was written after Marcus's death, it also helps to put the *Meditations* into a wider context.

Marcus the Stoic

In the light of what we have seen in this chapter, it seems clear that Marcus was well versed in and felt a commitment to Stoicism. So, should we call him a Stoic? Before trying to answer that question, we might want to reflect on what it really meant to be a Stoic in this period. The original community of Stoics in Athens was, by this point, a distant memory, having come to an end in the first century BC. Its demise was part of a wider decentralization of philosophy that happened in this period, with Athens no longer being the central geographical point of focus.[63] In the wake of this, there was a shift of focus away from communities of like-minded people living together and towards the study of texts. In the first and second centuries AD, it was no longer possible to travel to Athens and join the official Stoic community – not that it is clear precisely what that would have ever entailed – but it was certainly possible to read increasingly canonized Stoic texts and to identify with the ideas they contained. To be a Stoic in this period simply meant to be a part of what has been called a "textual community" of readers who read the same texts and accepted their central doctrines.[64] In this sense, Marcus was clearly a Stoic as much as anyone could be in this period.

The more substantive issue of the extent to which Marcus can be seen as a Stoic hinges on how close his ideas align with what one might take to be central Stoic doctrines. In antiquity the Stoics had a reputation for a certain freedom of thought, with Seneca famously proclaiming that, unlike the Epicureans, Stoics were free to think independently rather than slavishly follow the thoughts of the school's founder (*Ep.* 33.4). Indeed, the history of ancient Stoicism is full of figures who in one respect or other have been judged heterodox, from Aristo to Boethus, Panaetius, and Posidonius.[65] In the context of a decentralized textual community, the attempt to canonize the writings of Chrysippus may have been an attempt to offer a clear doctrinal standard of what counted as Stoic. The question concerning Marcus's philosophical alignment with Stoicism, then, will depend in large part on how one defines orthodox Stoicism and the degree of intellectual autonomy tolerated within the tradition. This will of course be our primary concern in the chapters that follow, but Marcus's education by Stoics and reading of Stoic texts is beyond doubt.

Notes

1 On the long history of this "sanctification" of Marcus Aurelius, see Richlin (2012).
2 In Xylander (1559), one of our two key witnesses for the text, this appears *within* Book 1. His Book 1 continues to include our 2.1-3 and his Book 2 opens with our 2.4. Casaubon (1643), based on Xylander's text, does the same.
3 The inscription "Written in Carnuntum" is usually placed at the end of Book 2, following the only complete manuscript, Vaticanus Graecus 1950, but in Xylander (1559) (the other key witness for the text), it is printed at the head of Book 3. Whether that was an editorial decision or accurately represents the lost Palatine manuscript on which Xylander's text was based, it is impossible to know.
4 For just one example of this not uncommon view, see Arnold (1911: 122–7).
5 The biography of Marcus Aurelius in the *Historia Augusta* (or *Scriptores Historiae Augustae*) is credited to Julius Capitolinus, with other biographies in the collection attributed to other authors. This is now widely disputed and the collection as a whole is thought to be the work of one (unknown) individual, perhaps writing in the 390s. While its authority as a historical source has often been challenged, especially for the later Emperors, the life of Marcus is thought to be fairly reliable. See further Barnes (1978: 13–18 and 25).
6 For further discussion of Hadrian's relationship with Epictetus, see Birley (1997: 58–61). The no doubt spurious dialogue, *Altercatio Hadriani Augusti et Epicteti Philosophi*, is edited and discussed in Daly and Suchier (1939).
7 On Apollonius see *DPhA* I, 285-6; Hadot and Luna (1998: xc–xcv). Gill (2013: 61) suggests that Apollonius was invited by Antoninus Pius to instruct Marcus "possibly when Marcus was about 30 years old". This is based on *HA* 3.10.4 (and cf. Lucian, *Demon.* 31), which recounts Antoninus summoning Apollonius. However, it is far from clear that this describes their first encounter. Instead it might be taken to refer to Antoninus calling an existing teacher back at a moment when assistance was needed. Birley (2000: 44) dates their first meeting to 136, when Marcus was around 15 years old.
8 Hout (1988: 79); Haines (1919–20: I, 235). Here "master" (*magister*) could be understood as a compliment or could simply be referring to his role as Marcus's teacher.
9 On Rusticus, see *DPhA* Vb, 1817–18; Hadot (1998: 8–11). See also Dio Cassius (72.35.1), who describes Rusticus as a follower of Zeno's doctrines.
10 Farquharson (1944: II, 443) connects this reference to *therapeia* of *êthos* with the wider use of a medical analogy for philosophy in antiquity and cites a number of parallel texts. Gill (2013: 59) makes a similar connection.
11 Plutarch's most important texts arguing against the Stoics are *Comm. not.* and *St. rep.*; his relationship with the Stoa is discussed at length in Babut (1969).

12 The identification of Marcus's teacher Claudius Maximus with Apuleius's man of the same name has been questioned by some. Butler and Owen (1914: 1), doubt it, writing "there is no reason to identify" them. However, later (ibid. 56) they take the phrase *austerae sectae* (*Apol.* 19) to suggest that he was a Stoic, which offers at least some reason to make the connection. Brunt (2013: 328) calls the identification "immensely plausible". See further *DPhA* IV, 363–5.
13 Champlin (1980: 119, with n. at 174) suggests that his name alone indicates that he was probably a senator. See further *DPhA* II, 399–400. Gill (2013: 67) suggests the same.
14 See Gill (2013: 67). On Severus, see further *DPhA* VI, 241-4.
15 On Fronto in general see Champlin (1980). On his relationship with Marcus see Kasulke (2005) and Griffin (2018: 707–21). For further references see *DPhA* III, 428–30.
16 See Mai (1815) for the first publication of the finds in Milan, and Mai (1823) for the combined finds from Milan and Rome. The most recent critical edition of the correspondence can be found in Hout (1988), and see Hout (1999) for a detailed commentary on the text. The only complete translation into English is in Haines (1919–20). A selection is translated in Richlin (2006) with helpful notes. There is also a selection translated by R. B. Rutherford in Farquharson (1989). On its rediscovery and its contents, see Fleury (2012).
17 Hout (1988: 24); Haines (1919–20: I, 136).
18 See especially Richlin (2006). For some reservations see Gill (2013: 65), Griffin (2018: 717–21). For an emphatic rejection, see McLynn (2009: 52–3, 579–80).
19 See, for example, Richlin (2012: 512) and Griffin (2018: 709).
20 For a similar conclusion see Gill (2013: 65).
21 Hout (1988: 230); Haines (1919–20: II, 10–11). Hout (1999: 521) takes Fronto to be mocking Marcus here.
22 Hout (1988: 140); Haines (1919–20: II, 62–5).
23 Hout (1988: 141); Haines (1919–20: II, 66–7. Hout (1999: 337) doubts whether Marcus would have still been interested in dialectics at this point in his life, even if he had been in his youth, but there is no obvious evidence either way.
24 Hout (1988: 142); Haines (1919–20: II, 68–9).
25 It is also worth noting that in another letter, *De eloqu.* 1.3 (Hout 1988: 134; Haines 1919–20: II, 48–51), Fronto mentions Zeno twice, although here he simply figures as one of a series of examples among many.
26 On Plutarch's references to Chrysippus see Babut (1969: 225–37) and, more briefly, Morford (2002: 222–6). On Galen and Chrysippus see Tieleman (1996). For Aulus Gellius and Chrysippus see Holford-Strevens (2003: 274–5).
27 See for example Epictetus, *Diss.* 1.17.13-18 and 2.17.34-40 as just two examples among many.
28 The ancient biography of the Stoic poet Persius (traditionally attributed to Suetonius but now credited to Valerius Probus) reports that he had a collection of around 700 works by Chrysippus (who is reported to have written 705 books) that, in his will, he left to his fellow-Stoic Cornutus. See further Boys-Stones (2018: 200–1) for text, translation, and discussion.
29 See Babut (1969: 15–18); Gould (1970: 13); Tieleman (1996: xxvii).
30 See for example Seneca, *Ep.* 36.3 (*SVF* 1.388); 94.1-18 (*SVF* 1.358–9); 115.8 (*SVF* 1.372).
31 Hout (1988: 67–8); Haines (1919–20: I, 216–17). This letter is also translated with notes in Richlin (2006: 139–41) and I quote her translation here. For discussion see Kasulke (2005: 230–41).
32 On Aristo's dislike of dialectic, see Diog. Laert. 7.161 (*SVF* 1.333). In the list of Aristo's works in Diog. Laert. 7.163, we find *Against the Rhetoricians* and, in three books, *Against the Dialecticians*.
33 See for example Haines (1919–20: I, 218) with reservations in, for example, Champlin (1980: 121), Griffin (2018: 715). See also Hout (1999: 188).
34 See Champlin (1974: 144). Both Haines (1919–20: I, 216) and Richlin (2006: 140), writing before and after Champlin, take Marcus to be referring to the Stoic Aristo of Chios. See also Hout (1999: 188). Fleury (2012: 72) lists the many others who have rejected the suggestion.
35 The ancient evidence for Aristo is in *SVF* 1.333–403. For an overview and references to further studies, see *DPhA* I, 400–3.

36 For further discussion of Marcus and Aristo, see Roskam (2012), who, 93, offers a brief survey of earlier views on the extent of Aristo's influence, and, 95–6, examines the topic of indifferents. For a more sceptical attitude see Hadot (1998: 11–14 and 71–2).
37 See Musonius Rufus 1 (Hense 1905: 4,5–5,2; *SVF* 1.611); Seneca, *Ep.* 107.11 and Epictetus, *Ench.* 53.1 (both *SVF* 1.527). On Cleanthes and Musonius see Harriman (forth.b).
38 Hout (1988: 140); Haines (1919–20: II, 63).
39 On microcosm-macrocosm parallels in Cleanthes, see Cicero, *Nat. D.* 2.40-1 (*SVF* 1.504), with Harriman (forth.b).
40 See Diog. Laert. 7.174 (*SVF* 1.481) and note also Eusebius, *Praep. evang.* 15.20.2 (*SVF* 1.519), discussed in Long (1975–76: 150–51).
41 These are the source for DK 22B71-75; cf. LM Her. R54-5.
42 On Fronto's attitude towards Seneca, and the suggestion that in some respects Fronto may have seen his relationship with Marcus as analogous to Seneca's with Nero, see Griffin (2018: 716–17).
43 On Fronto's attack on Seneca's style, placed within a wider context of similar attacks, see Holford-Strevens (2003: 276–7).
44 Hout (1988: 154); Haines (1919–20: II, 102).
45 These passages are Epictetus frr. 26–28a (Schenkl 1916: 471–2). The claim that the *Discourses* were originally in eight books is based on a statement in Photius, *Bibl.* cod. 58 (17b11-20 = test. 6 Schenkl 1916). That the surviving four books are incomplete is confirmed by Aulus Gellius's reference to and quotation from Book 5 (*NA* 19.1.14 = fr. 9 Schenkl 1916). See further Souilhé (1975: xi–xix). Marcus's quotations from Epictetus in Book 11 of the *Meditations* are discussed briefly in Sellars (2018a).
46 See further Farquharson (1944: II 446), Hadot and Luna (1998: lxxxvii–lxxxix), Gill (2013: 60). Although Farquharson translates the passage to suggest that Marcus borrowed a copy of Arrian's *Discourses*, in his commentary he suggests that it more likely refers to Rusticus's own notes on Epictetus, a suggestion taken up by Hadot.
47 See Rigo (2010: 339–344). The full list is: *Diss.* 1.28.4 (in 7.63), *Diss.* 3.22.105 (in 11.36), *Diss.* 3.24.86-7 (in 11.33), *Diss.* 3.24.88 (in 11.34), *Diss.* 3.24.91-2 (in 11.35), *Diss.* 4.6.20 (in *Med.* 7.36). Not mentioned by Rigo are fr. 26 Schenkl, from 4.41, and fr. 28b (added by Oldfather 1925–28), from 4.49.
48 This passage is Epictetus test. 26 (Schenkl 1916: viii). On the date of Origin's work, see Chadwick (1953: xiv–xv).
49 This is, in effect, the central thesis in Hadot (1998).
50 See for example Hadot (1978) and Hadot (1998: 43–7) where he suggests that Epictetus's three *topoi* (*Diss.* 3.2.1-2) "are the true key to the *Meditations*" (47).
51 For an overview of Galen's work see Hankinson (2008); for a recent biography see Mattern (2013). In referring to his works, I have followed the abbreviations listed in Singer (2013: 429–42). Many of the texts referred to here are translated in Singer (1997) or Singer (2013).
52 Galen, *Lib. Prop.* 3.1 (XIX, 17 Kühn), with Boudon-Millet (2007: 193–4) and Mattern (2013: 195).
53 Text and translation in Nutton (1979: 126–9). Note also the accounts of this episode in Birley (2000: 196–7) and Mattern (2013: 212–3).
54 For further discussion see Mattern (2013: 219–22).
55 Philopator, who was probably roughly contemporary with Epictetus, is remembered for his contribution to Stoic discussions of fate and compatibilism, on which see Bobzien (1998: 358–412). See also *DPhA* Va, 454.
56 Galen, *Lib. Prop.* 14.21 (XIX, 44 Kühn; Singer 1997: 20) and 18.1-2 (XIX, 47 Kühn; Singer 1997: 22). His work on Epictetus, *To Favorinus Concerning Epictetus*, was likely a defence against the attacks of Favorinus who had written a work entitled *Against Epictetus*, our only evidence for which also comes from Galen (*Opt. Doct.* 1.2, in Barigazzi 1991: 92; see also Barigazzi 1966: 191–2 and Amato 2010: 151–3).
57 Text and translation in De Lacy (1978–84). For a thorough discussion see Tieleman (1996) and, more briefly, Donini (2008). On Galen's complex relationship with Stoicism, especially on topics in psychology, see Gill (2010).

58 See Donini (2008: 197–8). Note also *Aff. Pecc. Dig.* 1.8.8, where he writes "I do not declare allegiance to any sect, rather subjecting them all to a thorough examination" (Singer 1997: 120).
59 See the discussion in Mattern (2013: 258–60 and 266–72).
60 This work is edited in De Boer (1937). It is translated in Singer (1997) and, revised and annotated, in Singer (2013). De Boer prints it as two distinct works, *Aff. Dig.* and *Pecc. Dig.*, but Singer treats it as a single work, *Aff. Pecc. Dig.* in two books, which I follow here; see his note in Singer (2013: 315). I have consulted both versions of Singer's translation and tend to quote from the earlier one, sometimes amended.
61 On the idea of *askêsis* in ancient philosophy, with a focus on the Roman Stoics, see Sellars (2003: 107–28). On the theme of constant attention and vigilance in Marcus and also Epictetus, see Sellars (2018b).
62 Galen's *Avoiding Distress* (*Ind.*) was only discovered in 2005 and published for the first time in 2007. I have used the edition in Boudon-Millot *et al.* (2010). It is translated, by Vivian Nutton, in Singer (2013). For further discussion, see the detailed introductions in both of those volumes and the essays in Petit (2019).
63 On decentralization of philosophy in the first century BC, see Sedley (2003).
64 I borrow this notion of a textual community from the very helpful discussion in Boys-Stones (2018: 9–13).
65 This image of early Stoicism has in part been challenged by Sedley (1989), who argues that in fact Zeno remained a canonical authority for the early Stoa, and that subsequent internal disputes were primarily about how best to understand what Zeno had said. A good example of this is the debate concerning the Stoic *telos*, on which see Chapter 8.

2

THE *MEDITATIONS*, A PHILOSOPHICAL TEXT

A notebook

The *Meditations* is a unique and idiosyncratic text, quite unlike a typical work of philosophy. It takes the form of a series of private notebook jottings that Marcus wrote to himself. The opening book is slightly different from the other 11 books: it has its own structure, serves a specific purpose of paying respects to individuals who had been formative influences, and may have been composed separately.[1] The subsequent books contain a series of thoughts, reflections, and quotations from other authors, all in no apparent order.[2] Themes and topics recur again and again, and there is little sense that the text was ever revised or edited after first being written down. It has all the appearance of being Marcus's private notebook rather than a work intended for publication. What we find is Marcus in dialogue with himself.[3]

The English title *Meditations* was effectively coined in the seventeenth century by Meric Casaubon when he published his translation in 1634 under the title *Meditations Concerning Himselfe*.[4] This was his attempt to render into English the title that he found printed in editions of the Greek text, *tôn eis heauton*, "to himself".[5] While subsequent translators rendered the title in other ways – *Conversation With Himself* (Collier 1708), *Thoughts* (Long 1890) – Casaubon's proved most popular and was often shortened to just *Meditations*, with the unfortunate consequence of losing the connection with the original Greek title. While some later translators tried to reverse the trend (e.g. Rendall 1898), it was too late: the title *Meditations* had stuck.[6] In other European languages, it has been given a variety of titles, including *Pensées*, *Reflexions*, and *Ricordi*.[7] None of these really capture the sense of the Greek title, *Ta eis heauton*, which might best be translated as *To Himself*.[8] Although it is fairly unlikely that this title was devised by Marcus himself,[9] it is nevertheless apt and offers a way in to thinking about what Marcus was doing when he was writing these notes.

Attending to oneself

With a private text like this it can be difficult to know for sure what the author was trying to do. Helpfully, in a particularly important passage (4.3), Marcus gives us his own extended account of what he was doing.[10] Some people look for escapes from the pressures of everyday life by retreating to the countryside but as a philosopher Marcus can simply retreat into himself (*eis heauton anachôrein*). He writes "Continually, therefore, grant yourself this retreat and repair yourself (*ananeou seauton*)". This is not a permanent retreat but simply a brief period of rest and reflection before returning to the business of everyday life. What is the purpose of this retreat? It is to reflect on "brief and fundamental truths" (*brachea kai stoicheiôdê*) already within the mind, in order to "wash away all distress" (*to pasan lupên apoklusai*), to attain "perfect ease" (*eumareia*), which he identifies with "good behaviour" (*eukosmia*). He then gives us a couple of examples of what he has in mind, such as reminding himself that he is by nature a social animal, in order to keep in check any anger he might feel towards people who behave poorly. He goes on to suggest that there are two fundamental ideas that must be kept "ready to hand" (*procheiros*): (i) that mental disturbances are the product not of things but of our judgements (*hupolêpsis*), and (ii) nothing is stable and everything passes, subject to universal flux (*metabolê*). He then summarizes these two principles as concisely as possible, presumably in order to aid memorization: *ho kosmos alloiôsis, ho bios hupolêpsis*, which we might translate expansively as "the cosmos is in continual change; the concerns of human life are the product of opinion" (4.3[12]).[11] When Marcus was writing the *Meditations* he was engaged in a practice of reminding himself of these and other central philosophical principles, in order (as he tells us) to overcome distress (*lupê*) and to cultivate a state of complete ease (*eumareia*).[12]

In a second, equally important, passage (potentially confusingly, 3.4), Marcus reminds himself to avoid distractions that might take him away from what he ought to be doing, namely paying close attention to his "governing self" (*hêgemonikon*). This involves attending to his impressions (*phantasiai*) and habituating himself (*ethisteon heauton*) to think only of things he would be unashamed to share with others if they asked. Someone who manages to reach this level of attention to one's internal mental processes will, he suggests, be "dyed with justice to the core" and will welcome "all that comes to pass". They will pay little attention to the opinions of others, which they cannot control, focusing squarely on their own thought processes, which they can.

This concern with paying attention to oneself probably reflects the influence of Epictetus. In his *Discourses* Epictetus says that "the first and greatest task of the philosopher is to test the impressions and discriminate between them" (*Diss*. 1.20.7). This is achieved by a continual attitude of attention to one's thought processes (*Diss*. 1.20.10). Elsewhere he exhorts an interlocutor to "pay attention to yourself" (*prosochê eph' hauton*), which he suggests primarily involves careful observation of one's impressions (*Diss*. 3.16.15). In his account of the ideal Cynic, he suggests that although such a person is indifferent to external circumstances, they pay considerable attention on their own impressions and judgements (*Diss*. 3.22.104).

Epictetus gives a fuller discussion in a chapter of the *Discourses* entitled "On Attention" (*Peri prosochês*, *Diss*. 4.12), which is the only extended discussion of this notion in any surviving ancient text. As such, it may be worth discussing in some detail. This chapter opens by insisting on the importance of attention for all human activities. Whatever we might intend to do, it will be better done with an attitude of attention. By contrast nothing is improved by inattention (*Diss*. 4.12.4). Epictetus illustrates this in his typical Socratic fashion by referring to examples of craftsmen:[13]

> Does the inattentive carpenter do his work more accurately? The inattentive helmsman steer more safely? And is there any other of the lesser functions of life which is done better by inattention?
>
> *Diss. 4.12.5*

So, attention improves everything. That is one reason to maintain an attitude of attention at all times. Another reason, Epictetus suggests, is that once we lose our attention and let our minds wander off, we are no longer easily able to recover it:

> When you relax your attention for a little while, do not imagine that whenever you choose you will recover it, but bear this in mind, that because of the mistake which you have made today, your condition must necessarily be worse as regards everything else.
>
> *Diss. 4.12.1; cf. 4.12.6*

Before long, he adds, a habit of inattention develops, which will require considerable work to undo. At first glance this might look like it is encouraging an attitude of attention to whatever task someone might be undertaking. However, the sort of attention he is concerned with is not on the task at hand, even if he claims that greater attention will improve whatever one happens to be doing at the present moment, but in fact on something else. The things to which we ought to pay attention are, he says:

> First, these general principles, and you ought to have them at your command (*procheiros*), and without them neither go to sleep, nor rise up, nor drink, nor eat, nor mingle with men; I mean the following: [1] No man is master of another's moral purpose (*prohairesis*); and [2] In its sphere alone are to be found one's good and evil. It follows, therefore, [3] that no one has power either to procure me good, or to involve me in evil, but I myself alone have authority over myself in these matters.
>
> *Diss. 4.12.7-8*

Epictetus is suggesting that in whatever task a person undertakes they ought to keep these three philosophical principles ready to hand (*procheiros*). The continual attitude of attention that Epictetus insists is vital is not to the task itself but to these principles that ought to inform everything a person does. The goal underlying and uniting these principles is autonomy or freedom (*eleutheria*), which for Epictetus is an essential component of a good life. If someone is able to live a life informed by these principles then no external agent or event will have the power to upset their equanimity. If anyone suffers from mental disturbance, this is simply due to a lack of training in developing the appropriate attention to these fundamental philosophical principles (*Diss.* 4.12.13). This is a skill that can be learned, like any other art or craft, echoing Epictetus's wider conception of philosophy as an art of living (*Diss.* 4.12.14; cf. *Diss.* 1.15.2).

In this spirit of training, Epictetus repeats the point he has just made and his three principles. We ought to keep these principles ready to hand (*procheiros*) and do nothing without them (*Diss.* 4.12.15). These principles should always come first. However he adds some further guidance that also ought to be continually kept in mind:

> And next we must remember [4] who we are, and [5] what is our designation, and [6] must endeavour to direct our actions, in the performance of our duties, to meet the possibilities of our social relations.
>
> *Diss. 4.12.16*

This second set of principles is concerned with our social roles and relations. Throughout the *Discourses* Epictetus says that one ought to conform to such roles. It is worth noting, though, that here he puts them in second place. He also insists on the primacy of the first set of principles by describing them as God-given (*Diss.* 4.12.11-12), which for a Stoic could equally be rephrased as given by Nature. The fundamental principles that ought to inform all our actions refer to our natural constitution, but we ought to pay attention to our social obligations as well.

Epictetus concludes by acknowledging that it is impossible for a human being to be completely free from fault. However it is possible to strive to be as free from fault as one can. In order to do that, one must never relax one's attention (*Diss.* 4.12.19). A continual state of vigilance is required. Yet as we have seen, this vigilant attention is not to oneself in a very general sense but specifically to the philosophical principles that ought to guide one's actions.[14]

We have already seen Marcus effectively putting this into practice in 4.3 where he summarizes the key principles that he wants to keep ready to hand (*procheiros*). There are further examples throughout the *Meditations*. Indeed, the *Meditations* as a whole might be read as a series of written exercises designed to remind the author of the central philosophical ideas that he wants to keep ready to hand. Like Epictetus, Marcus warns against the dangers of letting one's attention wander off:

> Do externals tend to distract you? Then give yourself the space to learn some further good lesson, and stop your wandering.
>
> *2.7*

He also takes up the analogy with craftsmen:

> Just as doctors always have their instruments and knives at hand (*procheiros*) for any emergency treatment, so you should have your doctrines (*dogmata*) ready for the recognition of the divine and human, and the performance of every action, even the smallest, in consciousness of the bond which unites the two.
>
> *3.13*

In one passage, particularly interesting in the present context, Marcus picks up on the fundamental principles outlined by Epictetus:

> Whenever you suffer pain, have ready to hand (*procheiros*) the thought that pain is not a moral evil and does not harm your governing intelligence (*dianoia*): pain can do no damage either to its rational or to its social nature. [...] Remember too that many things we find disagreeable are the unrecognized analogues of pain – drowsiness, for example, oppressive heat, loss of appetite. So when you find yourself complaining of any of these, say to yourself, 'You are giving in to pain.'
>
> *7.64*

Despite using different words (e.g. *dianoia*, in place of *prohairesis*), Marcus is making the same basic points as Epictetus: (i) pain, in so far as it is external, is neither good nor evil, and (ii) pain cannot damage or control the ruling part of the soul. If someone can attend to these principles at all times, then they will maintain their autonomy and freedom from mental disturbance.

A couple of paragraphs later, Marcus comments:

> The way nature has blended you into the compound whole [of soul and body] does not prevent you drawing a boundary around yourself and keeping what is your own in your own control. Always remember this: remember too that the happy life depends on very little.
>
> 7.67

Here Marcus is reminding himself to pay attention to some key philosophical ideas, taking up the content of Epictetus's basic principles, namely that: (i) the ruling part of the soul is completely within one's control, and (ii) that nothing else is required for a good life. Although Marcus and Epictetus formulate things slightly differently, the basic underlying ideas are the same.

An art of living

Throughout the *Meditations* Marcus makes a number of oblique references to the idea that he is engaged in an activity that is an art or craft. At 4.2 he tells us not to undertake any action that is not in accord with the principles of the art. By art (*technê*) it seems reasonable to assume he means philosophy, if philosophy embodies those principles according to which one ought to act, and a recent translation expansively renders *technê* here as "the art of life" (Hammond 2006: 23). At 5.1 Marcus draws a comparison between what he must do and what practitioners of other arts do, the implication perhaps being that he too is the practitioner of an art – one devoted to becoming a complete human being. At 6.16 we find a more explicit parallel between what Marcus is doing and what other craftsman do. Just as the horse trainer takes care of horses, for instance, making them fit for their task, so too Marcus must train himself to act or refrain from acting according to the appropriate principles. Like other arts and crafts, Marcus's task has a clear practical goal, and the reference to horse trainers and to taking care of oneself is reminiscent of the *technê* analogy drawn by Socrates in the *Apology* (esp. 25a–b). We find a similar parallel with other examples of craftsmen at 6.35. At 7.68 Marcus says that his art, the art of humankind, is the exercise of rational and social virtue, while at 11.5 he responds to the question "what is your art?" with the reply "to be good", adding that it is only with the aid of a theoretical understanding of both Nature and humankind that he will be able to achieve this.[15]

These passages indicate that Marcus conceived his own activity as some sort of craft-like activity with a specific set of closely inter-related goals, including making correct judgements, choosing the right actions, becoming virtuous, and fulfilling his proper function as a rational human being. We never find an explicit formal definition of philosophy as an art or craft devoted to these goals but it would perhaps be unrealistic to expect one in this sort of text. Instead what we find are a series of reminders and "notes to self" in which Marcus tries to keep in focus the nature of the task he has at hand.

Although Marcus may not be as explicit as we might like, Epictetus is a little more forthcoming. It is in the *Discourses* that we see Epictetus explicitly present philosophy as an art and, in particular, as an art concerned with how to live:

> Philosophy does not promise to secure anything external for man, otherwise it would be admitting something that lies beyond its proper subject-matter (*hulê*). For just as wood is the material (*hulê*) of the carpenter, bronze that of the statue maker, so each individual's own life is the subject-matter/material (*hulê*) of the art of living.
>
> *Diss. 1.15.2*

This notion that philosophy might be conceived as an art of living (*technê peri ton bion*) sounds as if it might be a very broad notion, potentially encompassing a wide variety of ancient philosophers, but almost all of the references to an art of living in ancient sources have some connection to the Stoics.[16] Beyond Epictetus there are references connected to Chrysippus, Posidonius, and Arius Didymus's epitome of Stoic ethics, while the only sustained analysis of this idea in antiquity is to be found in Sextus Empiricus, as part of his polemic against Stoic ethics.[17] The most obvious Latin equivalents (*ars vitae* and *ars vivendi*) can be found in Cicero and Seneca, again in contexts connecting the idea with the Stoics.[18] The idea that philosophy might be conceived as a *technê*, then, and in particular as a *technê* devoted to transforming one's *bios*, was a Stoic idea and one that Marcus would have learned from his reading of Epictetus and others.

The Stoic conception of philosophy as an art of living combines two ideas: first that philosophy is fundamentally concerned with how one should live, and second that it ought to be conceived in analogy with other arts and crafts. Both of these ideas were inherited from Socrates.

In Plato's *Apology*, Socrates makes clear that his philosophical mission is directed towards the transformation of his life: his divine mission is to *live* as a philosopher and this means subjecting his *life* to criticism because the unexamined *life* is not worth living (*Ap.* 28e, 39c, 38a). In order to complete this divine mission Socrates goes in search of those with a reputation for knowledge and, given his own practical goal, focuses his attention on practitioners of arts and crafts. This, of course, becomes a central concern throughout the early Platonic dialogues, but the most sustained analysis of arts and crafts appears in the *Gorgias*, where Socrates draws a distinction between arts that take care of the body and arts that take care of the soul (*Grg.* 463a–466a). This analysis lays the foundations for an analogy between medicine, the art that cures the body, and philosophy, the art that cures the soul. This analogy would prove to be an important influence on the Stoics and would gain a wider currency in the subsequent history of philosophy via Cicero's account in the *Tusculan Disputations*.

One of the central features of philosophy conceived as an art (of living or of curing the soul) is brought out well in the analogy with medicine. This analogy is highly appropriate because medicine is an art that is built upon a complex body of theoretical knowledge and yet is primarily concerned with delivering practical outcomes. Knowledge of medicine requires not only a grasp of the theoretical principles involved but also a period of training or exercise in which those principles can be digested or assimilated into oneself. When learning an art or craft like medicine it is necessary not only to study the formal principles underpinning the art but also to embark on a lengthy apprenticeship during which one learns how to apply those principles in practical situations. This applies to all those activities that are craft-like, as opposed to purely theoretical activities where understanding the key principles alone constitutes knowledge. Thus, the shoemaker, for instance, needs not only to grasp the principles behind his trade but must also train in order to master putting those principles into practice, during what we would naturally call his apprenticeship. The education of the shoemaker, or the doctor, or any other type of craftsman, will thus require two distinguishable stages: a theoretical education in the classroom followed by a period of practical training or apprenticeship. Mastery of any art or craft requires these two stages.

Philosophy conceived as an art will also presumably require these two stages: first, a period of learning or discovering philosophical ideas, and then a second stage designed to digest those ideas so that, just like in other arts and crafts, those ideas can be put into practice. In the *Gorgias* Socrates himself hints at the need for some form of training or exercise (*askêsis*) that would form this second stage (*Grg.* 514e, 527d).

These Socratic ideas were taken up and developed by the early Stoics. As is often the case, however, our knowledge of the early Stoic position is fragmentary and it is only in later texts that we find these ideas discussed in any detail. For example later Stoics such as Seneca and Epictetus took up and developed the idea that philosophy be thought of as an art of living, while the only extended critical discussion of the idea came a little later still from Sextus Empiricus, repeated in both his *Outlines of Pyrrhonism* (3.25) and *Against the Professors* (Book 11, also known as *Against the Ethicists*). However, the idea was clearly in circulation much earlier as numerous references in the works of Cicero attest. Indeed, it is in Cicero that we find an account of the way in which the Stoics took up Socrates' analogy between philosophy and medicine (*Tusc.* 3.1-21) and it has been suggested that Cicero's discussion draws directly on the works of Chrysippus.[19] We have further, explicit evidence for the claim that Chrysippus took up the Socratic analogy in Galen's *On the Doctrines of Hippocrates and Plato*, who reports that for Chrysippus philosophy is an art concerned with curing the diseased soul and that the philosopher is the physician of the soul (*PHP* 5.2.22-3). The idea of taking care of one's soul is of course also a central theme in the *Meditations* because, as Marcus puts it, "those who fail to attend to the motions of their own soul are necessarily unhappy" (2.8).

For the Stoics, then, philosophy was conceived as an art analogous to the art of medicine and, like medicine and other arts and crafts, mastery of philosophy conceived as an art will involve an education in two stages. While the first stage will be devoted to understanding the theoretical principles underpinning the art, the second stage will involve a period of training or exercise devoted to the assimilation and mastery of those principles. Thus, it will not be enough merely to grasp complex philosophical ideas in the classroom; one must also engage in a period of training in order to digest those principles so that one is ready to put them into practice. The point behind this is forcefully put by Epictetus when he laments that although many of his Stoic students will be able to express eloquently the central doctrines of the Stoic Chrysippus, few will be able to display those same doctrines in their behaviour (*Diss.* 2.19.20-5). He predicts that most will in fact turn out to be Epicureans, with perhaps a few feeble Peripatetics, but he doubts he will find any Stoics among these students who are nevertheless perfectly able to recite Stoic doctrine. Theoretical understanding on its own is not enough.

Epictetus's students read treatises by Chrysippus and presumably works by other canonical Stoic authors as well. These texts, so far as we can know, probably met many of our expectations about what a philosophical text should contain: the presentation of key doctrines supported by argument, perhaps responding to objections raised by others or responding to alternative views articulated in the works of earlier philosophers.

The *Meditations* clearly do not fall into this genre of philosophical writing. Indeed, at first glance the *Meditations* do not look much like what we usually think of as a philosophical text. What we encounter is a notebook containing private thoughts and reflections, along with a few quotations copied from other authors, with no immediately obvious structure or chain of reasoning, often repeating similar ideas across its different books. Via the quotations and other passing references we do find mention of a number of earlier philosophers, but their views are not subjected to any critical analysis or sustained commentary.

Although the *Meditations* might not take the form of a philosophical treatise that does not automatically mean it is not a serious philosophical text. If theoretical treatises correspond only to one half of the sort of philosophical education outlined above, there may well be other forms of philosophical writing associated with the second half. The *Meditations* look like a good candidate for an example of a text devoted to this second stage.

Assimilation and digestion

What exactly will this second stage of philosophical education involve? Seneca, Epictetus, and Marcus himself all offer some helpful analogies. For Seneca and Epictetus the preferred analogy is with digestion. Seneca suggests (*Ep.* 2.2-4) that in order to digest properly the ideas of an author one must read slowly and one ought not to jump too quickly from one author to another. If one is too greedy or has too varied or rich a diet one runs the risk of vomiting the whole lot up and failing to digest anything at all. Epictetus pursues this unsavoury image by comparing the hasty discourses of his students to vomit (*Diss.* 3.21.1-4), in which they throw up philosophical ideas out of their mouths before they have had the opportunity to digest them properly. If they had digested them properly then those same doctrines would not come back out of their mouths but rather would be expressed in their actions. Epictetus illustrates this with more palatable example:

> Do not, for most part, talk among people about your philosophical principles, but do what follows from your principles […] for sheep do not bring their fodder to the shepherds and show how much they have eaten, but they digest their food within them and on the outside produce wool and milk. And so you, therefore, make no display to people of your philosophical principles but let them see the results that come from the principles when digested.
>
> *Ench. 46*

Marcus himself takes up this theme, with a different analogy, probably borrowed from Seneca.[20] As we saw earlier in 3.4, he suggests that we should dye our souls in a manner akin to the way in which we might dye a piece of cloth a new colour. Our aim is to become "dyed to the core with justice" as he put it, and in order to produce such a complete transformation we shall need to repeat the process again and again. The more we think or reflect on a particular idea, the more that idea will become a permanent feature of our mind, just as a piece of cloth will permanently bear the colour of a dye the more it is exposed to it:

> As are your repeated impressions so will your mind be, for the soul is dyed by its impressions. Dye it, then, in a succession of impressions like these: for instance, where it

is possible to live, there also it is possible to live well: but it is possible to live in a palace, therefore it is also possible to live well in a palace.

5.16

Here we have an explicit philosophical explanation for the repetition of certain key ideas again and again in the *Meditations*. While this feature of the text has often been explained away as an unfortunate consequence of this being a private text never properly edited or prepared for wider circulation, we can now see that far from being a structural or stylistic fault, this may well be an essential and necessary characteristic of the text. If what Marcus was trying to do when writing in his notebooks was dye his soul by repeatedly reflecting upon key ideas, then it is inevitable that the text should be marked by repetition. Without the repetition Marcus would not be able to complete the task at hand. As Galen put it, when discussing the nature of the exercise (*askêsis*) involved in becoming a good human being, "in matters of the greatest importance, there is no harm in repeating the same things twice or even three times" (*Aff. Pecc. Dig.* 1.5.1).[21] And in his treatise on character, lost in Greek but preserved in the Arabic tradition (*Mor.*), Galen writes "a character is developed through being constantly accustomed to things that man sets up in his soul and to things that he does regularly every day".[22]

Spiritual exercises

So far we have seen that the *Meditations* ought to be approached as a private notebook in which Marcus tries to remind himself of key philosophical principles. This practice presupposed a conception of philosophy as an art of living and it formed a second stage in philosophical training, aimed at digesting and assimilating key principles. This second stage might be described as a process of training or exercise (*askêsis*), and earlier we saw Galen do just this. Famously, Pierre Hadot called this sort of training a "spiritual exercise" and he went to develop an interpretation of Marcus Aurelius shaped by the claim that the *Meditations* is in effect an extended spiritual exercise.[23] Hadot borrowed the phrase "spiritual exercise" from Ignatius of Loyola,[24] but the word "spiritual" has unsettled a number of commentators who have been concerned that it obscures the fundamentally rational nature of philosophy.[25] Despite those concerns, both the phrase and the sorts of practices it refers to have ancient precedent. This can be seen most clearly in one of the *Discourses* of Musonius Rufus, whose lectures in Rome were attended by, among others, Epictetus. Notes from those lectures were recorded by Musonius's student Lucius and the notes from one of those lectures have come down to us under the title *On Exercise* (*Peri askêseôs*).[26]

Musonius's interest in exercise (*askêsis*) stems from his conviction that philosophy is not merely a theoretical discourse but, fundamentally, an activity aimed at transforming one's life. The study of virtue, he suggests, ought to be conceived as something akin to the study of medicine or music, namely something we study in order to gain a practical skill.[27] Like a student of medicine or music, "a man who wishes to become good not only must be thoroughly familiar with the precepts which are conductive to virtue but must also be earnest and zealous in applying these principles".[28] This is where exercise comes in: first, one studies the principles or precepts (*mathêmata*); then one undertakes a period of training or exercise (*askêsis*), as we saw earlier.[29] Musonius goes on to claim that this period of exercise is more important for the student of philosophy than it is for the student of any other art or craft in so far as philosophy is the most difficult discipline to master.[30] By philosophy he means the task of becoming a good, virtuous person.

What form should this exercise take? Musonius notes that because human beings are comprised of both body and soul it will be necessary to undertake exercises appropriate to both. It is at this point that Musonius introduces the idea of what he calls *askêsis tês psuchês*, which we might translate as "exercise of the soul", "mental training", or, indeed, "spiritual exercise". We might expect this to be contrasted with a fairly straightforward notion of physical exercise but instead Musonius proposes a composite form of training: "there are two kinds of training, one which is appropriate for the soul alone, and the other which is common to both soul and body".[31] This second type of training works on both the body and the soul at once and includes things like avoiding physical pleasures, testing oneself in extremes of cold and heat, training to cope with thirst and hunger, and practising endurance in the face of suffering. These sorts of practices benefit the body and soul at once. But what of purely spiritual exercises? These work on the soul alone and, although Musonius thinks both types of exercise are essential for anyone who aspires to become a good human being, these spiritual exercises are, he suggests, fundamental to philosophy. Musonius gives us an extended definition of what these spiritual exercises involve:

> Training which is peculiar to the soul consists first of all in seeing that the proofs pertaining to apparent goods as not being real goods are always ready at hand and likewise those pertaining to apparent evils as not being real evils, and in learning to recognize the things which are truly good and in becoming accustomed to distinguish them from what are not truly good. In the next place it consists of practice in not avoiding any of the things which only seem evil, and in not pursuing any of the things which only seem good; in shunning by every means those which are truly evil and in pursuing by every means those which are truly good.[32]

The central task of spiritual exercises, then, is to keep philosophical principles (in this case, Stoic principles regarding what is and is not good) "ready to hand" (*procheiros*).[33] In so doing one will be better placed to become accustomed (*ethizesthai*) to acting in accordance with those principles. It will also involve the practice (*meletê*) of actions that embody those principles. In short, spiritual exercises offer the training necessary to transform oneself according to a set of philosophical ideas so that one consistently lives according to those ideas.

Musonius does not mention any sources for his account, although we might note that the distinction between mental and physical/mental exercises had been made well before by Diogenes of Sinope, who was eulogized at length by Musonius's pupil Epictetus.[34] We shall come back to this Cynic ancestry later. It is striking, though, that Musonius makes no mention of his near contemporary in Rome, Seneca. Yet Seneca also engaged in spiritual exercises and he tells us that this was a practice he learned from someone called Sextius:

> All our senses must be toughened: they have a natural endurance, once the mind has ceased to corrupt them; and the mind must be called to account every day. This was Sextius's practice: when the day was spent and he had retired to his night's rest, he asked his mind, 'Which of your ills did you heal today? Which vice did you resist? In what aspect are you better? Your anger will cease and become more controllable if it knows that every day it must come before a judge. […] I exercise this jurisdiction daily and

plead my case before myself. When the light has been removed and my wife has fallen silent, aware of this habit that's now mine, I examine my entire day and go back over what I've done and said, hiding nothing from myself, passing nothing by.

Ira 3.36.1-3

This is an example of keeping one's guiding precepts "ready to hand" and it also pre-empts the practice of self-dialogue that Marcus engaged in when writing the *Meditations*. The Sextius mentioned by Seneca is Quintus Sextius, founder of a philosophical school in Rome where two of Seneca's own teachers, Fabianus and Sotion, had studied.[35] The practice of daily self-examination that Seneca recounts and attributes to Sextius appears to have been Pythagorean in origin and it is described in the Pythagorean *Golden Verses*:

Do not welcome sleep upon your soft eyes
before you have reviewed each of the day's deeds three times:
'Where have I transgressed? What have I accomplished? What duty have I neglected?'
Beginning from the first one go through them in detail, and then,
If you have brought about worthless things, reprimand yourself, but if you have
    achieved good things, be glad.

Carm. Aur. 40-44[36]

As well as recommending this practice of evening self-examination, the *Golden Verses* also describe a series of mental and physical/mental exercises of the sort outlined by Musonius, exhorting the reader to become accustomed (*ethizesthai*) to acting in accordance with a series of moral precepts.[37]

A number of scholars have suggested that the *Golden Verses* is a relatively late text, perhaps dating from the Imperial Period.[38] However, as Thom has pointed out, there is evidence to suggest that the text is earlier than that and that it was known to early Stoics such as Cleanthes and Chrysippus, both of whom draw on it.[39] If the early Stoics did know this relatively short text then no doubt they would have been familiar with its recommendation of this spiritual exercise.

As well as appealing to these Pythagorean practices, Seneca also comments with approval on Cynic exercises. According to Seneca, Demetrius the Cynic held that it was far better to have just a few philosophical doctrines (*praecepta sapientiae*) ready to use than many of no practical purpose and so, like a wrestler, one ought to be carefully trained (*diligenter exercuit*) in just a handful of essential skills (*Ben.* 7.1.3-4). The beginning philosopher, says Demetrius, must make those few, essential doctrines "a part of himself, and by practising them daily (*cotidiana meditatione*) to get to the point that healthy thoughts come of their own accord" (*Ben.* 7.2.1).

We can see connections, then, between later Roman Stoic accounts of spiritual exercises by Musonius and Seneca on the one hand, and earlier Pythagorean and Cynic traditions of mental training on the other. Although it is difficult to be sure given the fragmentary nature of the evidence, the presence of both Pythagorean and Cynic influences on the early Stoics makes it not unreasonable to suppose that they too may have been concerned with spiritual exercises as an important part of philosophical education.[40] We do know that some early Stoics wrote books devoted to the topic of *askêsis*, notably Herillus and Dionysius (Diog. Laert. 7.166-7). If this is right then the concern with spiritual exercises that we find in Roman Stoics such as Musonius Rufus, Seneca, and Marcus Aurelius was not a late innovation but rather a theme running through Stoicism from the outset.

Spiritual exercises in the Meditations

While we find descriptions of spiritual exercises in a number of ancient texts, the *Meditations* stands out as a text that is itself an extended spiritual exercise. What we find is Marcus engaging in the sort of self-dialogue proposed in the *Golden Verses* and taken up by Sextius and Seneca. Rather than merely mentally rehearsing the difficulties of everyday life, Marcus's mode of self-dialogue involves writing his thought processes down. It may well be that others produced these sorts of written exercises as well, but the *Meditations* is unique as the only example of such writing to come down to us. In this sense the *Meditations* taken as a whole is an example of a series of written spiritual exercises. There are various features of the text that support this, such as the repetition of phrases like "always remember",[41] and it also helps to explain the lack of structure and the repetition of topics. Indeed, the repetitive character of the text, once judged a stylistic weakness, can now be seen as an essential feature of the work.[42]

As well as being able to consider the *Meditations* as a whole as a form of spiritual exercise, it is also possible to pick out a number of specific exercises in the text. Putting aside Book 1,[43] the *Meditations* open proper with the first chapter of Book 2, which begins: "Say to yourself in the early morning: I shall meet today inquisitive, ungrateful, violent, treacherous, envious, uncharitable men" (2.1; see also 5.1, 10.13). This mental rehearsal of potentially unpleasant events to come is an example of the premeditation of future evils, something that we saw earlier in Galen. This was a common theme in Hellenistic philosophy and discussed at length by Cicero, who reports that Chrysippus had made use of this technique.[44] Cicero notes that Chrysippus held the view that "what is unforeseen strikes us with greater force" than what we have already rehearsed in our minds (*Tusc.* 3.52). Although, as Cicero makes plain, the technique was not original to the Stoics, it was an established Stoic practice long before Marcus took it up in the *Meditations*.[45]

In Marcus's version here, he responds to his opening rehearsal of the difficulties he might expect to encounter in the coming day by reminding himself of a number of key Stoic doctrines that ought to inform his response. He opens with the thought that the behaviour of the unpleasant people he might encounter is ultimately the product of their ignorance (*agnoia*), and so not deliberate on their part. Marcus himself, however, is not ignorant of how he ought to behave so he has no justification to respond in kind. On the contrary, he knows that he and these others share the same nature and that all share in a divine nature, and so, no matter how they behave, he ought to treat them as kinsmen (*suggenês*). Using an analogy with parts of a single organism, Marcus suggests that to work against other people is to act contrary to Nature (*para phusin*), and he concludes by saying that to respond to the negative emotions of others with negative emotions of one's own would also be against Nature.

As we can see, Marcus is implicitly drawing on a range of Stoic ideas in a way that highlights the interconnectedness of the Stoic system. He appeals to: (i) central ideas in Stoic physics, to give him the resources (ii) to avoid jumping to rash judgements that might generate negative emotions, which will in turn mean that he can (iii) act towards those whom he meets in the ethically appropriate way. In particular, he presupposes a number of Stoic claims: that only virtue is good, that emotions are the product of errors in judgement, and that all humans are part of a single, rational community. By pre-rehearsing encounters with the worst sorts of people he might meet and reminding himself of both the appropriate way to behave in response and the philosophical principles that underpin that response, Marcus is training himself not to rush into making negative judgements about unpleasant people that would, in turn, generate negative emotions, lead to inappropriate behaviour, and, ultimately, compromise the integrity of his character and the rationality of his soul. This early morning reflection on the day ahead compliments the evening review of the day described by Seneca and both offer very practical examples of philosophical training in action.

Another specific exercise we find in the *Meditations* is often called "the view from above".[46] There are a number of examples throughout the text,[47] of which here is just one representative example:

> Watch and see the courses of the stars as if you ran with them, and continually dwell in mind upon the changes of the elements into one another; for these imaginations wash away the foulness of life on the ground. Moreover, when discoursing about mankind, look upon earthly things below as if from some place above them – herds, armies, farms, weddings, divorces, births, deaths, noise of law courts, lonely places, divers foreign nations, festivals, mournings, market places, a mixture of everything and an order composed of contraries.
>
> 7.47-8[48]

This passage and others like it appear to be doing a number of things at once. First, there is a meditation on universal flux and the impermanence of all things, designed to offer consolation for loss of various kinds and ultimately consolation for death. Second, there is an attempt to see Nature as a whole and to grasp it as a single interconnected system. Third there is an effort to put into a much wider context everyday human cares and concerns in order to minimize their significance.[49] This goes hand in hand with offering a series of dispassionate, physical descriptions of things that are often taken to be very important in everyday human life, again in order to downplay their significance. Thus, for example countries, over which wars are fought, are merely lumps of mud around a pond (6.36). This single mental exercise of viewing things from above does, then, a number of things at once, implicitly appealing to a range of claims from Stoic physics along the way. The frequency with which Marcus repeats or alludes to this vision from above in the *Meditations* highlights the significance he attached to it. In one passage, 12.24, he includes it among three things that he must keep "ready to hand" (*procheiros*), confirming its central place in his repertoire of spiritual exercises.

Marcus's reflections on "the view from above" also form an example of the way in which many of his spiritual exercises ultimately depend on doctrines in physics and, although his aim is entirely practical, it is potentially misleading to characterize his exercises as merely practical ethics, if that is taken to mean the practical application of ethical principles. In the *Meditations* it is the practical application of logical and physical doctrines that recur again and again.[50] In one particularly striking passage, Marcus reflects on the contrast between seeing objects from a purely physical perspective and seeing them overlaid with cultural significance:

> Surely it is an excellent plan, when you are seated before delicacies and choice foods, to grasp the impression that this is the dead body of a fish, that the dead body of a bird or a pig; and again, that the Falernian wine is grape juice and that robe of purple a lamb's fleece dipped in a shell-fish's blood [...]. Surely these are excellent impressions

(*phantasiai*), going to the heart of actual facts (*pragmata*) and penetrating them so as to see the kind of things they really are.

6.13

Elsewhere, Marcus offers a description of this technique of describing objects from a physical perspective, a technique clearly aimed at undermining excessive attributions of value to such things:

> Always make a figure or outline of the imagined object as it occurs, in order to see distinctly what it is in its essence (*kat' ousia*), naked, as a whole and parts; and say to yourself its individual name and the names of the things of which it was compounded and into which it will be broken up. For nothing is so able to create greatness of mind as the power methodically and truthfully to test each thing that meets one in life, and always to look upon it so as to attend at the same time to the use which this particular thing contributes to a Universe of a certain definite kind, what value it has in reference to the Whole, and what to man [...].
>
> *3.11*

This technique of physical description has the virtue not only of ensuring that objects are valued correctly but also of enabling one to grasp objects as they are in themselves, which is an important end in itself. Many of the spiritual exercises we find in the *Meditations*, including "the view from above", employ this kind of physical perspective on the world, both for its own sake and for its therapeutic benefits.[51]

Summing up

In this chapter we have considered what sort of text the *Meditations* is and what Marcus was trying to achieve in writing it. In order to do this we have considered the wider context of Stoic thinking about practical exercises in Seneca, Musonius, and Epictetus, while also touching on Pythagorean, Socratic, and Cynic ideas predating the Roman Stoics.[52] Yet it is worth stressing that these practical exercises come *after* the study of philosophical theories, upon which they are grounded. Philosophy remains an activity devoted to rational inquiry into what exists and what has value. The point that Musonius Rufus insisted upon is that the study of, say, virtue ought to be not merely for the sake of being able to supply a definition of virtue but ultimately for the sake of becoming a virtuous person.[53] In this he was at one with Socrates. Spiritual exercises to do not challenge or replace the sort of rational inquiry usually identified with philosophy; they supplement it. As we have seen, in the *Meditations* Marcus refers to philosophy as an art which, following Musonius and Epictetus, may be best understood as a two-stage process. First one studies philosophical theory and only after that does one undertake the exercises necessary to digest that information and so transform one's behaviour. Spiritual exercises are the practical training that forms just one part of philosophy conceived as an art of living.

As a book of such exercises, it is important also to remember that Marcus's *Meditations* is an idiosyncratic and partial book. It comprises a series of spiritual exercises about topics that were of particular importance to him at the time he was writing. It does not pretend to offer a complete or comprehensive account of all the possible spiritual exercises a Stoic philosopher might deploy, much less the theoretical principles upon which those exercises are grounded. In so far as these exercises are designed to put philosophy to work in order to overcome some of Marcus's personal problems, it inevitably focuses on a range of negative issues in his own life. These ought not to be taken as a complete account of either Marcus's outlook on life or his conception of Stoicism. Indeed, it would be a mistake for detractors or admirers to think that the *Meditations* straightforwardly presents us with Marcus's own version of Stoic philosophy. The philosophical precepts, doctrines, and arguments upon which Marcus's spiritual exercises depend remain on the whole unstated.[54] The task of the rest of this book is to try to unpack, so far as is possible, the philosophical views standing behind Marcus's notes to himself.

Notes

1 On the distinctive character of Book 1 see Rutherford (1989: 48–125), Hadot and Luna (1998: xli–clxxxiii), Gourinat (2012a: 318–20), Gill (2013: lxxv–lxxxiv).
2 See further Gourinat (2012a: 320–30). I do not subscribe to Hadot's view (1998: 232) that the *Meditations* is "organized in accordance with a threefold structure", namely the three *topoi* outlined by Epictetus (*Diss.* 3.2.1-2).
3 On the *Meditations* and self-dialogue see Ackeren (2011: I, 206–87).
4 See Casaubon (1634), who went on to publish an edition of the Greek text in 1643.
5 Casaubon prints the title as *tôn eis heauton* at the beginning of his "Notes Upon Antoninus" in Casaubon (1634).
6 One odd case is the translation by John Jackson which was issued simultaneously by Oxford University Press in 1906 under the titles *Thoughts* (in "The World's Classics") and *Meditations* (in the "Oxford Translation Series"). See Jackson (1906a and 1906b).
7 For titles of translations up to 1908 see Wickham Legg (1910).
8 The title is recorded in the *editio princeps*, which was based on the now lost Palatine manuscript (on which see Ceporina 2012: 55–6). Many have assumed that the title was taken over from the manuscript, although Ceporina (2012: 47) suggests that it may have been added by Xylander (however, see the next note). When translated into Latin it is usually, though not universally, rendered literally as *ad se ipsum*.
9 The title is first mentioned by Arethas of Caesarea (*c.* 850–935), *Schol. in Lucianum* 207,6-7 Rabe, quoted in Farquharson (1944: I, 158). An earlier mention of the text by Themistius, *Or.* 6.81c (dated 364; see Farquharson 1944: I, xv) does not use the title but instead calls the work *Precepts* or *Admonitions* (*paraggelmata*). In the *Meditations* Marcus refers to his own writings as *hupomnêmatia* (little notes), at 3.14.
10 For commentary on 4.3, see Farquharson (1944: I, 309–11), Gill (2013: 120–22). Brunt (1974: 3) says of this passage "Here surely is the key to the *Meditations*".
11 It is worth noting that these two fundamental principles that Marcus thinks he ought to keep ready to hand are not ethical principles relating to conduct. Instead one is logical (conceived broadly), the other physical. Marcus *is* interested in logic and physics – not logical and physical theory, but rather living in accord with a series of logical and physical claims central to Stoicism (*contra* Roskam 2012: 94–5). In 4.3, as a whole he shows us how reflecting on doctrines in Stoic epistemology and physics might contribute to the cultivation of a mind at complete ease and in good order.
12 Distress (*lupê*) is one of the four principal types of emotion (*pathê*) the Stoics sought to avoid. It is, on their account, a belief (or the product of a belief) in a present evil. See for example Diog. Laert. 7.110-11; Cicero, *Tusc.* 3.24-5 (*SVF* 3.385), 4.14 (*SVF* 3.393) where it is rendered into Latin as *aegritudo*, with discussion in Sorabji (2000: 29–32).
13 On Epictetus's admiration for Socrates and his debts to the early Socratic dialogues of Plato, see Long (2002) and Jagu (1946), respectively.
14 On this point I differ from the views in Bonhöffer (1894: 147) and Sorabji (2000: 13, 252).

15 Cf. Farquharson (1944: II, 860).
16 For a fuller discussion of the idea of an art of living, with further references, see Sellars (2003).
17 For a full list of ancient references see Sellars (2003: 5).
18 See Cicero, *Acad.* 2.23; *Fin.* 1.42, 1.72, 3.4, 4.19, 5.16, 5.18; *Tusc.* 2.12; Seneca, *Ep.* 95.7–9.
19 See further Sellars (2003, 64–5).
20 See Seneca, *Ep.* 71.31, with Newman (1989: 1507).
21 See De Boer (1937: 15,16–18) and Singer (2013: 256).
22 This is his *Peri êthôn* (*De moribus*) 31 Kr., translated in Mattock (1972: 241) and Singer (2013: 144).
23 On Marcus and spiritual exercises, see Hadot (1972). The idea is examined more widely in Hadot (1977) and both are reprinted in Hadot (1993).
24 See Hadot (1977), citing Rabbow (1954), with discussion in Sellars (2003: 110–18).
25 See for example Cooper (2012: 402).
26 The text is preserved in Stob. 3,648–51 and excerpted in Hense (1905: 22–7). The title may well have been added by Stobaeus. It is translated in Lutz (1947: 53–57). For discussion of this passage see Geytenbeek (1963: 40–50).
27 See Musonius Rufus 6 (Hense 1905: 22,7-9).
28 Musonius Rufus 6 (Hense 1905: 23,1-3).
29 Musonius Rufus 6 (Hense 1905: 23,14-16).
30 See Musonius Rufus 6 (Hense 1905: 23,17–24,1). He explains why this is the case: "men who enter the other professions have not had their souls corrupted beforehand […] but the ones who start out to study philosophy have been born and reared in an environment filled with corruption and evil, and therefore turn to virtue in such a state that they need a longer and more thorough training".
31 Musonius Rufus 6 (Hense 1905: 25,4-6).
32 Musonius Rufus 6 (Hense 1905: 25,14–26,5).
33 The topic of keeping principles *procheiros* recurs throughout the works of Musonius's pupil Epictetus (see e.g., the titles of *Diss.* 1.27 and 1.30) and is echoed in the title of Epictetus's *Encheiridion* compiled by Arrian (a connection noted by Simplicius, *in Ench.* Praef. 18-20 Hadot).
34 See Diog. Laert. 6.70, with Goulet-Cazé (1986: 195–222). Diogenes draws a distinction between mental and physical exercises but goes on to suggest, like Musonius, that physical exercises also benefit the soul. For Epictetus on Cynicism see *Diss.* 3.22.
35 On the school of Sextius see Lana (1992); on Seneca's teachers see Sellars (2014: 99–102).
36 As Thom notes (1995: 37), these lines are quoted or alluded to by a wide range of ancient philosophical authors, including Cicero (citing Cato the Elder as his source), Seneca, Plutarch, Epictetus, Galen, Porphyry, and Diogenes Laertius.
37 See for example, *Carm. Aur.* 9, 14, 35.
38 Thom (1995) suggests that Nauck's proposal of the fourth century AD is the *opinio communionis*.
39 See Thom (2001) elaborating on points first made in Thom (1995). For Chrysippus compare Aulus Gellius, *NA* 7.2.12 (*SVF* 2.1000) with *Carm. Aur.* 54, and for Cleanthes compare *Hymn to Zeus* 23-5 (*SVF* 1.537) with *Carm. Aur.* 55-6.
40 See in particular the previously unpublished essay "Chrysippus on Practical Morality" in Brunt (2013: 10–27). Brunt suggests that Chrysippus may have shared more in common with Epictetus than is usually supposed, and that "by systematically omitting homiletic material von Arnim induces a false conception of old Stoic morality" (11).
41 Brunt (1974: 3) (repr. in Brunt 2013: 365) notes that phrases such as "always remember" (*memnêso aei*) are repeated some 40 times; see the Index Verborum in Schenkl (1913) s.v. *memnêsthai, memnêso* to which Brunt refers, and Rigo (2010: 129) who lists 46 instances s.v. *mimnêskô*.
42 See further Giavatto (2012a: 339–42).
43 Some have suggested that Book 1 was composed separately from the rest of the work. It is far more coherent and structured than the subsequent books. Even so, a case can be made for treating it too as an example of spiritual exercise. See further Gill (2013: lxxv–lxxvii).

44 See Cicero, *Tusc.* 3.29. For the mention of Chrysippus, see *Tusc.* 3.52 (*SVF* 3.417). For further discussion see Newman (1989: 1477–78). On its prehistory see Hadot (1969: 60–2) referring to Pythagorean practices described in Iamblichus, *Vita Pythagorae* 196 (DK 58D6).
45 See for example Seneca *Ep.* 78.29, 91.3-4; *Vit. Beat.* 26.1. For further discussion, see Newman (1989), who contrasts Stoic *meditatio* with earlier versions.
46 See for example Hadot (1995: 238–50) discussing Marcus Aurelius alongside a wide range of other thinkers, and also Rutherford (1989: 155–61) focusing on parallels with earlier ancient literature. For this phrase in Marcus, see 9.30.
47 As well as 7.47-48 quoted below, see for example 3.10, 5.24, 6.36, 9.30, 9.32, 10.15, 11.1, 12.24.
48 In modern editions this passage is divided into two chapters but this dates back only to Gataker (1652). In the earlier edition by Casaubon (1643), they are printed as a single chapter, "7.27". There are no chapter divisions in the Greek text printed in Xylander (1559), although his Latin translation is divided into unnumbered paragraphs, where he prints 7.47-49 as a single paragraph. The earliest edition containing chapter divisions is Sally (1626).
49 In a number of passages (e.g., 3.10, 5.24, 6.36, 9.30, 9.32), human life is put into a wider temporal as well as spatial context.
50 Compare with the different view of Roskam (2012: 94–5).
51 For further discussion of this kind of physical description see esp. Hadot (1972), but note also Hadot (1998: 104–5) and Gill (2013: xl–xliv).
52 In this context, it is interesting to note that Marcus mentions Pythagoras, Socrates, and Diogenes the Cynic as role models at various places in the *Meditations*; see for example 6.47, 7.19, 8.3.
53 The same point is made throughout Epictetus; see for example *Diss.* 2.19, 3.21.
54 A similar view is expressed in Brunt (2013: 447).

PART II
Logic

3
IMPRESSIONS AND JUDGEMENTS

Marcus and logic

It is not uncommon to see the *Meditations* described as a work of practical ethics.[1] This is hardly surprising given the focus on techniques of self-transformation of the sort we have considered in the last chapter. Yet there is much in the *Meditations* that goes beyond the confines of ethics.[2] In this chapter and a number that follow we shall consider a range of themes that naturally fall under the headings of logic and physics. Ethics, physics, and logic were, of course, the three central parts of philosophy according to the Stoics.[3] At first glance, Marcus does not seem to have any interest in the logical part of Stoic philosophy; at least this is how it has seemed to a number of commentators.[4] In part this is because there are only a few places where he explicitly makes reference to logic as a subject. In one of these, 1.17[22], he expresses relief that he has not wasted time on syllogisms, while in another, 8.1, he reminds himself that he will not find the good life that he is seeking through the study of syllogisms. Yet these seemingly negative judgements are balanced by another passage, 7.67, where he expresses regret that he never managed to master dialectic. He was clearly not uninformed about the subject, though, as Fronto makes plain in one of his letters. There, Fronto notes Marcus's interest in logical problems such as horn dilemmas, heap fallacies, and the liar paradox (*De eloqu.* 2.13).[5] It is unclear whether this was just something that Marcus studied in his youth or if he retained this interest into later life.[6] Either way, there is little trace of any interest in that sort of thing in the *Meditations* which, as we have seen, is a very specific kind of text with a very different purpose.

In one passage that has confused some commentators,[7] Marcus says the following:

> Continually and, if possible, on the occasion of every impression (*phantasia*), test it by natural science (*phusiologein*), by psychology (*pathologein*),[8] by dialectic (*dialektikeuesthai*).
> *8.13*

This has sometimes been taken to be a clear reference to the Stoic division of philosophy into physics, ethics, and logic.[9] Indeed, the terms Marcus uses have sometimes been translated as "physics, ethics, logic" (e.g. Hays 2003: 103). But what does Marcus mean by it? Does he actually do anything approaching this in the *Meditations*? Before tackling those questions directly, it may be useful to say something about what the Stoics took the term "logic" (*logikê*) to cover.

Stoic logic

According to the account in Diogenes Laertius, Stoic logic was usually divided into the two branches of rhetoric and dialectic, with some adding further parts dealing with definitions and criteria (Diog. Laert 7.41). The Stoics, who seem to have relished detailed taxonomies, divided rhetoric and dialectic further into subsections. They divided rhetoric into deliberative, forensic, and panegyric, and dialectic into "what is signified and what is uttered" (ibid. 7.43).[10] Within what is signified fall impressions, sayables, propositions, and arguments, including the sorts of paradoxes and fallacies that, according to Fronto, had occupied Marcus's attention (ibid. 7.43-4). One striking element of Diogenes' summary is his report that the Stoics regarded dialectic as a virtue and a skill essential for a sage (ibid. 7.46-7).[11] As Diogenes puts it, overhastiness in assertion can lead one to fall into unseemly conduct.

This view was not restricted to the early Stoa and later Epictetus also insisted on the necessity of the study of logic.[12] Indeed, Epictetus is an interesting case in the present context because, like Marcus, he both warns against the dangers of being distracted by logical problems while at the same time insisting on the necessity of logic. To someone who says they want to learn about Chrysippus's work on the liar paradox, Epictetus replies "Go hang, you wretch! What good with knowing that do you?" (*Diss*. 2.17.34). Elsewhere he comments that there is nothing to prevent someone from "analysing syllogisms like Chrysippus, and yet being wretched, sorrowing, envying, disturbed, miserable" (*Diss*. 2.23.44). This is clearly in line with Marcus's comments on the futility of wasting time with syllogisms (1.17[22], 8.1). Despite these excessively harsh judgements, elsewhere Epictetus emphatically insists on the importance of logic. It supplies a standard of judgement against which the claims of others can be assessed, and this is an essential skill acknowledged not only by Stoics such as Zeno and Chrysippus but also by Antisthenes and Socrates (*Diss*. 1.17.1-12).[13] Many people, he notes elsewhere, do not realize that the study of arguments is essential for knowing how to live well (*Diss*. 1.7.1). To the interlocutor who says that making a logical error is unimportant compared to, say, acting unjustly, Epictetus recounts being rebuked by Musonius Rufus for saying just this at one of Musonius's lectures (*Diss*. 1.7.32; Musonius Rufus 44). By error in logic Epictetus says he means, among other things, failing to follow an argument, falling into inconsistency, and making poor use of impressions (*phantasiai*).[14] Attention to such things is, according to Epictetus, essential for anyone who is trying to learn how to live well.

Marcus is by no means neglectful of such things in the *Meditations*. As Giavatto has noted, there is a wide variety of argument forms throughout the text, including *modus ponens*, sorites, and disjunction (2012b: 415-18).[15] Indeed, there are probably far more arguments in the *Meditations* than readers might initially suppose.[16] Here is just one example:

> If mind is common to us all, then also the reason, whereby we are reasoning beings, is common. If this be so, then also the reason which enjoins what is to be done or left undone is common. If this be so, law also is common; if this be so, we are citizens; if this be so, we are partakers in one constitution; if this be so, the cosmos is a kind of state (*polis*).
>
> *4.4*

Although Marcus, like Epictetus, had no time for logical puzzles for their own sake, he certainly grasped and indeed made use of logical reasoning, even lamenting that he did not make further progress in this part of Stoic philosophy (7.67). Marcus's claim not to be a dialectician might be put into further context by noting that Alexander of Aphrodisias – writing perhaps just a few decades after Marcus – reported that the Stoics claimed that only a sage will be a real dialectician (*in Top.* 1,8-14). With that in mind, it is unsurprising that Marcus would resist claiming expertise in this part of philosophy.

Introducing impressions

As we saw earlier, Epictetus took the correct use of impressions (*phantasiai*) to be one of the things made possible by a proper grasp of logic. According to the summary of Stoicism by Diocles of Magnesia – a key source for Diogenes Laertius – the Stoic account of dialectic begins with their doctrine of impressions. Impressions are the foundation for everything else: "impression arises first; then thought, which is capable of discourse, articulates the subject's response to the impression" (Diog. Laert. 7.49). Marcus spent a lot of time thinking about the nature of impressions. In order to get a better sense of why he took them to be so important, we need to say a bit about the concept in general and the way in which it was used in the early Stoa. As we shall see, Marcus used the term quite differently to some of his Stoic predecessors.

In translations of Marcus Aurelius' *Meditations* into English, the term *phantasia* is often rendered by a number of different English words – including "impression", "conception", "imagination", "thought", "image", and "representation" – in part depending on the context in which it appears. In fact, all these different renderings can be found in just one translation (Farquharson 1944), obscuring the fact that a single term is being used in a variety of different contexts. Wider literature on Stoicism has also rendered *phantasia* as "appearance" and "presentation". What all these English words share is that they all refer to something mental, namely, something that is in the mind and is distinct from the external world. Some of these words suggest a mental item that is produced by and reflects accurately some feature of the external world, while others suggest a mental item produced by the mind itself. This variety of English translations for *phantasia* reflects the way in which the term can refer quite broadly to an impression that is either generated by something outside the mind or generated by the mind itself.

Marcus seems to use the word *phantasia*, or "impression", to refer to mental items in this broad way, generated either by something external to the mind or by the mind itself. That is why translators have sometimes felt the need to translate it as "imagination". In this he differs from some of his Stoic predecessors. Chrysippus, for instance, distinguished between impression (*phantasia*) and imagination (*phantastikon*). Our source, Aetius, says:

> An impression (*phantasia*) is an affection occurring in the soul, which reveals itself and its cause. Thus, when through sight we observe something white, the affection is what is engendered in the soul through vision; and it is this affection which enables us to say that there is a white object which activates us. [...] Imagination (*phantastikon*) is an empty attraction, an affection in the soul which arises from no impressor, as when someone shadow-boxes or strikes his hands against thin air; for an impression has some impressor as its object, but imagination has none.
>
> *Aetius 4.12.1-5, SVF 2.54, LS 39B*

In early Stoic sources, as Long and Sedley note (1987: I, 240), it is common to affirm the usual reliability of impressions. In normal conditions and for the most part, all other things being equal, we can trust and rely upon our impressions, which are the source of our knowledge of the external world. In Marcus, however, we find a quite different attitude. By using the notion of impression to cover mental items both externally generated and internally generated, his attitude towards impressions is much more cautious. Impressions are, for Marcus, something to be examined and interrogated. They demand our careful attention. While some can be approached quite positively, and can even be curative, others are seen as deceptive and not to be trusted. For Marcus, then, impressions are in themselves neutral; they can be either positive or negative, reliable and beneficial or deceptive and dangerous. And this is why he continually insists that they require careful examination.[17]

This is one reason why impressions are important to Marcus in the *Meditations*. A second reason is that impressions shape our minds. He writes:

> As are your repeated impressions (*phantasiai*) so will your mind be, for the soul is dyed by its impressions. Dye it, then, in a succession of impressions like these: for instance, where it is possible to live, there also it is possible to live well: but it is possible to live in a palace, therefore it is also possible to live well in a palace.
>
> 5.16

There are a number of things to note about this passage.[18] As we saw in the last chapter, there is a justification for the repetition of key ideas. In particular, it is the repetition of *phantasiai* that does the work. Because Marcus uses the term to cover internally generated items as well as externally generated ones, it means that individuals are able to create impressions that can, in turn, shape their soul (*psuchê*). The sort of impression he has in mind is, in this instance, a logical argument, and here we see Marcus making explicitly use of syllogistic reasoning to make his point.[19] It is once again worth remembering that this is not a case of Marcus trying to persuade anyone else; he is using this syllogistic argument to remind himself of the logical coherence of the conclusion that he wants to embrace.

So, if, for a Stoic, the condition of one's soul is of fundamental importance (i.e. whether it is virtuous or vicious), and if one's soul is shaped by impressions, then attending to impressions will also be of fundamental importance – especially if, as with Marcus, impressions are seen to be things that can be either reliable or deceptive.

Reliable impressions and first impressions

What does Marcus have to say about reliable impressions? As Giavatto has noted (2012c: 135), in general Marcus follows Stoic orthodoxy in holding a positive view of the epistemological relationship between humans and the external world. In 6.13 Marcus refers to excellent impressions that get "to the heart of actual facts, penetrating them so as to see the kind of things they really are".

Particularly interesting in this context are Marcus's references to what he calls "first impressions" (*proêgoumenai phantasiai*). This expression seems to be unique to him:[20]

> Do not say more to yourself than the first impressions report. You have been told that someone speaks evil of you. This is what you have been told; you have not been told

that you are injured. [...] In this way then abide always by the first impressions and add nothing of your own from within.

8.49

In his commentary, Farquharson defines these first impressions as "the immediate presentations which are the material *precedent* to your judgement" (1944: II, 777). In other words, they are neither composite impressions informed by judgements, nor impressions solely generated by the mind. Instead they are impressions as defined by Chrysippus: a perceptual impression of something external that makes plain its cause. However, as 8.49 makes clear, Marcus's concern is not with the straightforwardly epistemological question concerning the reliability of the senses, but rather a slightly different question about the way in which impressions can become infected with value judgements that we add to them before they are presented to the mind for assent or rejection.

So, the phrase "first impressions" helps us to distinguish between purely perceptual impressions and impressions informed by our judgements. This helps to restore *some* of the precision lost by Marcus's indifference to Chrysippus's distinction between impression and imagination, although as we have seen, here we are dealing with a slightly different distinction, namely one between impressions and judgements. As Hadot as noted, "Marcus has a frequent tendency to confuse judgment and representation [i.e. impressions]" (1998: 103). When Marcus uses a phrase like "Wipe out impressions" at 8.29, what he really means is wipe out impressions that have become infected by judgements, which is to say, wipe out judgements. Elsewhere, for example 8.40, he makes the same point referring directly to judgements. We ought not to be too surprised about this terminological imprecision given that Marcus was not a technical, professional philosopher, and that he was writing for himself. Hadot acknowledges that in passages such as 8.49 quoted above Marcus is "quite capable" of making the correct distinction. Indeed, it is interesting to note the order of these three passages within the *Meditations*. They are all from Book 8. In the first, 8.29, Marcus targets impressions as the problem. A few paragraphs later, in 8.40, he realizes that in fact judgements are the problem, not impressions. Then, in 8.49, he gives a fuller account distinguishing between impressions and judgements, and using the phrase "first impressions" in order to help himself do so. So, rather than simple confusion, perhaps what we see here is Marcus's developing thought process.

Although that may be the case, Marcus was not really innovating here. As Hadot notes (1998: 104), the essential point had already been made by Epictetus:

He was carried off to prison. What happened? He was carried off to prison. But the observation 'He has fared ill' is an addition that each man makes on his own responsibility.

Diss. 3.8.5

For Marcus, then, some impressions, namely first impressions, are reliable and trustworthy. The task thus becomes to distinguish between these trustworthy impressions and those that are not. Consequently impressions must be examined and tested. To return to a passage we considered earlier, Marcus writes, again in Book 8:

Continually and, if possible, on the occasion of every impression, test it by natural science, by psychology, by dialectic.

8.13

We can see how this sort of testing might help someone to distinguish between first impressions and impressions infected by judgements, and between impressions and imagination. Knowledge of nature and human emotions will enable someone to distinguish between bare statements of fact ("He was carried off to prison") and value judgements ("He has fared ill"). Statements about nature ought always to be value neutral; as such, they ought not to generate an emotional response. Knowledge of nature and dialectics will help one to distinguish between impressions and imagination, for both will be able to judge whether an impression could plausibly be the product of the external world rather than something created in the mind. These might not be definitive tests, but one can see how they might help in weeding out many potentially misleading impressions.

To sum up thus far, we can make a number of observations. Marcus remains committed, like Chrysippus, to the idea that perceptual impressions are reliable sources of knowledge. His central concern, however, is quite different, and this is not merely due to terminological imprecision. We have seen that Marcus conflates Chrysippean impressions and imagination under the single heading of impressions, but more important is his distinction between first impressions and impressions infected by judgements — a distinction that, as we have also seen, he probably inherited from Epictetus. This involves the claim that many impressions that might appear at first glance to be unproblematic perceptual impressions have in fact been tampered with by the mind.

Deceptive impressions

Reliable impressions are contrasted with deceptive impressions. As we have seen, these fall into two types: impressions infected by judgements and impressions completely generated by the mind (i.e. Chrysippean imagination). In both cases the problem arises from the activity of the mind; trustworthy first impressions, by contrast, remain untouched by the mind.

Marcus often warns himself to be wary of impressions. He writes:

> How simple to reject and to wipe away every disturbing or alien impression, and straightaway to be in perfect calm.
>
> *5.2*

> What are you doing here, impression? Depart, in God's name, the way you came; I have no need of you.
>
> *7.17*

Although not always explicit, in these sorts of passages Marcus is usually concerned with disturbing or upsetting impressions. Those sorts of impressions, by definition cannot be first impressions, for they presumably already include some kind of value judgement that makes them disturbing. So the deceptive impressions he seems concerned with here are impressions infected by judgements.

But he is also concerned about impressions that are solely the product of the mind:

> Do not allow the impression of the whole of your life to confuse you, do not dwell upon all the manifold troubles which have come to pass, but ask yourself in regard to every present piece of work: what is there here that can't be borne and can't be endured?
>
> *8.36*

These sorts of impressions – what we might call thoughts and memories – are quite different from the previous kind, in so far as they do not have an immediately present external cause.

To these we can add a third kind of potentially dangerous impression:

> Do not waste the balance of life left to you on impressions about other people [...] I mean if you imagine to yourself what so and so is doing, and why; what he is saying or thinking or planning, and every thought of the kind which leads you astray from close watch over your governing self (*hêgemonikon*)?
>
> *3.4*

Here the impressions that Marcus wants to reject are not deceptive or tainted in any way, it is just that they are distractions from the most important task at hand, namely attending to his own judgements. So this is a further, quite different, way in which Marcus urges us to be extremely cautious about impressions, separate from questions about their formation. Here Marcus might be following Epictetus, who, in the opening chapter of the *Handbook* (*Ench.* 1.5), urges people to reject impressions, and he says the criterion for rejecting impressions is whether they have to do with things "up to us" (*eph' hêmin*). Any impressions concerned with things not up to us ought to be nothing to us. As in Marcus, the issue seems to be one of distraction: do not devote too much attention to the opinions of other people, or the body, or material possessions; instead give one's focus squarely on the ruling part of the soul.

We now have three types of potentially deceptive impressions: (i) impressions infected by judgements, (ii) impressions generated by the mind, and (iii) distracting impressions. Opposed to these three types of deceptive impressions we have so far only encountered one type of positive impression, namely first impressions. We can try to redress the balance by pointing to a second type of positive impression in Marcus. These are like first impressions in so far as they are free from added judgements and accurately reflect the external cause that created them. But they differ from first impressions in an important way. It may be best to begin with some examples:

> Surely it is an excellent plan, when you are seated before delicacies and choice foods, to grasp the impression that this is the dead body of a fish, that the dead body of a bird or a pig; and again, that the Falernian wine is grape juice and that robe of purple a lamb's fleece dipped in a shell-fish's blood [...]. Surely these are excellent impressions, going to the heart of actual facts and penetrating them so as to see the kinds of things they really are.
>
> *6.13*

What is distinctive about the impressions Marcus has in mind here is that they come after the initial impression of seeing fine food or fine clothes. So they are not first impressions. Instead they require some work on the part of the mind, to dig behind the immediate superficial appearance of an object and to grasp its material nature. These impressions are, like first impressions, reliable, and trustworthy, but they are not immediate and unthinking; they require some mental effort, at least at first.

We might call this a second type of positive impression. There is also a third type. Consider the following two passages:

> Watch and see the courses of the stars as if you ran with them, and continually dwell in mind upon the changes of the elements into one another; for these impressions wash away the foulness of life on the ground.
>
> 7.47

> Let your impression dwell continually upon the whole of eternity and the whole of substance, and realize that their several parts are, by comparison with substance, a fig-seed; by comparison with time, the turn of a drill.
>
> 10.17

These passages share something in common with the previous one: they all involve adopting what we might call the perspective of physics. But these new ones are different in so far as they are simply the product of imagination. When Marcus sees a fine meal and trains himself to see merely a dead fish, he is seeing an object before him in a different way. But when he tries to grasp the immensity of space and time, adopting what is usually called a cosmic perspective, he is engaged in an act of imagination, and has an impression generated by the mind.

So we now have three types of potentially dangerous impression – (i) with added judgements, (ii) imaginations, and (iii) distractions – and three types of potentially beneficial impression – (iv) first impressions, (v) of objects stripped back, and (vi) from a cosmic perspective. These two sets do not neatly correlate with one another, but the fact that there are three negative and three positive types does underline the way in which Marcus sees impressions as potentially either good or bad, and not intrinsically one or the other (quite different from the early Stoic view). And that further underlines the importance to Marcus of paying close attention to impressions. Both of these thoughts are quite nicely expressed by Simplicius, in his commentary on Epictetus:

> Impressions are sometimes revelatory of truths, and of what is truly beneficial or pleasant, but are sometimes idle dream-fictions. So just by our being disposed to keep in mind straightaway that the object of the impression is not always such as it appears, the intensity of the impression is relaxed. As a result, it doesn't impede the judgement of reason.
>
> *in Ench. 6, 15-20 Hadot*

Here Simplicius, explicating Epictetus, offers a helpful parallel to Marcus's view that impressions can be either good or bad, and he explains the importance not just of attending to particular impressions but also developing a general, sceptical attitude towards impressions, something that Epictetus himself describes in *Discourses* 2.18.23-5 (and cf. 1.28). Elsewhere, in *Discourses* 1.27.1, Epictetus identifies four different types of impression, outlining two ways in which they can be reliable and two ways in which they might be deceptive, but his attempt at classification is quite different from Marcus's implicit distinction between impressions that can be dangerous and those that might be beneficial. Yet in the same chapter, Epictetus goes on to insist that the epistemological concerns of Pyrrho and the Academy are mere idle pursuits of leisure; what really matters is addressing those impressions that cause us distress, such as "death is a terrible misfortune". In fact, Epictetus's opening classification of "things that are and seem to be, things that are not and do not seem to be, things that are and do not seem to be, and things that are not but seem to be" should perhaps be taken as a parody of epistemological hair-splitting that he will go on to say is irrelevant for someone who is suffering from mental turmoil ("trembling and perplexed and whose heart is broken", *Diss.* 1.27.21).

Impressions and impulse

There is one final feature of Marcus's various references to impressions that is worth examining. In a good number of the passages where he refers to impressions, he does so in conjunction with mentioning impulse, *hormê* (see e.g. 2.7, 3.6, 4.22, 6.16, 8.7, 9.7). That he does so ought not to be a great surprise, given that both are central aspects of the *hêgemonikon*, the governing part of the human soul, and indeed are features of all animal souls.[21] Here are a few examples from Marcus:

> Those who are sick to death in life, with no mark on which they direct every impulse or in general every impression, are triflers, not in words only but also in their deeds.
>
> *2.7*

> Do not wander without a purpose, but in all your impulses render what is just, and in all your impressions preserve what you apprehend.
>
> *4.22*

> Wipe out impression: check impulse: quench desire: keep the governing self (*hêgemonikon*) in its own control.
>
> *9.7*

These show that attention to impressions ought to go hand in hand with attention to impulses. The fact that Marcus mentions these two aspects of the Stoic ruling part of the soul side by side in this way suggests that he did have the formal account of Stoic psychology in his mind when he was writing. If that is right, then it would suggest that when Marcus refers to impressions, not just in these passages but throughout the *Meditations*, he is taking it to be a technical Stoic term. Yet that sense is often obscured by translators who, as noted earlier, sometimes translate *phantasia* with half a dozen different English words, depending on context.

Introducing judgements

Alongside impressions, another key concept in Stoic dialectic that appears throughout the *Meditations* is judgement. In this case, Marcus's immediate debt was probably to Epictetus for whom judgement is also a key concept. In his *Handbook*, Epictetus famously said "It is not things that disturb people, but their judgements (*dogmata*) about things" (*Ench.* 5). In a similar spirit, Marcus writes:

> If you suffer distress because of some external cause, it is not the thing itself that troubles you but your judgement (*krima*) about it, and it is within your power to cancel that judgement at any moment.
>
> *8.47*

Epictetus used the term *dogma* here, while Marcus uses *krima*. Both of these words are often translated as "judgement". So is a third term, *hupolêpsis*, which is perhaps the most important of the three terms, and has sometimes been translated as "value-judgement".[22] Marcus uses the term *hupolêpsis* throughout the *Meditations*.[23] We also find it in the opening section of Epictetus's *Handbook* (*Ench.* 1.1) where *hupolêpsis* is listed as one of the few things that is "up to us" (*eph' hêmin*). It was already a technical term for the early Stoa and can be found in a number of reports of their views.[24]

Marcus on judgements

Marcus is emphatic about the importance of judgements: at 2.15 he writes "everything is judgement" (*hoti pan hupolêpsis*) and he more or less repeats these words at 12.8 and 12.26, suggesting that it was an idea he was keen to keep uppermost in his mind. In 4.3, a lengthy passage in which Marcus outlines what he is doing in the *Meditations* as a whole,[25] he writes that there are two fundamental ideas that must be kept "ready to hand" (*procheiros*): (i) that mental disturbances are the product not of things but of our judgements (*hupolêpseis*) and (ii) nothing is stable and everything passes, subject to universal flux. At the end of the passage he summarizes by saying *ho kosmos, alloiôsis; ho bios, hupolêpsis*, literally, "the cosmos, change; life, judgement" (4.3[12]). The concerns of everyday human life, he reminds himself, are simply the product of judgements. Here Marcus also makes explicit why judgements are so important: they are the source of mental disturbances (*ochlêsis*).[26]

Stoic epistemology

In order to put what Marcus has to say about judgements into context, it will be useful to say something about Stoic epistemology. The early Stoics outlined a three-stage process, involving impression (*phantasia*), assent (*sunkatathesis*), and belief or cognition (*katalêpsis*). First comes an impression, either from sensation or produced by the mind (Diog. Laert. 7.49-51). This impression is presented to the mind in the form of a proposition. The mind then accepts or rejects this proposition in an act of assent. That act of assent generates a belief, which can be either true or false. According to Cicero, this model was first developed by Zeno (*Acad*. 1.40). The resulting belief is thus the product of an impression over which we have no control and an act of assent over which we do. The challenge, of course, is to know which impressions are worthy of assent, and Zeno argued that some impressions present themselves as self-evidently true. These sorts of impressions are said to demand our assent. There was much debate between members of the early Stoa and sceptically-minded members of the Academy over how one could be sure that one was only assenting to reliable impressions.

Roman Stoic developments

The early Stoic theory was primarily epistemological. It was concerned with giving an account of how we generate beliefs and how they come to be either true or false. It was concerned more with matters of fact than ones of value and it does not seem to have been concerned with accounting for value-judgements. Yet as we have seen, Marcus and Epictetus were more concerned with examining the judgements that have some psychological or ethical impact. For example Epictetus was primarily concerned with how judgements generate value:

> The essence of the good is a certain kind of moral purpose (*prohairesis*) and that of the evil is a certain kind of moral purpose. What, then, are the external things? They are materials for the moral purpose, in dealing with which it will find its own proper

good or evil. How will it find the good? If it does not admire the materials. For the judgements (*dogmata*) about the materials, if they be correct, make the moral purpose good, but if they be crooked and awry, they make it evil.

Diss. 1.29.1-3

The early Stoic account does not seem to be able to account for this, or at least not the account that has come down to us.[27] Thus, what we find in both Marcus and Epictetus is, in effect, an expansion of the early Stoic view, adding further stages to the process. Both suggest that mental disturbances are produced by assenting to impressions that contain value-judgements, such as "this is good" or "this is terrible". But where do these value-judgements come from? They cannot come from external impressions, on the Stoic view, because those simply present matters of fact about the world. Thus, they must have been added to impressions by the mind before they are presented for assent. It is in this context that Marcus introduces his notion of "first impressions" (8.49) which, as we have already seen, enable him to distinguish between purely perceptual impressions and impressions infected by value-judgements. As we saw earlier, the basic idea expressed by this notion had already been articulated by Epictetus (*Diss.* 3.8.5). What both Epictetus and Marcus do is add two further stages to the early Stoic account in order to explain how some impressions come to contain value-judgements *before* they are presented to the mind for assent. If the early Stoic account goes from (i) impression to (ii) assent to (iii) belief, then the Roman Stoic account adds two new preliminary steps and goes from (i) first impression to (ii) value-judgement to (iii) impression to (iv) assent to (v) belief. Although the concern with value judgements in impressions can be found throughout Epictetus, it seems to have been Marcus who introduced the phrase "first impressions" in order to distinguish properly stage (i) from stage (iii) in the expanded version.[28]

It is possible that the difference between these two models is not quite so great. In the case of the early Stoa it is worth noting that before an impression is presented to the mind for assent, it is turned into propositional form. Thus, even for the early Stoa, the mind intervenes with impressions before they face assent. Of particular interest in the present context is a brief summary in Diogenes Laertius that says "For impression (*phantasia*) comes first; then thought (*dianoia*), which has the power of expression, articulates the subject's response to the impression" (Diog. Laert. 7.49). Thus, there is (i) the impression that comes first (or "first impression" as Marcus puts it), then (ii) the process of turning it into a proposition, then (iii) the presentation of that proposition to the mind, then (iv) assent, and finally (v) belief. Comparing this with the five-stage process outlined above might suggest that it is during the process of turning initial impressions, which in many cases will be sensations (*aisthêseis*), into propositions that value-judgements creep in.

Testing impressions and avoiding judgements

One of the consequences of this expanded model is that impressions need to be tested to see if they contain value-judgements before they reach the mind for assent. In a passage that we have encountered more than once already, Marcus writes, "continually and, if possible, on the occasion of every impression, test it by natural science, by psychology, by dialectic" (8.13). Elsewhere he adds "nothing is so able to create greatness of mind as the power methodically and truthfully to test (*elenchein*) each thing that meets one in life" (3.11). This is not primarily a matter of testing them to assess their epistemological reliability (although, of course, that also matters); instead it is an interrogation in search of value-judgements that might generate mental disturbances or lead one astray in what one values.

Part of the problem is that these first stages happen very quickly, almost unconsciously. Impressions already containing value-judgements can often appear as if they are straightforwardly the product of the external world, untouched by the human mind. The task of testing impressions, then, involves paying careful attention to this often rapid process. As Epictetus comments:

> Don't allow yourself to be dazed by the rapidity of the impact [of an impression], but say, 'Wait a while for me, my impression, let me see what you are, and what you're an impression of; let me test you out'.
>
> *Diss.* 2.18.24

If Marcus's use of the term *elenchein* brings to mind Socrates, Epictetus makes the connection explicit when he comments "just as Socrates used to tell us not to live a life unsubjected to examination, so we ought not to accept an impression (*phantasia*) unsubjected to examination" (*Diss.* 3.12.15).[29]

In the early Stoic context there was much discussion about what the criteria might be for distinguishing between true and false impressions. In this, slightly different context, one might equally ask by what standard does one test impressions in the way Marcus and Epictetus propose. The answer to this appears to be relatively simple: any impression that contains a value-judgement about an external object or state of affairs ought to look suspicious, given the Stoic view that such things are mere "indifferents" (*adiaphora*), without any inherent value. Thus, the claim that any given event is a misfortune will have "no basis in reality" and will necessarily rest upon a mistake, namely adding a "false value-judgement" (Hadot 1998: 85). Marcus puts it like this:

> Get rid of the judgement (*hupolêpsis*), and you are rid of 'I am hurt'. Get rid of 'I am hurt', and you are rid of the hurt itself.
>
> 4.7

Elsewhere he counsels himself not to resist a bodily sensation (*aisthêsis*), which will be natural, but to make sure that the governing part of his soul (*hêgemonikon*) does not add to it "the judgement (*hupolêpsis*) that it is either good or bad" (5.26). Thus what we have are value-neutral sensations provided by the body – what Marcus calls "first impressions" – and judgements made by the mind that add either positive or negative value. It is clear throughout the *Meditations* that Marcus sees human life – our everyday experience – to be the project of our judgements; these shape and colour how we experience the world and how we react to it. This was captured in Marcus's brief summation of, in effect, his entire philosophy, in 4.3[12]: "the cosmos, change; life, judgement" (*ho kosmos, alloiôsis; ho bios, hupolêpsis*). In 12.22 he writes that "all things are what we judge them to be"; if one can stop making such judgements, then things will be calm. The first part of this statement ought not to be taken too literally; Marcus does not think that all things are actually created by our judgements. As we can see from his line "the cosmos, change; life, judgement" he wants to draw a contrast between how things are in themselves and how they appear to people most of the time through a veil of value-judgements. There are a number of reasons why Marcus thinks one ought to avoid such judgements. One is simply that they involve making a mistake, attributing value to an "indifferent" that is in fact value neutral. Another, expressed in the second part of 12.22, is that by so doing one will attain a state of calm. Indeed, just a couple of paragraphs later he writes "cast out the judgement (*hupolêpsis*); you are saved" (12.25).[30]

Judgements, then, of the sort that Marcus is preoccupied with can be said to be against Nature in a number of ways: first, they misrepresent the external natural world, and second, they often lead to mental disturbances that undermine our rational nature as human beings. Thus, they inhibit our ability to live in harmony with Nature. Correct judgements, by contrast, are in accord with Nature:

> Venerate your faculty of judgement (*dunamis hupolêptikos*). For it depends entirely on this that there should never arise in your governing part (*hêgemonikon*) any judgement (*hupolêpsis*) that fails to accord with Nature or with the constitution of a rational being (*logikon zôon*).
>
> *3.9*

What techniques might one use to avoid such judgements? It is within this context that Marcus engages in the practice of re-describing things in purely physical terms. We have already considered some examples where Marcus outlines what he has in mind (6.13, 3.11). At 12.8 he suggests that by engaging in this kind of practice, trying to see things as they are in themselves, stripped of their usual value-judgements, it will be possible to see that all of the usual things that disturb people – pain, pleasure, death, fame – are in fact self-created. They are, in effect, self-inflicted wounds.

One can see in this practice the way in which aspects of Stoic logic, ethics, and physics all come together in a way that makes it difficult to separate them out. Marcus's concern with impressions and judgements, key concepts in Stoic dialectic (Diog. Laert. 7.49), is intimately bound up with trying to grasp Nature as it is in itself, the purview of Stoic physics, all done for the sake of an ethical goal of avoiding mental disturbances and leading a life appropriate to a rational animal. Although the logical element in this may seem somewhat limited compared to the prevalence of ethical and physics themes, it is in fact foundational.

Notes

1 See for example Edelstein (1966: 46) and Gill (2012: 383–8).
2 See esp. Giavatto (2012b), which surveys logical material in the *Meditations* but also, 409, acknowledges the ubiquity of topics from physics throughout the work. For a fuller account see Giavatto (2008) and also Ackeren (2011: II, 553–610).
3 See for example Diog. Laert. 7.39 (*SVF* 2.37). Strictly speaking, Diogenes reports that philosophical discourse was divided in this way, not philosophy itself. That this is accurate seems confirmed later at 7.41, where Diogenes reports that some later Stoics (he names Zeno of Tarsus) disputed this, claiming that it is philosophy itself that is so divided. See further Hadot (1991) and Ierodiakonou (1993). For a wide range of relevant ancient texts see Hülser (1987: I, 2–22).
4 Thus, Edelstein (1966: 46) who comments that Marcus was "not concerned with logic and physics" and Barnes (1997: 1) who writes "Marcus would love neither physics nor logic". A little later in his study of logic in the Roman Stoics Barnes adds "I shall say no more about Marcus, who is a hopeless case" (11).
5 Hout 1988: 141; Haines 1919–20: II, 66–7. For these three logical puzzles, see Diog. Laert. 7.187 (*SVF* 2.279), 7.82 (*SVF* 2.274), and Epictetus, *Diss.* 2.17.34 (*SVF* 2.280) respectively.

6 Hout (1999: 337) doubts whether Marcus would have been interested in dialectics at the time that Fronto was writing – the 160s – even if he had been in his youth. There does not seem to be any clear evidence on this either way.
7 See for example Barnes (1997: 11) who says that he does "not know what to make of" this passage.
8 I have simply followed Farquharson in using "psychology" here. It is usually taken to refer to the ethical part of Stoic philosophy. Thus, Long (1890: 39) "I have translated *pathologein* by using the word Moral (Ethic), and that is the meaning here"; see also Hays (2003: 103) "ethics" and Nickel (2010: 187) "ethische". It is also often taken to refer to the emotions (*pathê*); see for example Hard (2011: 72) "the passions", Trannoy (1925: 85) "des passions", Cassanmagnago (2008: 305), "alle affezioni", hence Farquharson's "psychology". However, the conjunction of the terms *phusiologein* and *pathologein* echo a passage in a text traditionally attributed to Galen but sometimes thought to be spurious, the *Introductio sive medicus*, which says (Chapter 8; XIV, 690–1 Kühn; Petit 2009: 15,16–23) "Giving an account of the natural course of things (*phusiologein*) is necessary, because it is not possible to know what is contrary to nature if one does not have prior knowledge of what is in accordance with nature, diseases being things that establish themselves contrary to nature. Giving an account of the causes and of the pathological aspect of these (*pathologein*), too, is necessary, the former in order that we see the causes of the pathological states against which we need to set up the treatment, the latter in order that we get to know the pathological states themselves" (trans. Eijk 2014: 470). In the light of this, we might simply translate *pathologein* here as "pathology", understood in a broader sense to cover the analysis of any disease, even if Marcus primarily has mental diseases in mind. Something like "psychotherapy" might fit better than either "ethics" or "psychology". Thus, Hammond (2006: 73) has "identify the emotion"; Rendall (1898: 110) opts for "subjective effect".
9 See for example Farquharson (1944: II, 759) and Hard (2011: 157).
10 On Stoic dialectic see further Gourinat (2000). All of the relevant ancient texts are gathered together in Hülser (1987).
11 On dialectic as a virtue see Long (1978), Gourinat (2000: 69–87), and Giavatto (2008: 65–88).
12 On Epictetus's attitude towards and interests in logic see Long (1978: 119–21), Barnes (1997: 24–125), and Crivelli (2007). Beyond the texts mentioned below, note also *Ench.* 52.
13 Epictetus takes Antisthenes and Socrates to be exemplars of philosophers primarily focused on living a good life. The chapter as a whole, as well as defending the necessity of logic, also defends the study of Chrysippus against the doubts of an interlocutor sympathetic to a broadly Cynic (or perhaps Aristonian) view, while at the same time warning against getting lost in the textual interpretation of Chrysippus. See further Dobbin (1998: 161–8).
14 On the "use of impressions" (*chrêsis tôn phantasiôn*) see also *Diss.* 1.6.13; 1.20.15; 1.28.11-12. For discussion see Bénatouïl (2009: 102–15).
15 These are also discussed in greater detail in Giavatto (2008: 207–34).
16 The following list is merely a random selection of examples: 4.4, 5.16, 7.75, 8.58, 9.39, 9.40, 10.33, 10.35, 11.1, 12.5, 12.14.
17 It would probably be a mistake to overstress the difference between Marcus and the early Stoa here. Note Diog. Laert. 7.46, where it is said that the Stoics held that there were two types of impression, reliable (*kataléptikê*) and unreliable. Unreliable impressions, he reports, either do not come from a real object or, if they do, are misleading.
18 Here I follow the very helpful analysis in Giavatto (2012b: 415).
19 The argument takes the form: if x then y; x; therefore y. This, as Bobzien (2003: 102) notes, is a "typical Stoic argument". Indeed, it is an example of the first Stoic indemonstrable syllogism (see Diog. Laert. 7.80; Sextus Empiricus, *Math.* 8.224).
20 The nearest thing to it I have found is in Diog. Laert. 7.49, which refers to an impression coming first (*proêgeitai gar hê phantasia*), before being turned into a proposition. We shall discuss this passage later on. I thank Jean-Baptiste Gourinat for alerting me to the parallel.
21 See for example Diog. Laert. 7.159, which identifies impressions (*phantasiai*), impulses (*hormai*), and reason (*logos*) as the three features of the *hêgemonikon*. As Inwood (1985: 22) notes, although animal souls do not possess reason, they also have impressions and impulse as key features. (In Hierocles, *El.*

Eth. 1.31-3 animals are defined as possessing sensation (*aisthêsis*) and impulse (*hormê*).) For more on both the *hêgemonikon* and the difference between human and animal souls in the scale of nature, see Chapter 6 below.

22 Both *dogma* and *hupolêpsis* are also sometimes translated as "opinion" or "belief". Hadot (1998: 110) translates *hupolêpsis* as "value-judgement" ("jugement de valeur"; cf. Hadot 1992: 128). In the context of the early Stoa is has also been translated as "assumption" (Pomeroy 1999: 158). Marcus uses both *hupolêpsis* and *dogma*, the former slightly more often, while Epictetus overwhelmingly prefers *dogma*. Bonhöffer (1894: 267) suggests that they are synonymous. Note also *Diss.* 1.11.33 where Epictetus uses them together to mean the same thing.

23 See 2.12, 2.15, 3.9, 4.3, 4.7, 5.26, 7.62, 8.40, 8.44, 9.6, 9.13, 9.21, 9.32, 10.3, 10.33, 11.16, 11.18, 11.21, 12.1, 12.4, 12.8, 12.22, 12.25, 12.26.

24 See Plutarch, *St. rep.* 1055f (*SVF* 2.994), Stob. 2,111,18–113,11 = Ar. Did. 11m (Pomeroy 1999: 94, *SVF* 3.548, LS 41G), Stob. 2,88,8–89,3 = Ar. Did. 10 (Pomeroy 1999: 56, *SVF* 3.378, LS 65C). It also features in the title of a book by Chrysippus (Diog. Laert. 7.201, *SVF* 2.17).

25 See Chapter 2 above.

26 This is the only place where Marcus uses *ochlêsis*. It appears just once among the fragments for the early Stoics, in a list of definitions from Pseudo-Andronicus's *Peri pathôn* (*SVF* 3.414), and just once in Epictetus, in one of the short sayings attributed to him (Schenkl 1916: 494). Neither are particularly reliable sources.

27 One of our principal sources is Cicero's *Academica* whose account is shaped by the debate between the early Stoa and the sceptical Academy and so focused on issues of epistemology. It is conceivable that other, non-epistemological aspects of the early Stoic position were omitted by Cicero because they were not relevant to that dispute.

28 Another key passage relevant here is the story in Aulus Gellius (*NA* 19.1.1-21) that surrounds his report of a passage from the now-lost fifth book of Epictetus's *Discourses* (fr. 9 Schenkl), discussed briefly in Sellars (2003: 155–7).

29 Compare with Plato, *Ap.* 38a and see also *Diss.* 1.26.18. On Socratic themes in Marcus Aurelius, see Sellars (2019).

30 Compare this with 4.3[2], discussed in Chapter 2 above, where this is said to lead to "perfect ease" (*eumareia*).

PART III
Physics

4
NATURE AND CHANGE

As we noted at the beginning of the previous chapter, it is not uncommon to see the *Meditations* described as a work of practical ethics. Yet as we have seen, there is certainly material in the *Meditations* that falls under the traditional Stoic heading of logic in their tripartite division of philosophy. The same can be said in the case of physics. To repeat a passage that we considered there, Marcus comments at one point:

> Continually and, if possible, on the occasion of every impression, test it by natural science, by psychology, by dialectic.
>
> *8.13*

What does he mean by testing impressions by natural science, or physics (*phusiologia*)? We shall come back to that idea towards the end of this chapter, once we have a better sense of his interests in physics. That interest permeates the *Meditations*. He describes himself at one point as a *phusiologêtos*, a student of Nature (10.9; see also 8.50, 10.11),[1] and topics in physics crop up again and again. Indeed, *phusis* is one of the most common words that Marcus uses.[2] Although, as with logic, Marcus does not claim any technical expertise, his insistence on the importance of at least some understanding of how Nature works is unambiguous. For example he writes:

> He who does not know that the comsos exists, does not know where he is. He who does not know the purpose of the cosmos, does not know who he is nor what the cosmos is.
>
> *8.52*

This implies that knowledge of Nature via the study of physics is a vital part of what we might call Marcus's ultimately Socratic project, in so far as it contributes to the development of self-knowledge.[3] The person who does not understand how Nature works is, he suggests, like a stranger in their own country (12.1; see also 12.13). Someone who is surprised or shocked by what happens to them during their lives reacts in this way because they do not adequately understand how Nature works. In this sense, the study of Nature, Marcus argues, has direct practical and therapeutic benefits.

We might also connect this with the Stoic *telos* of living harmoniously or consistently with Nature. Marcus alludes to this key element of Stoic doctrine a number of times (see 10.15, 12.1). According to the doxographical reports in Diogenes Laertius and elsewhere, there were a number of different elaborations of the *telos* formula put forward by different members of the early Stoa, and there has been some debate regarding whether these indicate doctrinal innovation or are simply different attempts to articulate more clearly the same underlying idea.[4] One of those formulations stresses the idea of living "in accordance with experience of the actual course of Nature" (Diog. Laert. 7.87), and Diogenes credits it to Chrysippus. This version of the *telos* – or perhaps one should say this aspect of what it was taken to entail – in particular resonates with the point that Marcus wants to emphasize.

Marcus also makes use of physics in his practice of examining impressions. In particular he draws on knowledge of how objects are constituted into order to challenge some of his own unwarranted value-judgements. He puts it like this:

> Always make a figure or outline of the imagined object as it occurs, in order to see distinctly what it is in its essence, naked, as a whole and parts; and say to yourself its individual name and the names of the things of which it was compounded and into which it will be broken up. For nothing is so able to create greatness of mind as the power methodically and truthfully to test each thing that meets one in life, and always to look upon it so as to attend at the same time to the use which this particular thing contributes to a cosmos of a certain definite kind, what value it has in reference to the Whole, and what to man [...]. What is this which now creates an image in me, what is its composition? how long will it naturally continue …
>
> *3.11*

Elsewhere, as we saw earlier, he gives examples of this procedure of supplying physical descriptions in action:

> Surely it is an excellent plan, when you are seated before delicacies and choice foods, to grasp the impression that this is the dead body of a fish, that the dead body of a bird or a pig; and again, that the Falernian wine is grape juice and that robe of purple a lamb's fleece dipped in a shellfish's blood; and in matters of sex intercourse, that it is attrition of an entrail and a convulsive expulsion of mere mucus. Surely these are excellent impressions, going to the heart of actual facts and penetrating them so as to see the kind of things they really are. You should adopt this practice all through your life, and where things make an impression which is very plausible, uncover their nakedness, see into their cheapness, strip off the profession on which they vaunt themselves.
>
> *6.13*

While this kind of re-description is partially motivated by a therapeutic desire to avoid making the sorts of value-judgements that will lead to excessive attachments, it is also worth stressing that there is – as importantly – a motivation simply to see things correctly, as they truly are in themselves. It is not that any alternative description will do, so long as it has a suitable therapeutic benefit. The goal is to comprehend things aright, and that requires a decent understanding of the physical world.

So, physics understood as the study of Nature is a vital part of Marcus's philosophical project. Given that the *Meditations* is not a technical treatise, he does not spell out the fine details of Stoic physical theory – indeed, why would he feel the need to do so if he was simply writing for himself? But he often mentions in passing, alludes to, or presupposes aspects of Stoic physics in his reflections. In the remainder of this chapter and ones that follow we shall unpack some of these connections.

The unity of Nature

Throughout the *Meditations* Marcus present Nature as a single, unified dynamic system:

> All things are woven together and the common bond is sacred, and scarcely one thing is foreign to another, for they have been arranged together in their places and together make the same cosmos. For there is one cosmos out of all, one God through all, one substance and one law, one common reason of all intelligent creatures and one truth, if indeed the perfection of creatures of the same family and partaking of the same reason is one.
>
> 7.9

Here Marcus makes reference to there being a single god running through all of Nature. Elsewhere he is more explicit in seeing Nature as a whole as not only a unified system but also a living organism:

> Constantly think of the cosmos as one living creature (*zôion*), embracing one substance and one soul; how all is absorbed into the one consciousness of this living creature; how it compasses all things with a single purpose, and how all things work together to cause all that comes to pass, and their wonderful web and texture.
>
> 4.40

Here Marcus follows the orthodox Stoic view, which claimed that the whole cosmos is an ensouled, rational animal (Diog. Laert. 7.139). This idea dated all the way back to Zeno, who offered a range of arguments for this view. One of these argued that if something possesses reason, then it is better than something that does not; nothing can be better than the cosmos, so the cosmos must possess reason (Sextus, *Math.* 9.104, *SVF* 1.111). Another argued that nothing devoid of sensation can produce things with sensation; the cosmos produces animals with sensation; therefore, the cosmos itself must also possess sensation (ibid. 9.110, *SVF* 1.113).[5]

Causal and material principles

When Marcus reflects on the physical world, he often refers to two fundamental principles out of which everything is comprised. He calls these the causal (*to aitiôdês*) and the material (*to hulikon*).[6] In a passage reflecting on questions related to the immortality of the soul, he concludes the discussion by writing that the only way to investigate the truth of the matter is by "distinguishing between the material and the causal" (4.21). Elsewhere, touching on more or less the same issue, Marcus writes:

> I am composed out of the causal and the material; and of these neither will pass away into nothingness, just as neither came to exist out of nothingness. Thus, every part of me will be assigned its place by change into some part of the cosmos, and that again into another part of the cosmos, and so on to infinity. By a similar change both my parents and I came to exist, and so on to another infinity of regression. For there is no reason to prevent one speaking so, even if the cosmos is governed according to finite periods.
>
> *5.13*

In another passage in which he lists to himself a series of fundamental exhortations – wipe away impressions, focus on the present moment – he includes the reminder to "divide and analyse any given object into the causal and the material" (7.29). This is, in effect, a reminder to himself to practise the use of physical descriptions of everyday objects of the sort discussed earlier, although here it is not a re-description in terms of physical components but instead a more basic one in terms of these two fundamental principles. Marcus describe this process himself:

> What is this by itself in its own constitution? What is its substance or material [component]? What is its causal [component]? What is its function in the cosmos? How long a time does it persist?
>
> *8.11; see also 9.25, 12.18*

This sort of analysis is, Marcus suggests, essential for anyone aspiring to live a satisfying life. It is also the mark of a philosopher and one of the things that distinguishes philosophers from other people.[7] In one passage he notes three necessary tasks: (i) this kind of physical re-description, (ii) acting justly, and (iii) speaking truthfully. This might be taken as an implicit reference to the three parts of Stoic philosophy, physics, ethics, and logic, and so a passage that ought to be read alongside 8.13, quoted above:

> The security of life is to see each object in itself, in its entirety, its material [component], its causal [component]; with the whole heart to do just acts and to speak the truth. What remains except to enjoy life, joining one good thing to another, so as to leave not even the smallest interval unfilled?
>
> *12.29*

Either way, this pair of fundamental principles, the causal and the material, crops up again and again throughout the *Meditations* and was clearly foundational for how he understood the physical world.

The Stoic principles

The claim that everything in the physical world is comprised of two fundamental principles was a core doctrine of early Stoic physics.[8] The doctrine, first articulated by Zeno, posited two principles (*archai*), the active (*to poioun*) and the passive (*to paschon*). The passive principle was identified with matter (*hulê*), while the active principle was identified with reason (*logos*) and with god (see Aetius 1.3.25, *SVF* 1.85). These two principles are ungenerated and indestructible. They are both bodies, for only bodies exist, and they are that out of which everything is made. The active principle, god, was further identified with intellect (*nous*) and fate (*heimarmenê*; see Diog. Laert. 7.135). Nature as a whole is governed by the active principle, which penetrates every part of the physical world, just as the human soul penetrates every part of the human body (ibid. 7.138). As another source puts it, god is mixed with matter, extending through it, shaping and forming it (Alex. *Mixt.* 225,1-2).

Some formulations connect the active principle with fire (*pur*), "an intelligent, designing fire" (Aetius 1.7.33). This primordial fire was taken to be distinct from the element of fire that stands alongside the other elements of earth, air, and water. It was closely associated with their doctrine of periodic conflagration (*ekpurôsis*), in which everything is destroyed back into this fire, before being reborn at the beginning of a new cosmic cycle.[9] Other accounts connect it with breath (*pneuma*), perhaps in order to make a connection with discoveries in contemporary anatomy.[10] In both cases, fire and breath were often associated with life; in primitive thought heat and breath were the characteristics that distinguished a living body from a corpse. The Stoic use of similar terms at a cosmological level reflects their desire to present Nature as a whole as a living creature, leading one commentator to describe their physics as a "cosmobiology".[11] Nature (*phusis*), the cosmos (*kosmos*), the whole (*to holon*) – these terms are used interchangeably – is a living creature, comprised of a body permeated with a soul. While some sources call the active principle permeating nature "God" (the soul of the world), others present Nature as a whole as "God", a combination of soul and body. Either way, Nature for the Stoics is alive, animate, and self-moving. There is nothing beyond or outside it, except infinite void.[12]

Marcus and the Stoic principles

The resonances between the early Stoic theory and Marcus's two principles are multiple and seem unambiguous. One principle is identified with matter, while the other is causal or active. In both cases the principles are ungenerated and indestructible, and in both cases a connection is drawn between these two wider principles in Nature and their expression as body and soul in an individual human being (cf. 5.13). Even so, one might raise doubts about whether Marcus really had the orthodox Stoic theory in mind, given that he did not use the standard Stoic terms.[13] Indeed, when he refers at 8.3 to great philosophers of the past who comprehended the world in terms of its matter (*hulê*) and cause (*aitia*), he names Diogenes, Heraclitus, and Socrates, none of whom were Stoics. Was he really thinking of the formal Stoic theory of principles when he referred to things being composed of matter and cause? In response to these doubts we can point to evidence in Seneca that explicitly makes the connection between the Stoic doctrine and Marcus's own way of putting it:

> Our Stoic philosophers, as you know, say that there are two things in nature from which everything is produced – cause and matter (*causa et materia*). Matter lies inert, an entity ready for anything but destined to lie idle if no one moves it. Cause, on the other hand, being the same as reason, shapes matter and directs it wherever it wants, and from matter produces its manifold creations. Hence a thing must be made *from* something, and *by* something. The latter is its cause, the former its matter.
>
> *Seneca, Ep. 65.2, LS 55E*

Here Seneca explicitly presents the Stoic account of principles using the language of cause and matter (*causa et materia*).[14] Given that we know Marcus was an admirer of Seneca, he may have taken this terminology from him, or they may have both been following some other common source.

Another objection that might be raised is that Marcus does not consistently hold on to this twofold distinction into fundamental principles. There is one passage in particular that might be taken as evidence for this:

> One light of the sun, even though it be sundered by walls, by mountains, by a myriad other barriers. One common substance (*koinê ousia*), even though it be sundered in a myriad individual bodies. One soul (*psuchê*), even though it be sundered in a myriad natural forms and individual outlines. One intelligent soul (*noera psuchê*), even though it appears to be divided.
>
> 12.30

Here Marcus appears to introduce a threefold distinction between substance, soul, and intelligent soul. The passage might be taken as a cosmic counterpart to other passages dealing with humans, which divide them in a similar threefold way into body, soul, and intelligence.[15] As we shall see later, in the case of humans, Marcus's threefold distinction can easily be accommodated with the early Stoic view. The passage here might equally be accommodated with the Stoic scale of nature, outlining a progression from cosmic substance (i.e. matter), to animal soul, to rational soul.[16] In short, this passage makes more sense when read in the light of the Stoic scale of nature than with reference to the Stoic principles.

Perpetual change

Nature, for Marcus, is in a continual process of change. It is, he writes on a number of occasions, like a river:

> Of man's life, his time is a point, his existence a flux, his sensation clouded, his body's entire composition corruptible, his vital spirit an eddy of breath, his fortune hard to predict, his fame uncertain. Briefly, all the things of the body, a river; all the things of the spirit, dream and delirium; his life a warfare and a sojourn in a strange land, his after-fame oblivion.
>
> 2.17; see also 4.43, 6.15

This river imagery brings to mind the earlier Greek philosopher Heraclitus,[17] who is famously associated with the phrase, "it is impossible to step into the same river twice".[18] He is also remembered for claiming the fundamental principle in Nature is fire. He is reported to have stated that the cosmos is ungenerated and indestructible, a "fire ever-living, kindled in measures and extinguished in measures".[19] In one extended doxographical account Heraclitus is credited with holding that fire is the fundamental principle, that all things come into being through a process of condensation and rarefaction, and that they dissolve back into fire, all of which happens according to a fixed necessity.[20] Some sources credit Heraclitus with the claim that everything is resolved back into fire at the same time, creating a moment of conflagration (*ekpurôsis*) that marks the end of one cosmic cycle and the beginning of the next.[21] As the ancient sources note, the Stoics would come to hold the same doctrine.

It should come as no surprise, then, that the Stoics had a particular interest in Heraclitus.[22] Cleanthes is reported to have written a four-volume commentary (*exêgêsis*) on his work and his own *Hymn to Zeus* is often said to echo Heraclitean ideas and language.[23] One of Cleanthes' pupils, Sphaerus, also wrote on Heraclitus.[24] It is not clear that Heraclitus was an influence on the development of Stoic thinking; instead they appear to have recognized him as a precursor, sharing some of the views they had arrived at independently. Again, it may have been Cleanthes who first recognized similarities between Heraclitus and the new philosophy developed by his teacher Zeno. Stoic admiration for Heraclitus continued into the Roman period. Both Musonius Rufus and Seneca refer to him, perhaps drawing on Cleanthes.[25] So too does Marcus. Indeed, Marcus seems to have had a particular interest in Heraclitus.[26] He mentions him as an eminent philosopher in a number of places alongside Socrates, Diogenes, and Pythagoras (6.47, 8.3). He also quotes from him a number of times, preserving fragments not known from other sources (at 4.46, 6.42).[27] It is conceivable – although there is no evidence for this – that he may have taken these passages from Cleanthes' commentary.

The most important passage on this topic is 4.46. It is worth considering this within its immediate context, for Marcus develops a string of closely related thoughts that highlight the way in which Heraclitean themes permeate this thought. As we saw earlier, at 4.40 Marcus describes the cosmos as a single living animal, embracing one substance (*ousia*) and one soul (*psuchê*), and given the context it seems plausible to take this as a reference to the two Stoic principles, with *ousia* standing in for *hulê*.[28] This sets the scene for a series of passages, from 4.42 to 4.46 all focused on the ubiquity of change.[29]

In 4.42 Marcus stresses the value-neutrality of processes of change: "what comes to pass in the course of change (*metabolê*) nothing is bad (*kakon*), as nothing is good (*agathon*)". This reflects the standard Stoic view that such value comes from judgements, a point often repeated by Epictetus (e.g. *Ench*. 5). This is primarily a claim about Nature, the province of physics, but the albeit implicit allusion to the role of human judgements touches on a theme in logic, while the references to what is good and bad connect with ethics. As such this brief remark nicely illustrates the way in which Marcus draws on all three parts of Stoic philosophy throughout the *Meditations*. The point behind it is clearly consolatory, and so it also shows how Marcus puts to work theoretical claims from all three parts of Stoic philosophy for his own psychological benefit. In the present context, though, the important point is that Marcus is reflecting on the nature of change.[30]

The next section, 4.43, is even more explicitly Heraclitean in so far as it draws on the river imagery that we have already seen elsewhere in the *Meditations*:

> There is a kind of river of things passing into being, and eternity is a violent torrent. For no sooner is each seen, then it has been carried away, and another is being carried by, and that, too, will be carried away.
>
> *4.43; also 2.17*

This image of continual change is combined with the consolatory tone of the preceding section in Marcus's next thought, 4.44, where he draws a parallel between the inevitable natural change from one season to the next and what can often seem to be challenging changes affecting human life. In particular he notes that some things belong to one season rather than another – "the rose in the spring and the grape in the summer" – and that this is a familiar fact that people accept without further thought, much less complaint.[31] He goes on to compare these with sickness and death which, like roses and grapes, have their own appropriate season within human life. Only the foolish, he concludes, are disturbed by these things. This is a good example of Marcus adopting what we have referred to elsewhere as the perspective of physics in order to devalue typical human anxieties. Although commentators have tended not to make an explicit connection with Heraclitus here,[32] one might note that one source attributes to him a reference to the "seasons which bring all things to birth" in the context of natural cycles of change.[33] Whether or not Marcus had this in mind, once again the ubiquity and inevitability of change is his primary theme.

In the next section, 4.45, Marcus extends this concern with change over time by connecting it back to his image of Nature as an organic unity in 4.40. Not only are the various parts of Nature united in a single organic unity, so too are the events that take place in Nature over time. They are not, he writes, isolated events connected together by necessity but instead they are in a rational combination (*eulogos sunapheia*) and inter-relation (*oikeiotês*). This is all standard Stoic doctrine.

It is with all these thoughts in mind – the organic unity of Nature, the inevitability of change, the organic unity of events – that Marcus then explicitly invokes Heraclitus:

> Always remember what Heraclitus said: 'the death of earth is the birth of water, the death of water is the birth of atmosphere, the death of atmosphere is fire, and conversely'. Remember, too, his image of the man who forgets the way he is going; and: 'they are at variance with that with which they most continuously have converse (Reason which governs the Universe), and the things they meet with every day appear alien to them'; and again: 'we must not act and speak like men who sleep, for in sleep we suppose that we act and speak'; and 'we must not be like children with parents', that is, accept things simply as we have received them.
>
> *4.46*

Marcus implicitly draws connections between these statements by Heraclitus and the Stoic view of Nature that he has been describing in the preceding sections. As has been argued in relation to the early Stoa, what we have here is probably less a case of influence and more Marcus simply recognizing shared themes running through Heraclitus's physics and his own Stoic physics. Rather than see Marcus as particularly Heraclitean, his attitude towards him simply appears to follow an already established Stoic practice of acknowledging him as a precursor and kindred spirit.

Reflecting on change

It has been suggested that Marcus's stress on perpetual change ought to be understood in the context of the rise of Platonism during the second century, which prioritized unchanging intelligible Forms over the impermanent physical world.[34] The contrast between Stoicism and systematic Platonism is well taken, but there does not seem to be much evidence in the *Meditations* to suggest that Marcus was paying much attention to those wider philosophical developments. Instead, his concern remains focused on himself and the ways in which he can draw on a physical theory of perpetual change for therapeutic ends.

Its central role seems to be to stress that any event one might think of as bad is simply part of a natural process of change. For example:

> Dwell upon everything that exists and reflect that it is already in process of dissolution and coming into being by change and a kind of decay and dispersion, or in what way it is born to die, in a manner of speaking.
>
> *10.18; see also 9.35, 12.21*

He repeatedly applies this to death and, more widely, to thinking about the transience of life:

> Through the matter of the whole, as through a winter torrent, all bodies are passing, connatural with the whole and cooperating with it, as our members work with one another. How many a Chrysippus, a Socrates, an Epictetus has eternity already sucked down! Let the same thought strike you in the case of any single individual or object.
>
> *7.19*

In many of these reflections on change Marcus's aim appears to be to present such transformations as value neutral: entities are formed, they develop, decay, and ultimately break back down into their constituent parts. This is a purely natural process, neither good nor bad in itself. This is how Marcus makes use of the doctrine of continual flux as a therapeutic tool to challenge the habit of making positive or negative value judgements about material entities or physical processes of change. This is all in accord with Stoic ethical theory, which argues that only virtue (*aretê*) is good, while external events and states of affairs are simply indifferents (*adiaphora*), even if some may be preferred over others.

However, elsewhere Marcus suggests that whatever happens is good, in so far as it is a product of divine providence. Thus, at 12.23 he says that whatever happens is good (*agathon*) "because it is in due season for the whole, benefiting it and itself benefited by it". At first glance there appears to be a tension between these two views. Are events value neutral or are they good? Is this an inconsistency and, if so, is it Marcus's or is it one that he has inherited from the Stoa? One way to think about the relationship between the two claims is that the first derives from Stoic value theory (i.e. ethics) while the second depends on their commitment to providence (i.e. physics). So, do these two claims imply a tension between Stoic ethics and Stoic physics? That may be an unhelpful way to put it. The tension can be explained better by connecting the two views to different stages of philosophical development and understanding. The person at an earlier stage of training will do well to adopt the first view that events are value neutral, in order to combat their existing habits of making unwarranted value judgements. Someone at a more advanced level, who has a better grasp of the workings of Nature, will see the interconnectedness of events and how they all contribute to the perfection of the Whole. Such an individual will not merely be indifferent about what happens but will welcome whatever comes to pass as a necessary and essential part of Nature's divine order.

Notes

1. It should be noted that *phusiologêtos* is a contested reading. Although it is found in the two principal witnesses for the text, Xylander (1559) and Vaticanus Graecus 1950, it was amended to *aphusiologêtôs* by Gataker (1652) in a marginal note and many modern editors have followed him (e.g. Dalfen 1987). However, some editors have kept *phusiologêtos* (e.g. Haines 1916).
2. See Rigo (2010: 235). Setting aside things such as articles, prepositions, and the like, *phusis* is the most common word with any substantial meaning.

3. On the Socratic nature of Marcus's project, see Sellars (2019).
4. For the Stoic *telos* formula see Diog. Laert. 7.87-9 and Stob. 2,75,11-76,23, with discussion in Chapter 8 below.
5. See also the account in Cicero, *Nat. D.* 2.21-2, with further discussion in Hahm (1977: 136–84).
6. For "causal" and "material" see 4.21, 5.13, 7.29, 8.11, 12.29 where both are used; note also 4.20, 9.9, 9.25, 12.2, 12.8, 12.18 where just one or the other appears.
7. See 8.3, where Marcus says that Diogenes, Heraclitus, and Socrates all saw the world in terms of its matter (*hulê*) and cause (*aitia*), unlike men of action such as Alexander, Julius Caesar, and Pompeius.
8. See for example Diog. Laert. 7.134 (*SVF* 2.299), with further texts in *SVF* 2.299-328 and LS 44. For discussion of the Stoic principles (*archai*), see Gould (1970: 93–9), Lapidge (1973), and Hahm (1977: 29–56).
9. On *ekpurôsis* see for example Stob. 1,171,2 (*SVF* 2.596), along with the other texts gathered in *SVF* 2.597-632. Some Stoics rejected this doctrine, notably Boethus, Panaetius, and Diogenes of Babylon; see Philo, *Aet. mundi* 76-7 (*SVF* 3.Diog.27, LS 46P). Marcus uses the word just once, in connection with Heraclitus at 3.3, but note also 11.1 where he refers to periodic rebirth.
10. See further Chapter 6 below. For a summary of these developments, with further references, see Sellars (2018c: 93–9).
11. See for example Hahm (1977: 136).
12. The Stoics drew a distinction between "the whole" (*to holon*) and "the all" (*to pan*). The former includes unified Nature while the latter includes both Nature and the surrounding infinite void. See for example Aetius 2.1.7 (*SVF* 2.522); Sextus Empiricus, *Math.* 9.332 (*SVF* 2.524). Marcus alludes to this Stoic doctrine at 11.1.
13. Marcus does use the words *poioun* and *paschon*, but in other contexts; see for example 6.8 and 12.1 respectively.
14. For commentary on this passage see Inwood (2007: 138–9) and the note in Graver and Long (2015: 535–6).
15. On this threefold division see further Chapter 6 below.
16. On the Stoic scale of nature, see Chapter 6 below. On the equivalence of substance and matter in Marcus, see Farquharson (1944: II, 898).
17. So Crossley (1882: 35) commenting on 4.43.
18. This is the formulation attributed to Heraclitus by Plato in *Cratylus* 402a (DK 22A6); other sources phrase it slightly differently. See the texts gathered together in LM Her. D65-6 (in vol. 3.2). For Heraclitus I supply references to what probably remains the standard collection of texts, DK, but I have primarily used the more recent collection in LM, which includes many texts not in DK.
19. Clement of Alexandria, *Strom.* 5.105.2 (LM Her. D85, DK 22B30).
20. See Simplicius, *in Phys.* 23,33–24,11 (LM Her. R45, cf. DK 22A5). This summary of Heraclitus has been taken to be a potentially unreliable account deriving from the doxography of Theophrastus, but that is an issue I put to one side here. See further Long (1975–76: 138–41).
21. See Simplicius, *in Phys.* 480,27-30 (LM Her. R62) and *in Cael.* 294,4-7 (LM Her. R63). In both passages Simplicius notes the parallel with Stoicism.
22. On Heraclitus and the Stoics see in particular Long (1975–76). The ancient evidence is gathered together in LM Her. R50-66.
23. See Diog. Laert. 7.174 (*SVF* 1.481, LM Her. R1d). On Heraclitus and Cleanthes' *Hymn* see Thom (2005: 22–4) and Harriman (forth.b).
24. See Diog. Laert. 7.178 (*SVF* 1.620, LM Her. R1e).
25. Musonius quotes Heraclitus in 18a (Hense 1905: 96,8-10, LM Her. D103, DK 22B118); note also 9 (Hense 1905: 47,7-9). Seneca refers to him in *Ep.* 58.23 (LM Her. D65d); he is also mentioned in passing at *Ep.* 12.7; *Ira* 2.10.5; *Tranq.* 15.2. On Musonius's debt to Cleanthes, who may have been his source here, see Harriman (forth.b).
26. On Marcus and Heraclitus, see for example Long (1975–76: 153) and Cortassa (1989: 41–54).
27. *Meditations* 4.46 is the source for DK22B71-4, while 6.42 is the source for DK 22B75. In LM they are Her. R54 and 55, respectively, and LM take only one of the five DK fragments to be genuine (DK

22B74, which they also print as Her. D7), preferring different versions of the same passages in other authors. Whether these are direct quotations or not is of less significance in the present context.
28 Farquharson (1944: II, 898) suggests the same, in the context of 12.30.
29 It is worth noting again that the division into sections currently in use only dates back to Gataker (1652). In Casaubon (1643), 4.43–45 are printed as a single numbered section, "4.28", while in Xylander (1559), it is all printed as continuous text.
30 Farquharson (1944: II, 628) draws a further connection between this passage and Heraclitus by referring to DK 22B102 (LM Her. D73), where Heraclitus contrasts god, who sees all things as just, with humans who see some things just and others unjust (and cf. Gill 2013: 139). The connection seems weak; the parallel with Epictetus is much stronger. Even so, the broader focus on the nature of change still brings Heraclitus to mind here.
31 Compare with Lucretius 1.174-9, who also refers to the produce appropriate to each season.
32 For example, Farquharson (1944: II, 629–30) and Gill (2013: 139).
33 See Plutarch, *Quaest. Plat.* 1007d-e (DK 22B100, not in LM), and discussed in Kahn (1979: 155–6).
34 See Sedley (2012: 399).

5
FATE AND PROVIDENCE

A proper understanding of the workings of Nature will, Marcus suggests, enable one to embrace whatever happens as both necessary and beneficial to Nature as a whole. This brings us on to our next pair of topics: fate and providence. Marcus refers to providence (*pronoia*) throughout the *Meditations*; he also regularly refers to fate (*heimarmenê*), although not quite as often.[1] There are also numerous other passages that touch on the same theme without explicitly using either term. Both terms are important technical terms in Stoic philosophy, so before turning to consider the passages where Marcus uses them, it will be useful to give a brief account of how Stoics before Marcus understood these two terms and how they relate to each other.

The Stoics on fate and providence

According to Cicero, the early Stoics defined fate (*heimarmenê*) as "an ordering and sequence of causes" (*Div*. 1.125-6); another source describes it as "an inescapable ordering and interconnection" (Aetius 1.28.4).[2] According to Aulus Gellius, Chrysippus said that "fate is a certain everlasting ordering of the whole: one set of things follows on and succeeds another, and the interconnection is inviolable" (*NA* 7.2.3). This view of fate was the standard early Stoic view, but was often associated with Chrysippus who, as the most influential of the early Stoics, probably did most to disseminate it. It was also Chrysippus, we are told, who identified fate so understood with providence (*pronoia*). Calcidius reports the following:

> Providence will be God's will, and furthermore his will is the series of causes. In virtue of being his will it is providence. In virtue of also being the series of causes it gets the additional name fate. Consequently everything in accordance with fate is also the product of providence, and likewise everything in accordance with providence is the product of fate. That is Chrysippus' view.
>
> *in Tim.* 144, *SVF* 2.933, *LS 54U*

We find further evidence in the works of Augustine, who grappled with the Stoic theory at length. He reports that, for the Stoics, fate is "the connected series of causes which is responsible for anything that happens" (*De civ. D.* 5.8). He goes on to say that "they ascribe this orderly series, this chain of causes, to the will and power of the supreme God [...] what is meant by 'fate' is principally the will of this supreme God, whose power extends invincibly through all things" (ibid.). Augustine then quotes from Seneca (*Ep.* 107.11), who was himself quoting Cleanthes, to whom we shall turn in a moment. According to Augustine, then, drawing on Seneca, the Stoics identified fate with providence and the will of God. Elsewhere Seneca also affirms the identification of fate with providence and God:

> Do you want to call him fate? You will not be mistaken: he it is on whom everything depends, the cause of causes. Do you want to call him providence? You will be right: he it is by whose deliberation provision is made for this world, so that it can advance unhindered and unfold its actions.
>
> *Nat. Quaest.* 2.45.2

This, then, was the more or less orthodox Stoic view, set out by Chrysippus and later restated by Seneca. However, not all Stoics agreed. Calcidius's report, quoted above, goes on to note that Cleanthes held a different view, admitting that some things that come about by fate may not be the product of providence (e.g. a natural disaster may be inevitable, but not part of the divine plan).[3]

Cleanthes is important in this context as the author of the *Hymn to Zeus* that describes God's governance of the cosmos,[4] and his shorter *Prayer to Zeus*, quoted by both Seneca and Epictetus (*Ep.* 107.11; *Ench.* 53.1), with Seneca's Latin version reappearing in Augustine's discussion of Stoic fate (*De civ. D.* 5.8). The shorter *Prayer* reads:

> Lead me, Zeus and Destiny, wherever you have ordained for me. For I shall follow unflinchingly. But if I become bad and am unwilling, I shall follow none the less.
>
> *SVF* 1.527

Cleanthes thus insists that we shall follow fate – the unbreakable order of causes – no matter what, but we do have a choice whether to do so willingly or resentfully. On this point he seems to have been in harmony with his fellow early Stoics, and a similar thought is attributed to Zeno and Chrysippus:

> When a dog is tied to a cart, if it wants to follow it is pulled and follows, making its spontaneous act coincide with necessity, but if it does not want to follow it will be compelled in any case. So it is with people too: even if they do not want to, they will be compelled in any case to follow what is destined.
>
> *Hippolytus, Haer.* 1.21, *SVF* 2.975, LS 62A

We might compare these early Stoic statements about the unavoidability of fate with what we find in Marcus's *Meditations*:

> Picture to yourself every person who gives way to pain or discontent at any thing at all as like a pig being sacrificed, kicking and squealing. Such also is the man who groans on his bed, alone and in silence. Think of the chain we are bound by, and that to the rational creature only is it given to obey circumstances of his own will, while mere obedience is necessary for all.
>
> *10.28*

What all these passages imply is a distinction between unwilling compliance and an attitude of acceptance. We might draw a further distinction between different types of acceptance, some more positive than others. A person with an attitude of what we might call resigned acceptance, for instance, might acknowledge that there is nothing they can do about what is happening to them, and so accept that there is no point in complaining, even if they judge it to be bad. Someone with a more positive attitude of acceptance, by contrast, might embrace whatever happens as, say, part of the divine providential order of Nature. The former might be a suitable response to blind fate, while the latter might be taken to imply a belief in providence. Yet, as we have seen, the majority of Stoics insist on the identification of fate with providence. As we saw at the end of the last chapter, perhaps the differences here correlate with different stages of philosophical development. The irrational creature – whether that be the squealing pig or the groaning human – is at the lowest level, comprehending nothing. A basic grasp of cause and effect and necessity of events will lead to an attitude of resigned acceptance, while a fuller understanding of the rational and providential ordering of things will generate a positive acceptance of whatever happens – *amor fati*, to borrow a phrase. The lowest level will correlate with a belief that some external events are genuinely bad; the intermediate level will see them as subjectively bad for the individual but value neutral in themselves; while the higher level will see them as good, in so far as they benefit the whole, and, as such, something to be welcomed. One might say that the person at the intermediate level accepts fate but does not yet comprehend providence, while the person at the higher level grasps that fate and providence are one and the same thing.

This sets out some of the Stoic background regarding fate and providence and how one might understand their relationship. It is now time to turn to Marcus and to consider those passages where he explicitly discusses these two key terms.

Marcus on fate

Marcus refers to fate (*heimarmenê*) a number of times in the *Meditations*, with a couple of instances standing out and worth looking at closely.[5] At 3.6 he refers to the importance of being satisfied with fate and, in particular, with "what is assigned to you and is not yours to choose". At 8.35 he goes further, suggesting not mere acceptance of what has been assigned, but turning whatever that might be into something useful:

> As each reasonable creature receives the rest of his abilities from the Nature of the Whole, so have we received this ability, too, from her. Just as she converts every obstacle and resistance, puts it into its place in the order of necessity (*heimarmenê*) and makes it a part of herself, so, too, the reasonable creature can make every obstacle material for himself and employ it for whatever kind of purpose he has set out upon.
>
> *8.35*

Far more significant however is 5.8, where he says that there is one connecting harmony running through Nature, and all the causes in Nature connect to create one interconnected cause, which is fate (*heimarmenê*).[6] We ought to accept fate even if it seems unpleasant, for the sake of the good of the whole but also for our own benefit: "Accordingly let us accept these orders as we accept what Aesclepius orders. Many of them, too, are assuredly severe, yet we welcome them in hopes of health" (5.8[7–8]). One might compare this with Seneca's claims about the benefits of adversity in his *On Providence*. Marcus goes on to state at length why one ought to embrace what happens according to fate:

> Thus there are two reasons why you must be content with what happens to you: first because it was for you it came to pass, for you it was ordered and to you it was related, a thread of destiny stretching back to the most ancient causes; secondly because that which has come to each individually is a cause of the welfare and the completion and in very truth of the actual continuance of that which governs the Whole. For the perfect Whole is mutilated if you sever the least part of the contact and continuity alike of its causes as of its members; and you do this so far as in you lies, whenever you are disaffected, and in a measure you are destroying it.
>
> 5.8[12-13]

There are, he says, two reasons why we must accept fate: (i) because whatever happens was necessarily due to happen to us, produced by the chain of causes and (ii) because it is necessary for the perfection of the Whole, and if we do not accept it then we shall damage the Whole. Compare the first thought with 10.5, which does not use the term "fate" but is nevertheless highly relevant: "Whatever befalls you was prepared for you beforehand from eternity and the thread of causes was spinning from everlasting both your existence and this which befalls you". It has been suggested that the first of these two claims ultimately turns out to be the same as the second.[7] While that is ultimately true – for reasons we shall see in a moment – it is also useful to hold on to the distinction. These two claims can be taken to relate to the distinction between fate and providence or, to be more precise, the distinction between the intermediate attitude of acceptance based on a grasp of fate and the higher attitude of affirmation based on understanding the identification between fate and providence. While for the Stoics these two positions are strictly speaking the same – fate is identified with providence – it is nevertheless still possible to draw a distinction between someone who only grasps (i) and someone with a higher understanding who grasps both (i) and (ii). Marcus is of course reminding himself of both reasons in his continued attempt to reach that higher level of comprehension, but one can easily imagine someone accepting one without necessarily accepting the other.

Alongside 5.8, another key passage is 12.14:

> Either the necessity of fate (*heimarmenê*) and an order none may transgress, or providence (*pronoia*) that hears intercession, or an ungoverned welter without a purpose. If then a necessity which none may transgress, why do you resist? If a providence admitting intercession, make yourself worthy of assistance from the Godhead. If an undirected welter, be glad that in so great a flood of waves you have yourself within you a directing mind; and, if the flood carry you away, let it carry away flesh, breath, the rest of you, for your mind it shall not carry away.
>
> 12.14

Here Marcus draws a threefold division between (i) necessary fate (*heimarmenê*), (ii) providence (*pronoia*) that can assist, and (iii) blind chaos. He goes on to say that if fate is true, there is no point resisting; if providence is true, act worthy of receiving assistance; if chaos is true, follow your own inner reason. While at first glance this distinction between fate and providence might seem to go against Stoic doctrine, it does not. The Stoic account of providence does not admit of divine intervention within the order of causes, something that would be a problem for some later Christian readers who wanted to retain space for miracles.[8] Within the terms of the division that Marcus makes, the Stoic position is squarely (i). We might identify (ii) with traditional Greek and Roman theology,[9] and (iii) with Epicurean atomism. The real point Marcus wants to make here, though, is that whichever of these positions might be true, simply complaining about what happens is never an appropriate response.

Marcus on providence

In 12.14 just considered, Marcus appears to be using the term providence (*pronoia*) in a way that is out of step with early Stoic theory. As we have seen, they identified providence with fate, understood as an unbreakable chain of causation that did not admit acts of divine intervention. In order to get a better sense of how Marcus understood the term, we shall need to consider the other passages where he uses the term.[10]

In the first of these, 2.3, Marcus wants to remind himself that events that appear to be the work of chance or fortune (*tuchê*) are in fact part of the divine providential order. All events flow – *panta rhei*, an allusion to Heraclitus – from providence (*pronoia*).[11] He also reminds himself of the two key ideas expressed in 5.8, namely the necessity of all things and that events are arranged for the sake of the wellbeing of the whole of Nature. In sum, he reminds himself that nothing escapes providence and he take this to be a consolatory thought.

Not long after, in 2.11, he contemplates the possibility that there is no providence. Reflecting on his own fear of death, he argues that (i) if the gods exist, there is no reason to fear death for they would not have planned anything unpleasant, but (ii) if they do not exist, why would one want to continue living in a world not governed by divine providence? Either way, there is no reason to fear departing his current life. But Marcus does not leave it there; he goes on simply to assert that the gods do exist and "do care for men's lives". He offers no argument here but it is clear that, despite the opening disjunction, he is committed to a belief in providence. If his references here to "the gods" (*theoi*) might seem to take him away from Stoic physics, it is worth noting that he quickly shifts to talking more impersonally about "the nature of the whole" (*tôn holôn phusis*) which he presents as the directing agent. His focus here, though, is on his own fear of death and he concludes with an argument along the following lines: (i) nature is providentially ordered; (ii) death falls to good and bad people alike; therefore, (iii) death is not inherently good or bad. There is no argument for the existence of providence here; it is presupposed as a premise in an argument about indifference towards death.[12]

Marcus's claim that death – along with a whole series of other "indifferents" (*adiaphora*) – is neither good nor bad in itself is picked up in another passage, 9.1, which is an extended reflection on what it means to live in harmony with Nature. For Marcus this means living sociably, given that we have been created by nature as social animals, but it also means not placing value on indifferents such as pleasure and pain, which Nature clearly judges to be neither good nor bad given the way it distributes them randomly. He then adds that the natural order comes from "an original impulse of providence" (*archaia tês pronoias*) and it is from this "original cause" (*archê*) that everything flows. As in 2.11, Marcus presupposes the existence of providence in order to make an argument about the lack of inherent value in pleasure and pain, life and death, and other things that the Stoics classify as "indifferents". While there has been much discussion about whether Stoic ethics depends upon Stoic physics, it is clear that

Marcus regularly appeals to claims in Stoic physics in order to buttress his own commitment to central claims in Stoic ethics.[13]

There is a flurry of references to providence in Book 12 of the *Meditations*. We have already considered 12.14. In 12.1 Marcus counsels himself to forget the past, entrust the future to providence, and focus on the present. In 12.24 he remarks that external events are the product of either chance (*epituchia*) or providence (*pronoia*), but chance cannot be blamed, and providence cannot be criticized. Here he does not, as he did earlier in 2.3, insist that the former are in fact a product of the latter; instead he just leaves the disjunction hanging. Although it does not explicitly mention providence, it is also worth noting 12.5, which opens with the claim that the gods ordered all things. Whatever comes to pass is thus necessarily just, and if things ought to have been other than they are, then they would have been: "therefore from its not being so, if indeed it is not so, you should believe that it ought not to come to pass" (12.5[4]). This is the closest Marcus comes to giving an argument for the existence of providence: given that the gods exist, the world must be providentially ordered. In this passage Marcus slides between referring to plural gods (*theoi*), a singular god (*theos*), and impersonal Nature (*phusis*), suggesting that theological precision was not uppermost in his mind. Even so, one thing comes through loud and clear, namely his commitment to the view that the world is providentially and justly organized.

Providence versus atoms

As we have seen, although Marcus does not go too far into the details of what providence is and he does not offer any independent arguments in favour of its existence, in these passages at least he does seem to be firmly committed to its existence. Yet there are a number of other places where Marcus has been taken to be far more sceptical about whether Nature is arranged according to some kind of rational, providential order. There are a number of passages where Marcus explicitly contrasts providence with chance or atomic chaos; other passages not explicitly mentioning providence make the same contrast as well.[14] In some of these passages, at first glance Marcus seems either indifferent or unsure about how Nature is organized: either a chaotic and indifferent swirl of atoms (i.e. Epicurean physics) or a rational and ordered unity (i.e. Stoic physics). Some commentators have used these passages to question Marcus's orthodoxy as a Stoic.[15] If he really were a Stoic, so the argument goes, there would be no residual doubt in his mind between these two options, and he would be fully committed to the Stoic doctrine of providence. But others have rejected this, arguing that it would be a mistake to base one's assessment on just a handful of anomalous passages taken out of context.[16]

It is also worth noting that this contrast was by no means new with Marcus and can be found in a number of earlier Stoics. In one of his letters, Seneca outlines a contrast between determined fate and unpredictable chance.[17] Either way, Seneca argues, philosophy can offer consolation, encouraging us to welcome a providential order, if there is one, or endure chaos, if that turns out to be the case. His nephew Lucan, pupil of the Stoic Cornutus, made a similar point too.[18] The theme also appears in Epictetus:

> What do I care, says Epictetus, whether all existing things are composed of atoms, or of indivisibles, or of fire or earth? Is it not enough to learn the true nature of the good and the evil [...]?
>
> *Stob. 2, 13, 5-7; Epictetus fr. 1 Schenkl*

This passage, as it continues, is quite complex to interpret, but for present purposes it at least also shows that reflection on competing physical explanations was not new with Marcus.[19] If reflections such as these call into question Marcus's status as a Stoic, then the same might be said for Seneca and Epictetus as well. Rather than being a peculiar and potentially heterodox theme in the *Meditations*, this was evidently a wider topic of reflection among Roman Stoics. In order to get a clearer sense of how Marcus handled this topic, we shall need to look at the relevant passages.

The first of these, 4.3, is a lengthy and particularly important passage in the *Meditations* as a whole and has been discussed already.[20] In it Marcus reminds himself of a series of "brief and fundamental truths" that he considers to be essential for his therapeutic project of overcoming sorrow. It is in this context that he reminds himself of the following: "Revive the alternative: either providence (*pronoia*) or atoms (*atomoi*), and the many proofs that the cosmos is a kind of city (*polis*)" (4.3[5]). Here Marcus considers the options of rational order or chaos and plumps firmly in favour of the former, appealing to (although not explicitly stating) arguments in favour of his choice. His reference to reviving or renewing (*ananeôsamenos*) this distinction suggests that it was already established rather than a new innovation, and we have already seen earlier Stoics make use of it.[21] Although the disjunction "providence or atoms" is now primarily associated with Marcus – and taken by some commentators as a mark of his philosophical indecision – he himself implicitly says that it was not new with him. In any case, there is no indecision here and Marcus is clear that there are good reasons why he ought to see the cosmos as a rationally ordered entity, governed by law like a city.

In 4.27 Marcus addresses the choice directly:

> Either an ordered cosmos (*kosmos*) or a medley heaped together mechanically, but still an order (*kosmos*); or can order (*kosmos*) subsist in you and disorder (*akosmia*) in the whole? And that, too, when all things are so distinguished and yet intermingled and sympathetic.
>
> 4.27

The choice here is between two types of order within Nature: (i) some kind of inherent organization (the Stoic position); or (ii) an order generated out of chaos (the Epicurean view).[22] That there must be some kind of order in the whole is shown by the fact that there is order within us, he claims. There is a play on words here: the *kosmos* by definition cannot be *akosmia* (disordered). But given that Marcus has acknowledged that the second view also embodies some kind of randomly generated order within Nature, that point on its own does not settle the matter. Although it is far from explicit, taking the final line into account as well, the passage as a whole might be taken to imply the following kind of argument: the *kosmos* is by definition ordered (it cannot be *akosmia*), and the order within us confirms this. The sympathy and interconnection between things adds further evidence for the order within Nature. Now, which is more likely, that this order is inherent within Nature or that it is the chance by-product of the interaction of atoms? The more reasons that Marcus can give why we ought to see Nature as ordered might be taken to weigh against the claim that this order could have simply come about by chance. In other words, Marcus is prepared to concede to an atomist opponent that their physics offers an account of the origins of order within Nature, but the extent and complexity of that order makes it far more likely that the order is inherent.

The disjunction comes up again in Book 6 in three passages all reflecting in slightly different ways on dissolution and death. In 6.4 Marcus comments that everything is subject to continual change; when objects are finally dissolved they either "pass into vapour" (*ekthumiathêsetai*) or they are "dispersed into atoms" (*skedasthêsetai*).[23] The passage ends there, with no further comment, although it is immediately followed in 6.5 with a reference to the controlling reason (*logos*) in Nature. The disjunction, then, does not seem to imply any wider indecision on Marcus's part. Indeed if one takes into account 6.3 as well, a fuller picture emerges. In 6.3 Marcus reminds himself to focus on what is within, and then in 6.4 that what is external will quickly be transformed. Taken together, his point is that one ought not to pay too much attention to externals. Leave those, he continues in 6.5, to the controlling reason that governs all things. Taken on its own, 6.4 might at first glance look like indecision with regards to physical theory, but if one reads 6.3-5 as a continuous text, a quite different impression emerges.[24]

In 6.10 Marcus opposes "a medley, interlacing, and scattering" to "unification, order, providence". If the former, he asks himself, why be concerned about anything (cf. 2.11 discussed above), but if the latter, one can be calm in the knowledge that there is an order. Marcus does not come down on one side or the other in this instance; his aim is to offer consolation whichever might be true.[25] Either way, there is no good reason to be troubled.

A similar suspension of judgement can be seen in the next passage:

> Alexander the Great and his stable boy were levelled in death, for they were either taken up into the same life-giving principle (*spermatikos logos*) of the cosmos or were scattered without distinction into atoms.
>
> *6.24*

His main point here is of course that death is the great leveller, no matter what death might actually involve. There is no further comment about which of these two outcomes is most likely. Yet this apparent suspension of judgement again needs to be placed in its immediate context: the very next passage, 6.25, describes the way in which all events take place within the cosmos, described as a single (*heis*) and united (*sumpas*) entity. Nature is a unified whole, not a conglomeration of atoms.

This primary concern with consolation continues in 7.75. Nature has created itself either according to a necessary plan or without any discernible reason. Marcus makes no explicit judgement either way but suggests that reflecting on this will enable him to remain calm. It has been suggested that the second option is plainly impossible:[26] how could the ruling principle (*hêgemonikon*) of the cosmos be devoid of reason? Therefore, the calmness is produced by seeing that Nature must clearly be arranged according to some rational principle. This would involve inserting an unstated argument into the middle of the passage: either the cosmos is rational or irrational; [but the cosmos clearly cannot be irrational; therefore, the cosmos is rational]; and thus there is no reason not to remain calm. The argument follows a standard Stoic form: either "a" or "b"; not "b"; therefore "a".[27]

In 9.28 we find something more complex, with two distinct disjunctions:

> Now either the mind of the whole has an impulse to each individual; and if that is so, welcome what it initiates; or else it had an impulse once for all and what follows is consequential upon that; and why are you anxious? And whether the whole be God, all is well – or whether it be chance, somehow molecules or atoms, be not yourself then ruled by chance.
>
> *9.28*

The first disjunction is between whether the mind of the whole (*dianoia tou holou*) is concerned with the wellbeing of each individual (cf. option (ii) in 12.14 above), or whether it had a single initial impulse from which everything else follows. The second disjunction is between whether the whole (*to holon*) ought to be identified with god or with chance. As Marcus presents them here, they are distinct, and he responds to them separately. It has been suggested that the first disjunction ought to be placed under the second, creating a single, complex argument.[28] It is certainly possible that this is what Marcus had in mind, but equally it may just be two related but unconnected thoughts.

A few paragraphs later, at 9.39, we find a similar line of thought again, this time probably with death in mind. Reflecting on change within Nature, he comments that either such change comes from a directing mind, and what happens does so for the good of the whole, or it is a mere mechanical movement of atoms. Either way, why be troubled, Marcus asks.[29]

The single longest discussion of this issue can be found in a pair of passages in Book 10 that are worth considering together and may have been composed at the same time.[30] These are 10.6 and 10.7. The first, 10.6, opens with the following:

> Whether there are atoms (*atomoi*) or nature (*phusis*), the first postulate must be: 'I am part of the whole (*to holon*) which is governed by nature'; the second: 'I am allied (*oikeiôs*) in some way to the parts that are of the same kind with me.'
>
> 10.6[1]

Although this appears to propose an open choice between Epicurean and Stoic physics, it immediately slides into insisting on two key Stoic principles, using technical terms from Stoic physics and ethics.[31] Marcus continues by reminding himself that if he holds on to these two postulates then he won't be disturbed by anything that is assigned by the whole because "nothing which benefits the whole is injurious to the part" (10.6[2]). He continues by adding "by remembering, therefore, that I am a part of a whole so characterized, I shall be well-affected to all that results from it" (10.6[3]). To this he adds a brief reminder of another key theme we find throughout the *Meditations*, namely that he shares a kinship with parts of Nature similar to him – other rational beings – and so ought always to act in manner appropriate to a social animal. He concludes by drawing a parallel with the behaviour of a citizen of a city, whose life is smooth when he "acts to benefit his fellow citizens and welcomes whatever his city (*polis*) assigns" (10.6[5]). The implication is clear: Marcus conceives "the whole" as something analogous to the city, and in particular as something (i) unified, (ii) that acts for the benefit of the whole, and (iii) in which the parts benefit when the whole is benefitted.[32] None of these claims are really compatible with the opening option that everything might be composed of atoms. Despite apparently offering an open-ended choice between two physical theories, the bulk of the passage emphatically endorses the Stoic view that Nature is a unified and organized whole.

In the passage that immediately follows, 10.7, Marcus reflects on the nature of dissolution, which he characterizes as simply a type of change. At one point he writes:

> For this dissolution is either a dissipation of the elements out of which they were compounded or else a turning of the solid into its earthy and of the vital spirit (*pneumatikos*) into its airy part, so that these too are caught up into the reason of the whole (*logos tou holou*), whether the whole returns periodically to fire or is renewed by eternal exchanges.
>
> 10.7[5]

Either way, he consoles himself, do not be indignant about what happens. But again this is not a real, open-ended choice. The opening of the passage has already affirmed that Nature would never injure its own parts or produce changes for the worse – all change in some way benefits Nature as a whole. Marcus is merely considering the possibility that this might not be so, only to make the point that either way there are no grounds to complain about anything that happens: change is either for the benefit of the whole or random and without meaning; in neither case can a change be described as inherently bad.

Given the clear priority assigned to Stoic physics in 10.6 and 10.7, we might wonder why Marcus even raises the possibility of an alternative view of Nature. Why does he consider, even hypothetically, the possibility that atomism might be true? Perhaps the answer to this question can be found by reflecting on the context in which Marcus makes these remarks. It is usually within the context of thinking about change, which in fact usually means dissolution, the most extreme case of which is death – either his own or the death of a loved one. This is what Marcus seems to be really thinking about in these passages: how to come to terms with those sorts of changes that have the potential to disturb one's equanimity. The point that Marcus really wants to make is that change of this sort is natural and inevitable. Now that very broad point is true whether one believes in either providence or atoms. Both Stoic and Epicurean physics embrace the constant flux of the material world, which for both is the only thing that exists. So, whether it be providence or atoms, change is inevitable, Marcus insists. But when he goes on to flesh out the precise working of change, he always draws on the Stoic view of Nature to which he is unambiguously committed.

Summarizing Marcus

In the preceding sections a fairly clear sense of Marcus's own views on fate and providence has emerged. Even so, it may be useful to conclude by summarizing the variety of different positions he entertains in the passages that we have considered. There appear to be five distinct positions:

  i. The *kosmos* is rationally ordered by a divine providence (2.3, 4.3, 4.27, 6.10, 10.7, 12.5, 12.24).
  ii. The *kosmos* is controlled by a divine providence that can intervene into the causal chain (2.11, 9.28, 12.14).
  iii. The *kosmos* was prompted by a providential first cause but subsequently runs mechanically (9.1, 9.28).
  iv. The *kosmos* runs mechanically according to fate or necessity (5.8, 7.75, 10.5, 10.7, 12.5, 12.14).
  v. The *kosmos* is completely random and chaotic (4.3, 4.27, 6.10, 7.75, 12.14, 12.24).

This list includes all the different positions that Marcus mentions, but what is his own view? In some passages Marcus emphatically affirms the existence of providence (2.3, 2.11, 5.8, 9.11, 12.1, 12.5). By contrast, there do not seem to be any passages where he explicitly affirms that the *kosmos* is in fact disorderly and chaotic. In passages where he mentions multiple possibilities, it is almost always to make the point that whichever way the *kosmos* is arranged, (i) we ought not be troubled by events, or (ii) that we ought nevertheless to act rationally. The principal motivation for his repeated references to both fate and providence is to remind himself that external events are out of his control. This is an application of Epictetus's dichotomy of control (*Ench.* 1.1): external events are not "up to us" (*eph' hêmin*) and so there is little to be gained from worrying about them, let along trying to resist them. Moreover, change is natural and inevitable, and so ought never to be seen as something inherently bad, and this applies whether Stoic or Epicurean physics is true. At the same time, he is also clearly committed to the view that whatever happens is for the benefit of the whole – a claim we might associate with a belief in providence – and that whatever happens to us is necessary and cannot be altered – a belief in causal determinism or fate (see e.g. 5.8, 10.5). Marcus's commitment to both providence and fate is, as we have seen, completely in line with orthodox Stoic doctrine.

Notes

1 For providence (*pronoia*), see 2.3, 2.11, 4.3, 6.10, 8.3, 9.1, 12.1, 12.14, 12.24. For fate (*heimarmenê*), see 3.6, 5.8, 5.24, 7.46, 8.35, 9.28, 12.14.
2 These passages are *SVF* 2.921, LS 55L and *SVF* 2.917, LS 55J respectively. For fuller selections of texts see *SVF* 2.912-1007 and the rest of section 55 in LS. For a detailed study of Stoic thought on this topic see Bobzien (1998).
3 It has been suggested that Posidonius also held a heterodox view involving a hierarchy of God, Nature, and Fate. However, Kidd (1988: I, 417) argues that this is merely a logical or explanatory order, not an ontological one, and he notes that it mirrors the order of exposition in Diog. Laert. 7.148-9. See further Posidonus fr. 103 EK (Aetius 1.28.5) with Kidd (1988: I, 414–18) for further discussion and references.
4 This is preserved in Stob. 1,25,3–27,4 (*SVF* 1.537, LS 54I). For a detailed study see Thom (2005).
5 Marcus refers to fate (*heimarmenê*) at: 3.6, 5.8, 5.24, 7.46, 8.35, 9.28, 12.14. Of these, 3.6, 5.8, 8.35, and 12.14 will be discussed here (but note that Dalfen brackets *heimarmenê* in 12.14). Of the others, 5.24 will be quoted at the beginning of the next chapter, 7.46 is in a quotation from Plato's *Gorgias* 512d-e, and at 9.28, the text is corrupt and the instance of *heimarmenê* is merely a conjecture put forward by Rendall. (See Rendall 1898: 192 who suggests it "provisionally". It was not adopted by Farquharson but is by Dalfen. For a fuller argument in favour of the emendation, drawing a parallel with 12.14, see Rendall 1895: 150–51.) It is also worth noting that some translations hide this technical Stoic term by not translating it consistently. For example, Farquharson (1944) translates *heimarmenê* as "destiny" at 3.6, "the order of Nature" at 5.8, "the chain of causation" at 5.24, and "the order of necessity" at 8.35. This can contribute to the mistaken impression that Marcus was not engaging with the details of Stoic doctrine.
6 On 5.8, see the commentary in Gill (2013: 149–51) and note also Ackeren (2011: II, 412–20).
7 See Gill (2013: 150).
8 This was raised as an objection against Stoicism by Justus Lipsius in his dialogue *De Constantia* (1.20), published in 1584, although Lipsius himself was sympathetic to the Stoic view.
9 It is equally compatible with a broadly Christian theology that admits of miracles, but it is highly unlikely that Marcus had that in mind.
10 Marcus refers to providence (*pronoia*) at: 2.3, 2.11, 4.3, 6.10, 8.3, 9.1, 12.1, 12.14, 12.24. We have already discussed 12.14. We shall come back to 4.3 and 6.10 later, in the next section. We shall pass over 8.3, which uses the word in a different sense.
11 Farquharson translates *panta ekeithen rhei* in 2.3 as "all flows from that other world" and Rutherford, in his note in Farquharson (1989: 152) takes this as evidence for a Platonic element in Marcus's thought. But *ekeithen* might better be rendered as "from there", with "there" referring to providence, not some supernatural realm. The point being made is that there are no events outside the providential order of Nature. In his commentary, Farquharson (1944: II, 503) glosses it as "from the divine reason", which is closer to the mark and, in a Stoic context, does not imply anything supernatural.
12 For more on the topic of death, see Chapter 7 below.
13 On the relationship between Stoic physics and ethics, see Inwood (2009) containing further references. It is worth noting that the Stoics do give independent arguments for their central ethical

claims, including their views about "indifferents" (see Diog. Laert. 7.103-4, LS 58A-B), so the appeal to physics does not seem to be essential. Even so, Marcus gives good examples of the way in which claims in the different parts of the Stoic system inter-relate and mutually support one another.

14 See esp. 4.3, 4.27, 6.4, 6.10, 6.24, 7.75, 9.28, 9.39, 10.6, 10.7, 12.24. Ackeren (2011: II, 429) also notes 6.44, 7.32, 8.17, 11.18, 12.14.
15 See for example Rist (1982: 28–30) and Cooper (2004: 346–7). Annas (2004: 111) takes it to be a case of Marcus suspending his commitment to Stoicism.
16 See for example Gill (2013: lxix–lxxiv). For a recent discussion see Harriman (forth.a).
17 See Seneca, *Ep.* 16.4-6. On these Stoic precursors to Marcus's contrast, see Reydams Schils (2012b: 115) following Gourinat (2012c: 79) who is, in turn, following Hadot (1998: 151).
18 See Lucan's *De bello civile* 2.7-15.
19 This passage as a whole (Epictetus, fr. 1 Schenkl) opens with the part quoted here. As it continues, it turns into a dialogue with an interlocutor. Even if knowledge of Nature is not essential, surely self-knowledge is required, Epictetus argues. But humans are social animals, part of society, created by Nature and trying to live in harmony with Nature. The line of argument points to the conclusion that knowledge of Nature may well be required after all. Oldfather (1925–28: II, 443, and cf. Hard 2014: 279) translates the final line as "What Nature is, and how she administers the universe, and whether she really exists or not, these are questions about which there is no need to go on to bother ourselves." This is an odd conclusion to draw from the preceding line of argument and, as Gill notes (in Hard 2014: 344), it is out of step with what Epictetus says elsewhere. It would make much better sense if it were taken as a rhetorical question: is there really no need to bother ourselves about the study of Nature? Indeed, this last line is punctuated as a question in Schenkl (1916: 456). (For a quite different construal of the text see Wachsmuth and Hense 1884–1912: II, 14.) It is also worth noting that in the part quoted I follow Oldfather and Hard in printing "says Epictetus" but the Greek is simply *phêsi*, and it may make better sense of the passage as a whole to attribute this opening statement to the interlocutor, a statement that Epictetus then argues *against*. Both points are taken into account by Reydams-Schils (2012b: 115–16), who gives a good account of the passage. For a similar interpretation, see Barnes (1997: 25–7) but resisted by Long (2002: 149–51).
20 See Chapter 2 above.
21 Gourinat (2012c: 77–9) argues that it may well go back to Chrysippus's *On Providence*. He also notes that disjunctions were a standard argument form in Stoic logic, in which one of the two options would be expected to be true, the other false.
22 Farquharson (1944: II, 616) notes what he calls the two senses of *kosmos* in this passage, citing Aristotle, [*Mund.*] 391b9-12 as a parallel.
23 I follow Farquharson's translation here, who comments on his rendering of these two terms at Farquharson (1944: II, 677–8). He takes them to be clear references to Stoic and Epicurean processes, respectively. See also Gill (2013: 169).
24 In Casaubon (1643: 133–5) our 6.3 and 6.4 are printed together as a single passage. The wider point worth stressing once again is that the modern subdivisions of the *Meditations* date back only to Gataker (1652); in Xylander (1559) based on one of the two primary witnesses for the *Meditations*, this passage is all printed as continuous text.
25 Compare with Seneca, *Ep.* 16.4-6.
26 See Rutherford in Farquharson (1989: 169).
27 In the Stoic schema of arguments, this is the fifth indemonstrable syllogism. See Diog. Laert. 7.81. On Stoic disjunctive arguments in connection with Marcus's discussions of "providence or atoms", see Gourinat (2012c: 77). It is also worth noting that the reason why the additional argument remained unstated is that it might have been taken to be obvious, for by definition the *kosmos* cannot be *akosmia* (cf. 4.27, discussed above).
28 See Hadot (1998: 151–2). Although Hadot's analysis is rich and suggestive, I am not entirely convinced. He divides the first disjunction into three distinct positions rather than two, which does not seem warranted. Having said that, I am in agreement with his broader line of interpretation of these passages.

29 We shall come back to Marcus's reflections on death in Chapter 7.
30 As I have commented elsewhere above, the current divisions into chapters dates back only to Gataker (1652) and the first printed edition, Xylander (1559), based on one of the two key witnesses for the text, does not contain numbered divisions.
31 Thus, *to holon* in Stoic physics refers to all of Nature (cf. *SVF* 2.522-5); *oikeiôs* refers to the theory of *oikeiôsis*, the foundational doctrine in Stoic ethics (cf. *SVF* 3.178-89).
32 We shall come back to the idea of the cosmos as a city later in Chapter 9.

6
SOUL AND EMOTION

There are a number of central themes in the *Meditations*, each of which is tempting to highlight as the most important. One candidate for this would be the relationship between the individual and Nature.[1] Many of Marcus's comments dealing with aspects of physics or ethics are primarily concerned with the place of the individual within a larger entity, whether that be wider society or the cosmos as a whole. Here is just one of many examples:

> Call to mind the whole of substance (*ousia*) of which you have a very small portion, and the whole of time (*aiôn*) whereof a small hair's breadth has been determined for you, and of the chain of causation (*heimarmenê*) where of you are how small a link.
>
> *5.24*

Given the personal nature of the text, what Marcus is primarily reflecting on is his own place within these larger entities. So, how did Marcus understand himself, and how did that bear on how he understood his place within Nature? In this chapter we shall approach these questions by looking at Marcus's reflections on notions of the self and how he conceived himself as an embodied human being. This will involve looking at this passing remarks about the nature of the soul and in particular the ruling part of the soul. As we shall see, as well as seemingly downplaying himself by contrasting his smallness against the immensity of Nature, he also often seems to valorize and isolate himself, such as when he counsels himself to turn inwards, retreating into what he calls his citadel (*akropolis*). At first glance, there might appear to be a tension here. In what follows we shall try to make sense of this.

A note on terminology

Before starting, a brief note on terminology. We noted earlier that Epictetus was an important influence on Marcus and it has sometimes been claimed that he was Marcus's most important point of reference.[2] Indeed, we have already seen a number of ways in which Marcus echoes themes in Epictetus. A key concept in Epictetus, especially in the context of discussions about the nature of the self, is *prohairesis*.[3] This means something like "choice" or "will", but is sometimes translated as "moral purpose", "mind", or even "self".[4] For Epictetus, our *prohairesis* is the only thing that is "up to us", the only thing that is truly free. In a sense, you are your *prohairesis*, even if you are also an embodied human being.[5] Epictetus argued that all our attention ought to be directed towards our *prohairesis*, because: (i) that's where all good and evil reside (i.e. virtue and vice), and (ii) it is the only thing within our control, so by doing so we can avoid frustration and disappointment.

It might be natural to think that Epictetus's reflections on the self, understood as *prohairesis*, would be an important influence on Marcus's own thoughts on the topic. Perhaps surprisingly, the word *prohairesis* appears just once in Marcus Aurelius (11.36), and that is in fact a quotation from Epictetus (*Diss.* 3.22.105).[6] When Marcus talks about the self, he tends to use a different term, *hêgemonikon*, which appears over 40 times in the *Meditations*.[7] This is a technical term in early Stoic psychology. Before looking more closely at the role that this notion plays in the *Meditations* (and its relationship with the notion of *prohairesis*), it may be useful to begin by considering the wider background of Stoic psychology.

Stoic psychology

As we have seen, the Stoics held that there are two fundamental principles in Nature, the active and the passive.[8] The same applies in the case of human beings, who are of course merely fragments of Nature as a whole. A human being is thus a combination of portions of the two principles in Nature, active and passive. These are *pneuma* and matter, which in the context of a human being refer to the soul (*psuchê*) and the body. The soul is the *pneuma* or "breath" that permeates and animates the whole body.

According to early Stoic theory, the *pneuma* that is present in all things in Nature can exist at varying degrees of tension (*tonos*). Different levels of tension account of the different properties that material objects can have. This led the early Stoics to outline a scale of nature, running from simple entities up to the most complex. In particular, they are reported to have posited four different levels of pneumatic tension: (i) cohesion (*hexis*), the power or force that holds physical objects together giving them their unity; (ii) nature (*phusis*), the power of growth associated with biological organisms such as plants; (iii) soul (*psuchê*), the powers of perception and movement associated with animals; and (iv) rational soul (*psuchê logikê*), the power of rational deliberation enjoyed by humans.[9] There is thus no difference in kind between inanimate and animate entities, and no difference in kind between animals and humans, just varying degrees of tension within the same fundamental principle permeating all things.[10]

In the light of this, one can see that for the early Stoics the soul proper (*psuchê*) is not comprised of all the *pneuma* in the human body, but only that portion of *pneuma* that is at the appropriate degree of tension. According to Diogenes Laertius, the Stoics claimed that the soul has eight parts: the five senses, the powers of speech and reproduction, and the power of reasoning.[11] Other sources identify the last of these with the commanding faculty or ruling part of the soul (*hêgemonikon*).[12] The ruling part (*hêgemonikon*) was itself said to have its own parts or capacities: impression, impulse, and assent.[13] The last of these corresponds more or less to what Epictetus calls choice (*prohairesis*). There was some debate about the physical location of the ruling part of the soul. Chrysippus argued that it was located in the heart, which he took to be the seat of the emotions, but others argued that it was located in the brain.[14] The rest of the soul – the other seven parts – were said to "grow out of the leading part and extend to the body, just like the tentacles from the octopus".[15] It is tempting here to think of a brain connected to the nervous system spreading out through and controlling the body, and it may be that early Stoic thought was shaped by developments in the study of human anatomy in the Hellenistic period.[16]

A threefold division?

Having briefly outlined the early Stoic view of the soul, the first question to ask is whether Marcus shared it. This question has been raised in the past because in a number of passages Marcus appears to commit himself to a threefold distinction between body, mind, and soul, rather than the twofold distinction described by the early Stoics.[17] Here are a couple of examples:

> This whatever it is that I am, is flesh (*sarkia*) and vital spirit (*pneumation*) and the governing self (*hêgemonikon*).
>
> 2.2

> There are three things of which you are compounded: body (*sômation*), vital spirit (*pneumation*), mind (*nous*).
>
> 12.3

Such passages might be taken to imply some sort of Platonic influence on Marcus, whereby the ruling part of the soul (*hêgemonikon*) is seen as something distinct (and so potentially separable) from the spirit (i.e. *pneuma*) and flesh (i.e. the body).[18] That Marcus sometimes uses *nous* in place of *hêgemonikon* (as in 12.3 above; see also 3.16) might add to this impression. However, it has been argued that it would be a mistake to take this as an attempt to articulate some new hybrid Platonic–Stoic account of the soul.[19] Instead, Marcus makes these distinctions in order to underline Stoic ethical views to which he is committed. Thus, as 2.2 continues, Marcus adds dismissive remarks about the body or flesh compared with the soul, reflecting the fact that the body is an "indifferent" (*adiaphoron*) in the language of early Stoic ethics and "not up to us" (*ouk eph' hêmin*) according to Epictetus. The further distinction between soul or *pneuma* and the *hêgemonikon*, on which Marcus also elaborates in 2.2, is not an attempt to claim that the latter is not in fact part of the former, but rather simply an attempt to highlight the importance of paying attention to the *hêgemonikon* above all else.[20] Indeed, elsewhere, 5.26, Marcus acknowledges the standard Stoic view when he refers to the *hêgemonikon* as the ruling part *of the* soul (*psuchê*). Our other passage, 12.3, continues after making its threefold division by adding "Two of these are your own in so far as you must take care of them, but only the third is in the strict sense your own". The contrast Marcus wants to make here is again the Epictetean one between things that are and are not "up to us". The *hêgemonikon* is singled out from the other parts of the soul not in order to make an ontological point about the constitution of the individual but instead simply to highlight where his attention ought to be directed.

A further passage, 3.16, is more complex. This opens with a threefold distinction: *sôma*, *psuchê*, *nous*. These are then associated with sensation (*aisthêsis*), impulse (*hormê*), and doctrines (*dogmata*), respectively. The body is connected with sensations, and to be overwhelmed by these is no different from being an animal. Base humans are dominated by their impulses, while even rational humans, able to grasp doctrines, might use these in immoral ways. At first glance this looks as if it might map on to the Stoic scale of nature, although it fails to do so in its details. For that to work properly, sensation would have to be aligned with the soul, not the body, alongside impulse. The point Marcus goes on to make is that what matters most is not merely avoiding the puppet strings of sensations and impulses, but also becoming a good person, whom he describes as someone who embraces whatever fate brings. Once again, his aim in this passage as a whole is not to make a claim about the nature or structure of the soul but instead to focus attention on how one ought to act.

It looks as if it would be a mistake, then, to place too much weight on the few passages where Marcus draws this threefold division. If they serve any purpose within the context of thinking about human psychology, in general they simply underline the centrality of the *hêgemonikon* as the most important part of the soul.

The *hêgemonikon*

So, the *hêgemonikon* is the ruling part of the soul. As we noted earlier, the Stoics claimed it was divided into parts dealing with impression (*phantasia*), impulse (*hormê*), and assent (*sunkatathesis*). As such, it is that from which our beliefs, desires, and actions spring, and so the most important thing to which we can attend. As Marcus puts it in 4.39, our own *hêgemonikon* is of paramount importance because that is where good and evil reside, namely in our judgements. In so far as it refers to the ruling part of the soul, the term *hêgemonikon* has sometimes been translated as "mind" (e.g. Staniforth 1964). As we can see, this is something broader than Epictetus's *prohairesis*, which corresponds to just one part of the *hêgemonikon*, namely assent. In this sense, Marcus's focus on the *hêgemonikon* is broader in scope than Epictetus's much narrower concern with just *prohairesis* or choice. This is in part borne out by Marcus's regular reflections on impressions that we considered earlier.[21]

It has been argued that because Marcus uses *hêgemonikon* with reflexive pronouns, similar to the way in which we might now with the word "self", this is what he really had in mind when he used the term.[22] Similar arguments have often been made about Epictetus's use of *prohairesis*.[23] In a sense, what we truly are is the ruling part of the soul, claims Marcus, or, even more restrictedly, our power of choice, claims Epictetus. However, it is also worth noting that when Marcus does this, he talks about the *hêgemonikon* as if it were a thing, not as if it were himself. For example:

> What is my ruling part (*hêgemonikon*) to me, and what sort of thing am I making it now, and for what purpose am I employing it now?
>
> *10.24; see also 6.8, 12.33*

If he really thought of himself as his *hêgemonikon*, why would he talk about it in this way as a thing distinct from himself? (A similar question applies to Epictetus's use of *prohairesis*, which he sometimes refers to as a thing; see e.g. *Diss*. 1.2.33.) The answer (in both cases) is fairly simple: Marcus is not his *hêgemonikon*; he is an embodied human being, a psychophysical unity of body and soul, in line with the standard Stoic view.[24] One might compare passages such as 10.24 quoted above with colloquial phrases such as "my mind is playing tricks on me", and it would perhaps be a mistake to try to take that kind of phrase as evidence for a particular conception of the self.

There is one especially interesting passage where Marcus comments explicitly on the relationship between the *hêgemonikon* and himself conceived as a psychophysical unity:

See that the governing and sovereign (*hêgemonikon kai kurieuon*) part of your soul (*psuchê*) is undiverted by the smooth or broken movement in the flesh, and let it not blend therewith, but circumscribe itself, and limit those affections within the (bodily) parts. But when they are diffused into the understanding by dint of that other sympathy, as needs must be in a united system, then you must not try to resist the sensation, which is natural, yet the governing part (*hêgemonikon*) must not of itself add to the affection the judgement that it is either good or bad.

5.26

This is an important passage in the present context because it makes a number of relevant points: (i) the *hêgemonikon* is a part of the soul, in line with the standard Stoic view;[25] (ii) it is part of a single united system with the body, following Stoic psychophysical holism, even if it ought to circumscribe itself; (iii) it will inevitably receive impressions from the body, but must resist making unwarranted value judgements about them. It is precisely because the ruling part of the soul is intimately connected with the body, via the tentacles of the soul's nervous system, so to speak, that it must be careful not to be overwhelmed by the sensations of pleasure and pain that it receives. It is, as he puts it in 10.24, "melted into and blended with the flesh", although not to the extent that it is controlled by the movements of the body (it is, after all, the *ruling* part). The *hêgemonikon* can never isolate itself from the rest of the psychophysical unity of which it is a part; but what it can do – what is within its own power – is avoid making mistaken judgements about the impressions it receives over which it has no control.

Emotions

One reason why Marcus is concerned about the *hêgemonikon* making mistaken judgements is that they can generate emotions (*pathê*). The Stoics were of course famous for their analysis of emotions. Our most important sources report the way in which Chrysippus distinguished between four basic types of unwanted emotions, all of which are the product of mistaken judgements.[26] Thus, the judgement that something good or bad is present will generate the emotions of pleasure (*hêdonê*) or distress (*lupê*), while the judgement that something good or bad may come along in the future will generate the emotions of desire (*epithumia*) or fear (*phobos*). By avoiding making mistaken judgements it is possible to avoid the negative emotions that they produce, reaching a state of *apatheia*.[27]

Marcus alludes to the Stoic account a number of times.[28] In 11.19 he mentions four aberrations of the *hêgemonikon*, and in 11.20 he describes these as a severance from Nature.[29] In particular he mentions anger (*orgê*), distress (*lupê*), and fear (*phobos*), alongside the vices of injustice and intemperance. At 6.16 he refers to *apatheia*, contrasting it to being pulled around on puppet strings.[30]

Perhaps the most interesting passage in this context is 11.18, immediately before 11.19 and 11.20 just noted. This is primarily concerned with dealing with other people and, in particular, with Marcus's own emotional responses arising out of his interactions with others. It is not, he reminds himself, what other people do that matters (that belongs to their *hêgemonikon*, not one's own), but rather his own judgements about other people's actions.[31] It is these judgements that generate emotions such as anger (*orgê*).[32] If he can change his judgement, then he can avoid his feelings of anger. Towards the end of the same passage Marcus reflects on the thought that not getting angry might look like a sign of weakness to others. He reminds himself that there is nothing manly about losing one's temper. On the contrary, the most admirable human trait is strength of character, and it is *apatheia* that expresses this far more than emotions such as anger (*orgê*) or distress (*lupê*), which are ultimately signs of weakness.

Another string of passages where emotions are uppermost in Marcus's mind are 2.10-13. The first of these draws on material from the Peripatetic Theophrastus.[33] Marcus describes, seemingly with approval, Theophrastus's claim in his account of emotions that some vices are worse than others, and at first glance this looks as if Marcus is rejecting the Stoic view that all vices are equal. However, it has been argued that if anything Marcus re-describes Theophrastus's view using Stoic terminology.[34] Either way, this excerpt from Theophrastus on emotions prompts Marcus in the subsequent sections to reflect on the same theme. In 2.11 he considers his own fear of death and in 2.12 he warns against fear of inevitable and natural change. Then, in 2.13 he exhorts himself to remain untouched by emotion. In general Marcus warns himself against responding in anger (*orgê*) towards other people and experiencing fear (*phobos*) or distress (*lupê*) in the face of natural events out of his control. His goal is to attain a state of Stoic *apatheia*.

An inner citadel

In places Marcus presents the *hêgemonikon* as a place of retreat into which one can and ought to withdraw:

> Withdraw into yourself: the governing part (*hêgemonikon*) is by its nature content with its own just actions and the tranquillity it thus secures.
>
> 7.28[35]

> Remember that the governing part (*hêgemonikon*) becomes invincible when it withdraws into itself and is satisfied with itself, doing nothing which it does not will to do [...] On this account the understanding free from emotions (*pathê*) is a citadel of refuge (*akropolis*); for man has nothing stronger into which to retreat and be thereafter unassailable.
>
> 8.48

This image of turning oneself into an *akropolis* or "inner citadel" has become a powerful one in the wider reception of Marcus's thought, despite the fact that he only uses the word once, in the passage quoted above.[36] It is an interesting, but potentially misleading, image. First, Marcus is sometimes thought to be advocating a permanent retreat inwards, turning his back on the external world. In the important passage 4.3 discussed earlier,[37] Marcus also outlines a process of retreat inwards but there he is explicit that this ought to be a period of rest and repair before returning to the affairs of everyday life. Second, it is worth thinking about what is *in* the *hêgemonikon*, so to speak. As we have seen, it is the seat of impressions (of the external world) and judgements (about the external world), along with impulses (to act in the external world). Although a focus on the *hêgemonikon* certainly involves a shift of emphasis, from external objects to our judgements about those objects, it would be difficult to sustain the claim that this "turn inwards" implies turning one's back on the external world in any significant way at all. Instead it might better be described as developing a new relationship with the external world. The distinction at work here is not between the internal and the external, but instead Epictetus's distinction between what is and is not "up to us" (*eph' hêmin*).

This way of understanding what Marcus is proposing here effectively takes the *hêgemonikon* to be the "mind" rather than the "self": the aim is not to retreat into oneself, but instead to attend to the impressions, judgements, and choices within one's mind. As we have seen, he often writes about the *hêgemonikon* as if it were a thing, his mind, but not himself. He remains an embodied human being, fully part of the world.

Expanding the scale of nature

In order to underline the fact that Marcus's wider reflections on the self ought not to be taken as excessively self-obsessed or inward looking, there is one further passage worth considering. Earlier we saw the Stoic scale of nature, comprised of four different levels reflecting different degrees of tension within *pneuma*. These were cohesion (*hexis*), nature (*phusis*), soul (*psuchê*), and rational soul (*psuchê logikê*). In one passage where Marcus explicitly alludes to this theory,[38] he extends it by adding a fifth level:

> Most of the objects which the vulgar admire may be referred to the general heads of what is held together by 'cohesion' (*hexis*), like minerals and timber, or by 'nature' (*phusis*), like figs, vines, olives; those admired by slightly superior folk to things held together by '[animal] soul' (*psuchê*), for instance flocks and herds or bare ownership of a multitude of slaves; those by persons still more refined to things held together by 'rational spirit' (*logikê psuchê*), not, however, rational as such but so far as to be technical or skilled in something else. But one who reveres spirit in its full sense of reasonable and political (*logikê kai politikê psuchê*) regards those other objects no longer, but above all continually keeps his own soul rational and sociable in itself and in its activity, co-operating with a fellow being to this end.
>
> 6.14

There are a number of ways in which one might take this: (i) to see *politikê psuchê* as a fifth level above *logikê psuchê*; (ii) to see *logikê kai politikê psuchê* as a fifth level above *logikê psuchê* on its own, or (iii) to see *logikê kai politikê psuchê* as simply an elaboration of the existing fourth level of *logikê psuchê*. The second of these options seems to be what Marcus has in mind, distinguishing what one might call mere instrumental reason from rationality in the fuller, Stoic sense of the word. But Marcus is quite explicit that this higher sense of rationality is at once social as well. It is co-operation with other human beings that Marcus takes to be the highest stage in the scale of nature, the highest stage of development in a human being. The ideal Stoic sage with perfect rationality, he implies, is not locked away in isolated contemplation, but is actively engaged in the world, working with other people. That is the highest goal towards which Marcus thinks he ought to aspire.[39] If at the same time he stresses the importance of turning inwards in order to attend to the judgements made by the ruling part of his soul, it is precisely because these judgements shape his ethical character and his actions.

Notes

1 Thus, Stephens (2012) devotes two of his five chapters (3 and 4) to this theme broadly conceived.
2 See especially Hadot (1978) and, at greater length, Hadot (1998).
3 On *prohairesis* in Epictetus see Dobbin (1991), Asmis (2001), and Sorabji (2007).

4 Oldfather (1925–28) has "moral purpose"; Hard (2014) has "choice". Dobbin (1998: xxiv) suggests "moral character", while Long (2002) opts for "volition". On the idea of *prohairesis* as "self" (with qualifications), see Sorabji (2007).
5 Although in places Epictetus appears to identify *prohairesis* with the self (e.g. *Ench.* 9), other passages count against this (e.g. *Diss.* 1.2.33). It is not literally the self, but simply the most important part of oneself: the part over which one has control, the location of good and evil, and so where all one's attention ought to be directed.
6 This is one of a string of quotations from Epictetus at the end of Book 11, on which see Sellars (2018a).
7 See Rigo (2010: 91). Epictetus also uses this term (although not as frequently as *prohairesis*); see Schenkl (1916: 587).
8 See Chapter 4 above.
9 See Philo, *Leg. alleg.* 2.22-3 (*SVF* 2.458, LS 47P); note also the texts in LS 47Q, 53A, and 53B, and further passages in *SVF* 2.439-62.
10 See further Long (1982) who glosses differing degrees in tension as differences in organizational complexity.
11 See Diog. Laert. 7.157 (*SVF* 2.828).
12 See Aetius 4.21.1-4 (*SVF* 2.836, LS 53H).
13 Our source, Aetius (see previous note), also mentions sensation (*aisthêsis*), but for present purposes we might subsume that under impressions.
14 For Chrysippus's view see for example Galen, *PHP* 3.1.25 (*SVF* 2.886, LS 65H).
15 Aetius 4.21.2 (*SVF* 2.836, LS 53H); see also Calcidius, *in Tim.* 220 (*SVF* 2.879, LS 53G).
16 For further discussion, including the wider context of Hellenistic anatomy, see Sellars (2018c: 93–99), which contains further references.
17 As well as 2.2 and 12.3 quoted below, see also 3.16, 5.33, 7.16, 8.56, 12.14. For discussion, prompted by 2.2, see Gill (2013: 88–90).
18 See for example Asmis (1989: 2240). For an extended discussion of the issue see Ackeren (2011: II, 479–502).
19 See in particular Gill (2007: 192–206).
20 Annas (1992: 63) notes that earlier Stoics sometimes distinguished between two senses of "soul" along similar lines.
21 See Chapter 3 above.
22 See Long (2012: 469).
23 See for example Long (2002: 28).
24 On Stoic psychophysical holism see Gill (2006).
25 Marcus's use of *kurieuon* here also has early Stoic precedent: Chrysippus used it in passages quoted by Galen, where he referred to "the sovereign part of the soul" and "the sovereign and ruling part of the soul". See Galen, *PHP* 2.5.16 (*SVF* 2.894) and 3.5.28 (*SVF* 2.896).
26 See Cicero, *Tusc.* 3.24-5 and Stob. 2,88,8–89,3 = Ar. Did. 10 (*SVF* 3.378, LS 65A). For a full discussion see Graver (2007).
27 The Stoics also acknowledged a series of *eupatheiai*, "good emotions", produced by correct judgements. See for example Diog. Laert. 7.116 (LS 65F).
28 On emotions in Marcus see Engberg Pedersen (1998), Hadot (1998: 115–17), Ackeren (2011: II, 660–69), and Gill (2013: xlvii–xlix).
29 Compare this with Stob. 2,88,6 (*SVF* 3.378), where an emotion is described as "a movement of the soul against nature".
30 Compare this with 3.16, discussed above, and also 12.19. On puppet string imagery in Marcus see Berryman (2010).
31 Compare this with Epictetus, *Diss.* 1.15.1-5, also dealing with anger.
32 According to the Stoic classification, anger (*orgê*) is a species of desire (*epithumia*); see Stob. 2,90,19–91,1 = Ar. Did. 10b (LS 65E), with Graver (2007: 56).

33 Thus, 2.10 is Theophrastus fr. 441 in Fortenbaugh *et al.* (1992). It is discussed in Farquharson (1944: I, 288–9), Fortenbaugh (2011: 261–3), and Gill (2013: 94–5).
34 See Fortenbaugh (2011: 261–3).
35 The transmitted text has *to logikon hêgemonikon* but I follow Dalfen in bracketing *logikon* as it seems redundant here.
36 The phrase "inner citadel" was taken up as the title of Hadot (1998).
37 See Chapter 2 above.
38 As both Farquharson (1944: I, 343) and Gill (2013: 175) note, Marcus's main aim in 6.14 is to contrast different types of objects valued by different people, with the vulgar admiring objects at the lower end of the scale of nature.
39 For more on Marcus's stress on being a social animal, see Chapter 9 below.

7
TIME AND DEATH

Our place in nature

As we saw at the beginning of the last chapter, a central theme in the *Meditations* is the place of the individual within the larger whole. Marcus approached this theme both spatially and temporally. Thus, a recurrent theme in the *Meditations* is the relationship between the lifespan of the individual and the immensity of time. Marcus repeatedly reminds himself of the relative shortness of his own life and the futility of worrying about future posterity.[1] For example:

> Of man's life, his time is a point, his existence a flux, his sensation clouded, his body's entire composition corruptible, his vital spirit an eddy of breath, his fortune hard to predict, his fame uncertain. Briefly, all the things of the body, a river; all the things of the spirit, dream and delirium; his life a warfare and a sojourn in a strange land, his after-fame oblivion.
>
> *2.17*

Indeed, this is often seen as a distinctive feature of the *Meditations*, an idiosyncratic concern setting it apart from other ancient Stoic texts. However, here too Marcus was working within an established tradition of thought. One might compare passages such as the one above with the following extract from one of Seneca's letters, which Seneca appears to present as a quotation from Cato the Younger:[2]

> The whole race of man, both that which is and that which is to be, is condemned to die. Of all the cities that at any time have held sway over the world, and of all that have been the splendid ornaments of empires not their own, men shall someday ask where they were, and they shall be swept away by destructions of various kinds. [...] Why then should I be angry or feel sorrow, If I precede the general destruction by a tiny interval of time?
>
> *Seneca, Ep. 71.15*

Seneca prefaced this passage with his own reflections on the same theme.[3] Everything is born, grows, and is then destroyed. This applies to all things, even the earth and the stars. Given this, everything that now exists must at some point perish, which in fact means being broken down into its constituent elements. Life and death are merely these inevitable processes of generation and destruction.

These reflections from Cato and Seneca stress transience and the shortness of human life. They highlight the way in which doctrines from physics – in this case universal flux – can play their role in ethical reflections, broadly conceived.[4] Both of these themes, along with the wider idea that physical doctrines have their own practical, existential consequences, are ever present in the *Meditations*. Human life, Marcus writes at one point, is little more than a single breath:

> Some things are hastening to be, others to have come and gone, and a part of what is coming into being is already extinct. Flux and change renew the world incessantly, as the unbroken passage of time makes boundless eternity ever young. [...] Truly the life of every man is itself as fleeting as the exhalation of spirit from his blood or the breath he draws from the atmosphere. For just as it is to draw in a single breath and to return it, which we do every moment, so is it to render back the whole power of respiration, which you acquired but yesterday or the day before, at birth, to that other world from which you first drew it in.
>
> *6.15*

We have already considered the role that reflections on flux play in the *Meditations*;[5] here we shall focus on Marcus's treatment of time and death.

Thinking about time

Time is an ever-present theme in the *Meditations*, approached in a variety of ways: the length of human life, its brief length in comparison to the vastness of what we might call cosmic time, continual change through time, to name the most common. In the passages just quoted and others like them, Marcus uses two different words to refer to time, especially when he is reflecting on the immensity of cosmic time. These are *chronos* and *aiôn*, which are best translated as "time" and "eternity", respectively.[6] When referring to the length of a human lifespan, he sometimes refers to it as a point or pinprick (*stigmê*).[7] In one passage we see all three of these words together: *pan to enestôs tou chronou stigmê tou aiônos* (6.36), which is translated by Farquharson as "every instant of time, a pinprick of eternity" and Hard as "the whole of present time is but a point in eternity". That might lead one to think that Marcus intended to draw a distinction between time (*chronos*) and eternity (*aiôn*), with "time" referring to the present moment and "eternity" referring to what I earlier called cosmic time.

Indeed, a number of commentators have suggested just that. In particular, Goldschmidt argued that Marcus's use of the terms *chronos* and *aiôn* was a deliberate attempt to clarify a distinction in earlier Stoic thinking (1953: 39). According to him, Chrysippus had already begun to distinguish between time understood as the present moment and time understood as the past and future stretching infinitely backwards and forwards, but had failed to introduce terms to make this distinction clear. By using *chronos* to refer only to the present and introducing *aiôn* to refer to the infinite past and future, Marcus helped to clarify and make explicit the Stoic position. If that were the case, Marcus might be seen to pre-empt Plotinus, who also drew a distinction between time and eternity, although to make a quite different point.[8]

Goldschmidt's claim that both Marcus and the earlier Stoics were committed to, in effect, two distinct ways of thinking about time has been taken up by a number of subsequent commentators, such as Hadot and Brunschwig.[9] In order to assess this claim properly, we shall need first to get a clearer sense of early Stoic views about time. In the light of that, we can consider in more detail passages where Marcus refers to time and eternity. These will be the tasks of the next two sections.

Early Stoic accounts of time

As I have noted, Goldschmidt's account of Marcus's approach to time involves the claim that he was responding to earlier Stoic thinking about time. In particular, it involves the claim that the Stoics held what we might call a dual theory of time, conceiving it in two different ways at once. The first way focuses on the idea that there is an extended present moment that we all experience. The second way focuses on the idea that time extends infinitely into the past and future, with the two separated by a limit. In the first case, the present moment is extended in some sense, while in the second it is conceived as a durationless, mathematical limit.

Is this how the early Stoics understood time? The most common interpretations of the evidence for the early Stoa focus on the second of these two ways of thinking about time, rejecting the idea that there might be some kind of extended present moment as specious.[10] So was Goldschmidt correct to claim that the early Stoics, and following them Marcus, held a dual theory of time? In order to answer this question, we shall need to consider the ancient evidence.

There are three main sources for our knowledge of early Stoic thinking about time. The first is a very brief remark in Diogenes Laertius stating that time (*chronos*) is something incorporeal (*asômatos*) which is the measure or dimension (*diastêma*) of the change or motion (*kinêsis*) of the cosmos. The past and future, it continues, are infinite or unlimited (*apeiron*), while the present is finite.[11] The first part of that description is repeated by the second source, Stobaeus, this time explicitly attributed to Chrysippus.[12] It continues by saying that, like the unlimited void, time too is unlimited on either side, the two sides being the past and the future. Chrysippus claimed that no time is ever wholly present, for continuous things are infinitely divisible and time is itself something continuous. Thus, any period of present time can in fact be divided into part of the past and part of the future. Having said that, Stobaeus continues his account of Chrysippus's view by adding that while the past and future merely subsist (*huphestanai*), the present moment belongs (*huparchein*) in some stronger sense. This is explicated by drawing an analogy with predicates: the predicate "walking" belongs to someone when they are walking, but not when they are lying down or sitting.

One can immediately see the problem with this report by Stobaeus. On the one hand, the present moment does not really exist at all, for it is really just part of the past and part of the future; on the other hand, the present moment exists in a way that the past and future do not. The third source, Plutarch, also thought that the Stoic view was problematic.[13] It is at odds with common sense, he commented, to hold that the past and future exist, but not the present. Whenever one thinks they have grasped the present, he continued, it turns out that all they have is part past and part future, according to the Stoics. The present moment, then, is not a period of time but instead simply a limit between past and future. This they called "now" (*nun*), "a kind of joining and meeting of the past and future", which is not itself part of time but simply a limit of time.[14] Plutarch also credits to Chrysippus the view reported by Stobaeus, namely that while the past and future subsist (*huphestêkenai*), only the present belongs (*huparchein*). He goes on to neatly summarize the tension in these various statements:

> It turns out that he [Chrsyippus] divides the existing part of time [i.e. the present] into parts that are non-existent [i.e. the past and future] and what does exist, or rather that he leaves absolutely nothing of time existing if what is present has no part that is not future or past.
>
> *Plutarch, Comm. not. 1082a*

Unsurprisingly, there have been a number of different attempts to reconstruct a plausible theory from these bits of evidence. One view proposes an extended present moment in between an unlimited past and unlimited future; another holds the same view, adding that the extended present can be divided by a mathematical limit into part of the past and part of the future.[15] However, the most common interpretation rejects both of those views, arguing instead that for the Stoics the present moment has no real extension at all, and when one talks about the present moment in such terms this is merely specious.[16] Although talking about the present in this way is perfectly common, under strict analysis one can see that in reality what one is talking about is in fact part past and part future. Thus, any talk about an extended present moment is ultimately mistaken and not part of a formal theory of time.

There is, however, one piece of the ancient evidence that this interpretation does not take into account. It is the claim reported by both Plutarch and Stobaeus that while the past and future "subsist" (*huphestanai*), the present moment "belongs" (*huparchein*).[17] This word translated as "belong" (*huparchein*) has sometimes been translated as "exist".[18] The present moment belongs or exists in the same sense that the statement "I am walking" belongs to me when I am actually walking but not when I am sitting. The important point is that the present is said to have a greater ontological status than the past and future, and this seems at odds with the claim that the present is merely specious.

Goldschmidt's way out of this problem, as we have noted, was to claim that the early Stoics held a dual theory of time. The seemingly opposed ideas of an extended present moment and a durationless limit between past and future were both held by Chrysippus, just as the ancient sources imply.[19] Chrysippus's error, Goldschmidt argued, was not to be philosophically inconsistent, but merely to be unclear in his use of terminology and not adequately to differentiate between two distinct ways of conceiving time. In Chrsyippus's defence one might also add that the evidence is thin, to say the least, and one of our key sources, Plutarch, was deliberately trying to present him in an unfavourable light. This is where Marcus comes in. Goldschmidt argued that by introducing *aiôn* as a new technical term, Marcus was able to distinguish between two quite distinct ways of thinking about time: *chronos* understood as an extended present and *aiôn* referring to the unlimited past and future separated by a limit. All this looks like one possible way to explain what is going on in the evidence for Chrysippus and the early Stoa, although as we have seen this interpretation by no means secure and is rejected by many other commentators. The more important question in the present context is whether it captures something important at work in the *Meditations*.

Marcus on time and eternity

How does Marcus use the terms *chronos* and *aiôn*? In particular, does he use them in a consistent manner to refer respectively to the present moment and an infinite past–future? In support of his claim that Marcus does, Goldschmidt cited *Meditations* 4.3, in which *aiôn* is linked with infinity (*apeiros*):

> Shall mere glory distract you? Look at the swiftness of the oblivion of all men; the gulf of infinite eternity (*apeiros aiôn*),[20] behind and before; the hollowness of applause, the fickleness and folly of those who seem to speak well of you, and the narrow room in which it is confined. This should make you pause. For the entire earth is a point (*stigmê*) in space, and how small a corner thereof is this your dwelling place, and how few and paltry those who will sing your praises here.
>
> *4.3[7-8]*

However, there are other passages where Marcus conjoins *chronos* with the idea of infinity (*apeiros*), suggesting that he did not have in mind a strict distinction between a finite present time (*chronos*) and an infinite past–future labelled eternity (*aiôn*):

> Always remember, then, these two things: one, that all things from everlasting are of the same kind, and are in rotation; and it matters nothing whether it be for a hundred years or for two hundred or for an infinite time (*apeiros chronos*) that a man shall behold the same spectacle; the other, that the longest-lived and the soonest to die have an equal loss; for it is the present alone of which either will be deprived, since (as we saw) this is all he has and a man does not lose what he has not got.
>
> *2.14*

> For in this way you will continually see that man's life is smoke and nothingness, especially if you remind yourself that what has once changed will be no more in infinite time (*apeiros chronos*).
>
> *10.31*

There are many other passages where Marcus uses the terms *chronos* and *aiôn*, but just these two passages here are enough to show that Marcus was not using these terms in a consistent technical way to explicate the theory of time that Goldschmidt attributed to the early Stoics. In particular, his references to the vastness of infinite time, stretching back into the past and forward into the future involve as we have just seen the use of both *aiôn* and *chronos*, without any obvious discrimination between the two. Instead, he uses them synonymously and interchangeably.

So, what is Marcus doing in these passages? As we can see, his principal aim is to stress how small a portion of time each person is allotted when compared with the infinite expanse of cosmic time. These passages serve to highlight the brevity and relative insignificance of a human lifespan, but there is no evidence to suggest any engagement with a more technical theory of time, of the sort alluded to by the fragments for the early Stoa. We can see this in one further passage where Marcus uses both terms:

> Let your impression dwell continually upon the whole of eternity (*aiôn*) and the whole of substance (*ousia*), and realize that their several parts are, by comparison with substance (*ousia*), a fig-seed; by comparison with time (*chronos*), the turn of a drill.
>
> *10.17*

Here, *aiôn* and *chronos* are both used to refer to the totality of time, and many translators have rendered both terms as "time" in their versions of this passage.[21] Once again, Marcus's real concern here is with stressing the brevity of human life. This is confirmed by the passages that immediately follow the one above:

> Dwell upon everything that exists and reflect that it is already in process of dissolution and coming into being by change and a kind of decay or dispersion, or in what way it is born to die, in a manner of speaking.
>
> *10.18; see also 10.19*[22]

In defence of Goldschmidt's thesis, one can point to passages that use *chronos* to refer to a human lifespan in contrast to the immensity of cosmic time,[23] but again the primary motivation in these passages seems to be to highlight the transience and brevity of human life. As we have already noted, there are other passages that use *chronos* to refer to infinite cosmic time as well.[24]

The present moment

Marcus may not have been engaging with early Stoic thinking about time, but nevertheless reflections on time remain a recurrent theme throughout the *Meditations*. Alongside passages reflecting on the transience and brevity of human life, Marcus also often exhorted himself to keep his focus on the present moment. This is a central theme in Hadot's account of the *Meditations*, which also picks up on aspects of Goldschmidt's account.[25] Hadot suggested, following Goldschmidt, that what we find in the evidence for the early Stoa are "two diametrically opposed conceptions of the present": on the one hand, the present is merely a limit between past and future, without any extension; on the other hand, the present does have a certain duration, reflecting the intention and attention of the individual subject.[26] Rather than dismiss the idea of an extended present moment as specious, as the majority of commentators have done, Hadot flipped the order of priority, treating the extended present as more real than the limit between past and future. Taking inspiration from the philosophy of Henri Bergson, Hadot takes the present conceived as a mathematical limit as pure abstraction; it is the lived present moment that we experience that is truly real.[27] In effect he prioritizes the ancient report that the present "belongs" to us over the other ancient report that the present can be dissolved into part of the past and part of the future.

Hadot, again following Bergson, suggested that the lived present moment can expand and contract, depending on our focus or attention. When Marcus exhorts himself to pay attention to the present, he is referring to this expandable and contractible present, Hadot argued. On this view what one refers to as the present can vary considerably: this year, this week, this day, this minute, and all the way down to right now. One way in which Goldschmidt had connected the two ways of thinking about the present moment was to suggest that with suitable attention the present moment can be reduced right down to an instant without duration, namely the mathematical limit between past and future.[28] His evidence for this in Marcus came from the following passage:

> Remind yourself that it is not the future or the past that weighs heavy upon you, but always the present, and that this gradually grows less (*katasmikrunetai*), if only you isolate it and reprove your understanding, if that is not strong enough to hold out against it, thus taken by itself.
>
> 8.36

There is nothing here to support the claim that the present can be reduced to a durationless instant. It is true that Marcus does often refer to the present moment as a point or pin-prick (*stigmē*) in order to indicate its smallness, but that still might be taken to imply some degree of size.[29] Thus, Hadot rejected this part of Goldschmidt's interpretation, insisting that the present moment for Marcus was always a lived, extended present.

What ought we to make of all this? Marcus is indeed keenly interested in the present moment, but he seems to have little interest in these more theoretical concerns about the ontology of time. His prioritization of the present moment is motivated by two thoughts. The first is to avoid dwelling on the past and future if so doing might generate negative emotions. The second is to focus on the present because that is where we have the ability to act. These two thoughts are naturally quite closely inter-related. There is no point dwelling on what has happened in the past, or feeling anxious about what might happen in the future; instead one ought to focus on what we can do right now, because only that is within our control. That, combined with his reflections on the brevity of human life, shapes his reflections on time.

Death

Closely connected to Marcus's reflections on the transience and brevity of human life are his comments about death. At first glance he appears to offer a number of competing accounts of death at various points in the *Meditations*. For instance, in some places he presents death as a welcome release from the troubles of life:

> Death is rest from the recalcitrance of sensation, from the stimulus of impulse, from intellectual analysis, and the service of the flesh.
>
> 6.28; see also 9.2, 9.3

Elsewhere, in a more dispassionate frame of mind, he contemplates three possible options for what happens at death: (i) atomic dispersal, (ii) extinction, or (iii) movement to another place (7.32). This threefold division is noteworthy because it is one of the few places where Marcus appears to entertain the possibility of some kind of afterlife. Elsewhere (4.21), he considers the possibility that after death souls "pass on and continue for so long" before being fully reintegrated into the generative principle (*spermatikos logos*) of Nature. In this he was following Stoic doctrine, which, as it is reported, claimed that the souls of perhaps only the wise survive their separation from their bodies, at least for a while, presumably due to being held together by greater tension than typical souls.[30] However, despite this being an established Stoic position, in general Marcus discounts it. His focus of attention is mainly on the other two options: death is either (i) a dispersal of atomic elements or (ii) extinction, understood as reabsorption into

Nature. These of course echo his wider reflections on the choice between atoms or providence when thinking about Nature as a whole.[31] As we saw earlier, it is fairly clear that Marcus decides against atomism. In the present context, then, it seems that Marcus is committed to the idea of death as extinction, conceived as a reabsorption into Nature. As he puts it:

> You came into the world as a part. You will vanish in that which gave you birth, or rather you will be taken into its generative principle (*spermatikos logos*) by a process of change.
> 4.14; cf. 10.7

The *spermatikos logos* mentioned here and in 4.21 noted above is a technical Stoic concept, and in the passages where Marcus contrasts this sort of reintegration into Nature with atomic dispersal he is clearly alluding to his commitment to Stoicism.[32] However, in general his reflections on death are less concerned with the details of physical theory and more simply reminders of the inevitability of change. Death is no more than a natural process of transformation,[33] innocuous, and uninteresting when approached dispassionately. This is one of the contexts where he makes use of physical descriptions to describe things that are often heavily invested with value:

> Universal Nature out of its whole material, as from wax, models now the figure of a horse, then melting this down uses the material for a tree, next for a man, next for something else. And these, every one, subsist for a very brief while. Yet it is no hardship for a box to be broken up, as it was none for it to be nailed together.
> 7.23

Marcus also stresses that the time of our death is out of our control, drawing an analogy with an actor taking stage directions:

> Mortal man, you have been a citizen in this great City; what does it matter to you whether for five or fifty years? For what is according to its laws is equal for every man. Why is it hard, then, if Nature who brought you in, and no despot nor unjust judge, sends you out of the City – as though the master of the show, who engaged an actor, were to dismiss him from the stage? 'But I have not spoken my five acts, only three.' 'What you say is true, but in life three acts are the whole play.' For He determines the perfect whole, the cause yesterday of your composition, today of your dissolution; you are the cause of neither. Leave the stage, therefore, and be reconciled, for He also who lets his servant depart is reconciled.
> 12.36

This analogy with an actor taking directions was probably inspired by Epictetus, who makes the same point in very similar terms: "Remember that you are an actor in a play, which is as the playwright wants it to be: short if he wants it short, long if he wants it long" (*Ench*. 17).

Echoes of Epicurus

Marcus's echo of Epictetus is hardly surprising. Perhaps less expected is his engagement with Epicurean ideas about death.[34] Marcus mentions Epicurus just twice in the *Meditations*: at 7.64 he acknowledges the value of Epicurus's reflections on coping with pain (cf. 7.33), and he picks up the same theme at 9.41, where he quotes an otherwise unknown fragment.[35] There are numerous other allusions to Epicurean doctrine throughout the *Meditations*, the most obvious of which are his references to atomism. Marcus also echoes aspects of Epicurean thinking about death, and there is one passage (8.58) where it seems fairly clear that he was familiar with the Epicurean doctrine, even though he does not name Epicurus explicitly. Marcus was certainly not alone among Roman Stoics in drawing on Epicurean material when he found it useful. A similar approach can be found in Seneca, and especially in his correspondence with Lucilius.[36]

The Epicureans were well known for reflecting on death. Epicurus himself famously argued that death ought to be "nothing to us", for we shall never *be* dead in order to experience it. In particular, he argued that because all good and bad come via sensation (*aisthêsis*), the absence of sensation can be neither good nor bad in itself (*Ep. Men.* 124). He insisted that we ought not to fear death because "when we exist death is not present, and when death is present we do not exist" (*Ep. Men.* 125). Nor, he argued, is there any reason to be concerned about the length of one's life: one only ever lives in the present moment, so adding further time cannot increase one's wellbeing in the here and now. This last thought was elaborated upon by a later Epicurean, Philodemus, who argued that when assessing one's life, quality is more important than quantity.[37] His argument involved reference to the Epicurean account of static pleasures, which were thought to be not the sort of thing that can be increased by addition. If that is the case, then a life enjoying static pleasures in the here and now is complete in itself and cannot be improved upon by increasing its duration. As Epicurus himself had claimed, finite time and infinite time contain equal pleasure, if one understands pleasure correctly (*Rat. Sent.* 19).

Marcus echoes these Epicurean arguments at a number of points. He stresses that the length of life is unimportant, for at death all one loses is the present moment:

> Even were you about to live three thousand years or thrice ten thousand, nevertheless remember this, that no one loses any other life than this which he is living, nor lives any other than this which he is losing. Thus the longest and the shortest come to the same thing. For the present is equal for all, and what is passing is therefore equal: thus what is being lost is proved to be barely a moment. For a man could lose neither past nor future; how can one rob him of what he has not got? Always remember, then, these two things: one, that all things from everlasting are of the same kind, and are in rotation; and it matters nothing whether it be for a hundred years or for two hundred or for an infinite time that a man shall behold the same spectacle; the other, that the longest-lived and the soonest to die have an equal loss; for it is the present alone of which either will be deprived, since (as we saw) this is all he has and a man does not lose what he has not got.
>
> 2.14; see also 3.7, 6.49

He also more or less repeats Epicurus's argument that one ought not to fear death because death is the absence of sensation (*aisthêsis*), and the absence of sensation is neither good nor bad:

> He who fears death fears either total loss of sensation (*anaisthêsia*) or a change of sensation. Now if you should no longer possess sensation (*aisthêsis*), you will no longer be

aware of any evil; alternatively, if you possess an altered sensation, you will be an altered creature and will not cease from living.

8.58

A number of translators have rendered *aisthêsis* in this passage as "consciousness", which captures well the point that Marcus wants to make, but has the unfortunate consequence of obscuring the connection with Epicurus.[38]

It would be a mistake, however, to see these allusions to Epicurean arguments about death as a sign of philosophical eclecticism on Marcus's part. Another passage makes a further reference, this time more explicit, but in part in order to highlight his own philosophical distance from Epicureanism: "This is a stirring call to disdain of death, that even those who judge pleasure to be good and pain evil, nevertheless disdain death" (12.34). If even a hedonist like Epicurus can overcome fear of death, then a Stoic like Marcus should have no problem in cultivating the appropriate attitude of indifference. One might say that Marcus is happy to take something from Epicurus when it serves as a useful reminder for his own Stoic purposes, but that is as far as it goes. We might compare this practice with Seneca's use of Epicurean material. In his correspondence with Lucilius, Seneca insisted that one ought to think of Epicurean sayings as common property of all, rather than belonging to a particular school (*Ep.* 8.8). Elsewhere, Seneca was often openly hostile towards Epicureanism, and he described his ventures into Epicurean material as an expedition into an enemy camp (*Ep.* 2.5). In short, Seneca was happy to take from Epicurus or to acknowledge common ground where it suited him, while remaining firmly sceptical about Epicurean philosophy as a whole. A similar approach may well be in play in the *Meditations*: on the topic of death Marcus can find some valuable thoughts in Epicurus without feeling compelled to identify with Epicureanism any further. Indeed, this might help to explain why in these passages Marcus does not name Epicurus directly. Like Seneca, Marcus appears to approach this material as common property rather than something distinctively Epicurean.

Why think about death?

Like Epicurus, one reason for Marcus to think about death is to try to overcome anxiety about his own mortality. He also thinks that it concentrates the mind, prompting him to focus attention on things that matter most, rather than getting distracted by trivialities. In this sense, reflecting on death is a positive mental exercise.

We can see this especially clearly in one passage where all these ideas are expressed together along with the suggestion that one ought to focus on the present moment. In 10.11, he exhorts himself to develop a proper understanding of the way in which all things change and then to exercise himself in this. One starts with a theoretical understanding of the way in which Nature changes, and then one pays attention and engages in training, in order to digest that understanding. This is a fairly explicit example of a physical exercise, based on physical theory. With this grasp of the transience of all things properly digested, Marcus suggests that one will abandon pursuit of ephemeral external things, including other people's opinions, and instead focus on acting justly. This can only be done in the present moment (*to nun*). The person who fully grasps and digests the fact that everything is continually changing will, he suggests, be content with focusing on two things: acting justly in the present moment and accepting whatever happens in the present moment.

Many of the ideas in 10.11 recur throughout the *Meditations*. The suggestion that one ought not to worry about the opinions of others is closely tied to Marcus's evident preoccupation with his posthumous reputation. This was clearly something often on his mind, given how often he touches on it, although this is perhaps unsurprising given the preeminent public role he held.[39] Here is just one example:

> The man in a flutter for posthumous fame fails to picture to himself that each of those who remember him will himself also very shortly die, then again the man who succeeded him, until the whole remembrance is extinguished as it runs along a line of men who are kindled and then put out. And put the case that those who will remember never die, and the remembrance never dies, what is that to you?
>
> *4.19*

Once again, the key to overcoming excessive concern with one's reputation, either now or in the future, is to grasp fully the physical doctrine of continual flux. His reflections on death, then, are simply part of a wider strategy of reflecting on the transitory nature of all things. As we saw in 10.11, this can also contribute to a better grasp of the Stoic ethical attitude towards "indifferents" (*adiaphora*). Stoic ethical theory offered arguments for the claim that externals such as wealth and health ought to be seen as mere "indifferents", because they do not consistently benefit people; only virtue does that, and so only it deserves to be called good.[40] Epictetus later added another reason not to attend too much to externals, namely that they are not "up to us" (*eph' hêmin*), and so pursuit of them is likely to lead to frustration and disappointment.[41] Now Marcus adds a third reason: these externals are merely ephemeral, destined to be destroyed before too long, and so it would be misguided to invest them with great importance. Thus, it is not merely his own death that he is reflecting on, or the mortality of other humans, but the "death" of all physical things, which are presented as but momentary conglomerations of matters within the vastness of cosmic time.

Living in the present moment

The most substantial lesson that Marcus takes away from his reflections on death is that one ought to live in the present moment. As we saw in 10.11, this was the conclusion of his line of thought there. Elsewhere, he reminds himself that although he might appear to be concerned by events in the past or the future, in fact on closer examination all of his concerns relate to the present moment (e.g. 8.36). What matters is how one acts in the present moment, which thankfully is the one thing within one's control. By analysing concerns and reducing them to matters that can be attended to in the here and now, Marcus suggests that it is possible to transform what at first might look like insurmountable problems into things that can be acted upon.

Part of Marcus's strategy here it to highlight the fact that, in a sense, the past and future do not exist: "each of us lives only in the present, this brief moment; the rest is either a life that is past, or is in an uncertain future" (3.10). Consequently, one ought to limit one's attention to the present moment (7.29). In one passage, 12.3, he comments that one ought to strive to live only the life that is one's own, namely the present moment. Although these sorts of reflections might seem a world away from the details of early Stoic accounts of time that we considered earlier, Marcus is in effect saying that the past and the future do not really exist;

only the present moment belongs to us, echoing the claim made by Chrysippus. This ontological devaluation of the future in particular also leads Marcus to suggest that one ought to treat each day as if it were one's last (7.56, 7.69).

Thus, Marcus has two reasons to propose focusing one's attention on the present moment. The first, drawing on lessons from Epictetus, is that only the present moment is within our control or, to put it more precisely, it is only in the present moment that we are able to act, and there is little to be gained by directing one's attention at things where one is unable to effect a change. The second, echoing Chrysippus, is that only the present moment belongs to us; it exists in a way that the past and future simply do not.

Actions not outcomes

As we have seen, death highlights the pointlessness of pursuing fame and posthumous reputation, while the transitory nature of all things highlights the same for the pursuit of "indifferents". The goals of fame or wealth are directly challenged by Marcus. These thoughts, combined with his focus on the present moment, lead him to the conclusion that one ought to focus attention on one's actions rather than the outcomes or consequences of one's actions. As we saw earlier in 10.11, Marcus suggests that acting justly ought to be one's main concern (also 4.37), and we can probably take this reference to justice as simply one example of ethical action in general. It is the quality of our actions – completely within our control in the present moment – that matters, and not the longer-term consequences of those actions. In this, Marcus is completely in line with Stoic ethical thought.

Probably the best-known illustration of this is the archery analogy credited to Antipater.[42] The goal (*telos*), Antipater argued, ought to be not attaining certain ends but doing all one can to reach those ends. Like an archer, one ought to do everything one can to hit the target, without making one's success dependent on hitting the target. One's focus of attention ought to be not on whether the arrow hits the target – a goal that is ultimately out of one's control – but instead on shooting as well as one can. This places the goal within one's control, and shifts the focus of attention from the outcome to the action itself.

Although there is no evidence to suggest that Marcus had this analogy in mind, it is clearly in line with his own focus on shifting attention from outcomes to actions. In both cases, this is ultimately a consequence of the Stoic claim that real goodness lies in virtuous actions rather than external goods. The difference is that Marcus reaches this conclusion not with reference to Stoic ethical theory but via his reflections on Stoic physics.

Dealing with time and death

On first encounter, some readers may find passages such as the one with which this chapter opened (2.17) pessimistic or even nihilistic. Indeed, some commentators have used these passages as the basis for diagnoses of depression or even drug abuse.[43] Yet, in general Marcus develops a thoroughly dispassionate approach to death by treating it as but one more natural, physical process of change, using his technique of physical descriptions. He also draws ethical conclusions from his reflections: do not value transitory "indifferents" (*adiaphora*) or future outcomes; instead focus on acting virtuously in the here and now.

It is also worth noting that the passage with which this chapter opened, 2.17, ought not to be read in isolation. In fact, the part quoted then is just the beginning of a longer section in the *Meditations* which goes on to offer a remedy for the situation it describes. The transitory nature of human life might at first look like a problem, but there is a cure for such thoughts:

> What then can be his escort through life? One thing and one thing only, Philosophy. And this is to keep the spirit within him unwronged and unscathed, master of pains and pleasures, doing nothing at random, nothing falsely and with pretence; needing no other to do aught or to leave aught undone; and moreover accepting what befalls it, that is, what is assigned to it, as coming from the other world from which it came itself. And in all things awaiting death, with a mind that is satisfied, counting it nothing else than a release of the elements from which each living creature is composed. Now if there is no hurt to the elements themselves in their ceaseless changing each into other, why should a man apprehend anxiously the change and dissolution of them all? For this is according to Nature; and no evil is according to Nature.
>
> 2.17

It is through knowledge of the workings of Nature that it becomes possible to accept the shortness of human life when measured against the vastness of cosmic time and the inevitable transformation from life to death.

Notes

1 See, for example, 2.17, 5.24, 7.10, 8.21, 9.32, 10.17, 12.7, 12.32.
2 Seneca's precise intention here is unclear, due to a textual difficulty, discussed in Inwood (2007): 191–2. Gummere (LCL) presents this passage as the words of a sage following what Cato *would* say; Inwood (2007) has it as what a mind like Cato might say; Graver and Long (2015: 217–8) present it as a block quote from Cato.
3 See Seneca, *Ep.* 71.13-14, with commentary in Inwood (2007: 190).
4 Inwood (2007: 190–1) suggests one might see this as a reintegration of physics and ethics. Alternatively, one might present it as highlighting the practical, existential consequences of physics.
5 See Chapter 4 above.
6 For *aiôn* see 2.12, 4.3, 4.21, 4.43, 4.50, 5.24, 5.32, 6.15, 6.36, 6.59, 7.10, 7.19, 7.70, 9.28, 9.32, 9.35, 10.5, 10.17, 11.1, 12.7, 12.32; for *chronos* see 1.17, 2.4, 2.14, 2.17, 3.7, 3.11, 4.6, 4.32, 4.48, 5.10, 6.15, 6.18, 6.23, 6.25, 6.36, 6.49, 7.29, 7.35, 7.46, 8.5, 8.7, 8.11, 8.44, 9.14, 9.25, 10.1, 10.17, 10.31, 12.3, 12.18, 12.35.
7 See 2.17, 4.3, 6.36, 8.21.
8 See Plotinus, *Enn.* 3.7.1: "Eternity and time, we say, are two different things, the one belonging to the sphere of the nature which lasts for ever, the other to that of becoming and of this universe" (trans. Armstrong, LCL). The contrast that Plotinus has in mind is thus different from the one that Goldschmidt attributes to Marcus.
9 See Hadot (1998: 135–6), and Brunschwig (2003: 214–15).
10 See for example Sorabji (1983: 21–6), Long and Sedley (1987: II, 307), and Schenkeveld (1999: 191).
11 See Diog. Laert. 7.141 (*SVF* 2.520).
12 See Stob. 1,106,5-23 (*SVF* 2.509, LS 51B).
13 See Plutarch, *Comm. not.* 1081c-1082a (*SVF* 2.517-19, LS 51C). On this passage, and many of the issues it raises, see Schofield (1988).
14 See Plutarch, *Comm. not.* 1081e. Plutarch credits this point to the Stoic Archedemus, and so this passages is Archedemus fr. 14 in *SVF* 3. A similar view is credited to Posidonius by Stob. 1,105,17–106,4 (fr. 98 EK, LS 51E).
15 See Sorabji (1983: 25), who describes these views as "two rival interpretations of Chrsyippus". Kidd (1988: I, 400) credits the first of these views to Zeno.

16 See for example Sorabji (1983: 21–6), Long and Sedley (1987: I, 307), Schenkeveld (1999: 191).
17 On this distinction see for example Long (1971: 89–93), Goldschmidt (1972), Sandbach (1985: 79–80), and Long and Sedley (1987: I, 164).
18 See for example Long (1971: 89) and Sorabji (1983: 22).
19 See Goldschmidt (1953: 36–40).
20 Farquharson (1944) translates *apeiros aiôn* as "endless time"; Haines (1916) has "infinite time"; Hard (2011) has "boundless time". Clearly, none of them thought that a contrast between *aiôn* and *chronos* is implied here.
21 This is the case in Haines (1916), Farquharson (1944), and Hard (2011). Trannoy (1925) renders both as "durée"; Cassanmagnago (2008) uses "tempo" for both.
22 10.17-19 all address the theme of transience and perhaps ought to be read together. In editions predating Gataker (1652), they are often printed together as a single section; see for example Sally (1626), where they are "10.22", and Casaubon (1643), where they are "10.19".
23 Marcus uses *chronos* to refer to a finite human lifespan at 2.4, 2.17, 3.7, 4.48, 6.49, 7.46.
24 Marcus uses *chronos* to refer to infinite time at 2.14, 10.17, 10.31.
25 See Hadot (1998: 131–7).
26 See Hadot (1998: 135). On the idea of an extended present, distinct from the present conceived as a mathematical limit, see Augustine, *Conf.* 11.26.33, perhaps inspired by Plotinus, *Enn.* 3.7.11. Hadot in effect sees Marcus as a precursor to this Neoplatonic way of thinking about time.
27 See Hadot (1998: 136). Hadot draws on a lecture given by Bergson in Oxford, which was first published in Bergson (1911), reprinted in Bergson (1934: 143–76), and is translated in Bergson (1946: 153–86).
28 See Goldschmidt (1953: 195).
29 See 2.17, 4.3, 6.36, 8.21. It is worth noting, however, that Aristotle used *stigmê* to refer to a mathematical limit; see for example *Phys.* 4.13, 222a10-19. But there is nothing to indicate that Marcus had this usage in mind.
30 See for example Eusebius, *Praep. evang.* 15.20.6 (*SVF* 2.809, LS 53W); Diog. Laert. 7.157 (*SVF* 2.811); Sextus Empiricus, *Math.* 9.71-4 (*SVF* 2.812); with further texts in *SVF* 2.809-22. Diogenes Laertius credits to Chrysippus the view that only the souls of the wise survive separation from the body.
31 See Chapter 5 above.
32 On *spermatikos logos* see for example Diog. Laert 7.135 (*SVF* 1.102, 2.580, LS 46B) and Aetius 1.7.33 (*SVF* 2.1027, LS 46A).
33 See for example 2.12, 4.5, 4.14, 4.21, 5.13, 7.19, 7.50, 8.18, 8.25, 9.3, 9.21.
34 On Marcus and Epicurus, see further Cortassa (1989: 147–62).
35 *Meditations* 7.64 (with 7.33) is fr. 447 in Usener (1887); 9.41 is fr. 191 in Usener (1887) and fr. 259 in Arrighetti (1973).
36 This has attracted a variety of interpretations. For a brief overview, with further references, see Sellars (2014: 106–7).
37 Philodemus's treatise *On Death* is edited and translated in Henry (2009).
38 See for example Farquharson (1944) and Hard (2011). Among other options, Hays (2003) opts for "experience"; Grube (1983) has "awareness". Older translations, such as Jackson (1906a) and Haines (1916), use "sensation".
39 See for example 2.17, 3.10, 4.6, 4.19, 6.47, 7.21, 7.34, 8.21, 8.44, 9.30, 10.34.
40 For these arguments, see Diog. Laert. 7.101-5 (*SVF* 3.117, 119, LS 58A-B), more or less repeating arguments made in Plato's *Euthydemus* 278e-281e.
41 See for example Epictetus, *Ench.* 1.1, *Diss.* 1.22.10.
42 See Cicero, *Fin.* 3.22 (*SVF* 3.18, LS 64F). This is usually taken to be an attempt to illustrate Antipater's formulation of the Stoic *telos* (Stob. 2,76,9-15, LS 58K). For brief discussion see Sellars (2018c: 111–12).
43 See for example Africa (1961), discussed and debunked in Hadot (1984) (and cf. Hadot 1998: 95–114).

PART IV
Ethics

8
VIRTUE AND JUSTICE

Marcus's *Meditations* is often taken to be primarily a work of ethics, a guide to how to live. The previous chapters have tried to show the role played by logical and physical themes in the *Meditations*, although the practical consequences of those themes have never been far away. Indeed, one of the striking features of the work is the way in which logical, physical, and ethical themes are closely interwoven together. In this chapter, we turn to look directly at some of the explicitly ethical material in the *Meditations*.

Living consistently with Nature

In Book 1 of the *Meditations*, Marcus thanks his Stoic teacher Sextus for teaching him "the notion of life according to Nature (*ennoia tou kata phusin zên*)" (1.9). This idea of a life according to Nature was one of the core doctrines in Stoic ethics. As we shall see shortly, it was often expressed using the word *homologoumenôs*, "consistently", and Marcus uses this term to capture the same idea elsewhere. For instance, in 3.4 he reminds himself "to cling not to the opinion of all men, but only of men who live consistently with Nature (*homologoumenôs têi phusei*)". But, in general, he prefers to use the shorthand *kata phusin*. At 7.11 he writes, "for a reasonable creature the same act is according to nature (*kata phusin*) and according to reason (*kata logon*)". This reflects the Stoic view that what following Nature actually involves is following the right reason (*orthos logos*) pervading all things, which they identify with universal law (*koinos nomos*) and Zeus.[1] At 7.56, he imagines wiping the slate clean of his life up to the present moment and then proposes that he "use the balance remaining to live henceforward according to Nature". At 10.15, he exhorts himself to live as a true human being (*alêthinos anthrôpos*), which he then defines as one who lives according to Nature (*kata phusin*). At 12.1, he lists living according to Nature (*kata phusin zên*) as one of a handful of things to which one ought to aspire. It seems fairly clear, then, that the idea of living in tune with Nature was central to Marcus's thinking about how he ought to live his life.[2] But what precisely did it involve? What did Marcus think it involved? Before we turn to those questions, it might be useful to consider how this idea was formulated by the early Stoics and what they took it to mean.

It is fairly common to see the statement that the goal (*telos*) of human life for the Stoics was to live in agreement with Nature. In fact, we find the early Stoics offering number of different versions of this *telos* formula. Our principal sources of evidence for the Stoic *telos* formula are the Stoic doxography appended to the biography of Zeno of Citium in Diogenes Laertius, and the epitome of Stoic ethics attributed to Arius Didymus and preserved in the anthology of Stobaeus.[3] Diogenes Laertius reports that Zeno, in his book *On the Nature of Man* was the first person to define the *telos* as "living in agreement with Nature" (*to homologoumenôs têi phusei zên*). Diogenes goes on to report that Cleanthes, Posidonius, and Hecato all defined the *telos* in this way. Chrysippus, he tells us, glossed this by saying that living virtuously (*kat' aretên zên*) is equivalent to "living in agreement with experience of the actual course of Nature" (Diog. Laert. 7.87). Diogenes continues with an explication of what he takes the Stoic *telos* to mean, which probably derives from Chrysippus, before then noting slightly different formulations by Diogenes of Babylon and Archedemus (ibid. 7.88), and then signalling a potential difference between Chrysippus and Cleanthes. According to Diogenes, Chrysippus took "Nature" (*phusis*) in the formula "living in agreement with Nature" to refer to both universal (*koinê*) Nature and human nature (*idiôs tên anthrôpinên*), whereas Cleanthes took it to refer to universal (*koinê*) Nature only (ibid. 7.89). Although there were some later innovations, Diogenes' account suggests that Zeno, Cleanthes, Chrysippus, and Posidonius all defended the same *telos* formula as "living in agreement with Nature" (*to homologoumenôs têi phusei zên*).

When we turn to Arius Didymus (6a), we find a broadly similar account, with some minor but significant differences. He reports that Zeno defined the goal as simply "to live in agreement" (*to homologoumenôs zên*), which he glosses as living according to a single reason (*kath' hena logon*) and in harmony (*sumphônon*).[4] Arius then comments:

> Those after him, adding further detail, expressed it thus: 'to live in agreement with Nature', assuming that Zeno's statement was insufficient as a predicate. So Cleanthes, the first to take over the sect after him, added 'with nature' and interpreted it thus: 'the goal is living in agreement with Nature'. Chrysippus, wanting to make this clearer, expressed it in this way: 'to live in accord with experience of what happens naturally'.
> Stob. 2,76,1-8, SVF 1.552, 3.12

The significant difference with the report in Diogenes Laertius is of course the different *telos* formulation attributed to Zeno. But Arius agrees with Diogenes in suggesting that the three early heads of the Stoa – Zeno, Cleanthes, and Chrysippus – were in broad *philosophical* agreement about what the Stoic *telos* was. Where they differed was in how best to express and explicate it.

Here we come to a key question: what was the shared *telos* that they were all trying to express? Was it "to live in agreement" (*to homologoumenôs zên*) or was it "to live in agreement with Nature" (*to homologoumenôs têi phusei zên*)? According to Arius, the addition "with Nature" (*têi phusei*) was added by Cleanthes, who did so because "Zeno's statement was insufficient as a predicate" (Stob. 2,76,2-3). This might be taken to imply that Zeno's original formulation, as reported by Arius, was thought to be grammatically incomplete and so required revision. As Pomeroy puts it in his notes on this passage, "the predicate 'in agreement' (with what?) was therefore expanded by Zeno's successors to give a more complete definition" (1999: 113, n. 75). This takes us to the grammatical use of the key word in the all the different formulations: *homologoumenôs*. Can this word be used on its own – i.e. is it complete by itself – or is it necessarily incomplete, demanding a noun to complete its sense? Pomeroy thinks it is incomplete. In this he is following the statement by Arius, who may himself have been following Cleanthes (it is unclear whether Arius is attributing the expansion of the formula to Cleanthes' judgement that Zeno's formulation was incomplete, or whether that is Arius's (or some intermediate source's) attempt to explain the reason for the expansion). Grammatical rules are of course simply attempts to codify existing use, so the question effectively becomes whether other authors before or around the time of Zeno used the word *homologoumenôs* on its own without further specification. Some, including Xenophon and Plato, certainly did.[5] The word was used both with the dative and on its own (see LSJ 1226). Perhaps, the best way to take Arius's comment that *homologoumenôs* was "insufficient as a predicate (*katêgorêma*)", then, may simply be that Cleanthes thought it was insufficient to convey fully the idea that Zeno had in mind.[6]

All this bears on how best to understand the Stoic *telos* and also how to translate it. If Zeno did indeed use *homologoumenôs* on its own, then we ought to translate it in a way that can work both with and without anything further. In that case, translating the fuller version as "to live according to Nature" won't do. The slightly more neutral "in agreement with Nature" is also far from ideal. Better would be "to live consistently with Nature", because the first part, "to live consistently" can work equally well with or without the addition "with Nature". However, one can also immediately see why it might have been judged too concise and might benefit from further expansion, hence the additions and expansions by Cleanthes and Chrysippus: "to live consistently with Nature", "to live consistently with universal and human nature", "to live consistently with the experience of what happens naturally". These are all glosses on a single idea, rather than innovations in doctrine. The core idea, expressed by Zeno, is to live consistently.[7]

This account of the Stoic *telos* involves a number of assumptions. It prioritizes Arius's version of Zeno's formulation over Diogenes's. At the same time, it rejects Arius's claim that the reason for Cleanthes' expansion of Zeno's formulation was due to its incompleteness, because it rejects the claim that *homologoumenôs* is incomplete. While I have tried to justify the second of these, it is difficult to justify the first, especially when Diogenes names one of Zeno's books where he (or more likely his source) claims to have found the fuller formulation. Yet Arius's report is clearly no mere slip, given that he explicitly comments on the formulation straight afterwards. A little later in his account he adds that "they", the Stoics, say that "agreement is the goal (*tên homologian legousi telos einai*)" (Stob. 2,76,18-19), again stressing doctrinal unity despite the various expansions and glosses on the first version. No doubt much could be said about the potential unreliability of both of these doxographical accounts.[8] In its defence, however, this interpretation makes sense of the Stoic position, and it makes sense of the various reformulations, understood as clarifications rather than modifications of Zeno's original statement. While the Stoic *telos* formula makes reference to Nature in its expanded forms, the core of the idea is to live consistently. When we read that the *telos* is "to live consistently with Nature", perhaps the stress ought to be on "consistently" rather than "Nature".

What we have, then, are a number of different formulations all taken to express a single fundamental idea. Each formulation expresses a different aspect of the basic idea. These are: (i) internal consistency, (ii) consistency with human nature, and (iii) consistency with external, universal Nature, often understood as an acceptance of what happens.

We find all three of these aspects throughout the *Meditations*. With regard to the first, the desire to avoid inner disturbance is a constant theme throughout the work. With the second, as we shall see in due course, Marcus places considerable emphasis on living in harmony with human nature. For Marcus humans are rational, social animals, and a good life is one in harmony with these characteristics. Reflecting on social virtues, Marcus writes at 7.74 that "to benefit another is to act according to Nature (*kata phusin*)". As for the third, reflections on accepting what comes to pass according to Nature are also ubiquitous.

The virtues

As well as engaging with the Stoic *telos* of living consistently with Nature, Marcus also takes up the Stoic account of the virtues. Central to the Stoic account is the claim that virtue or excellence (*aretê*) is the only good, its opposite, vice, is the only thing inherently bad, and everything else falls into the category of "indifferents" (*adiaphora*), some of which we naturally pursue and others we prefer to avoid.[9] Virtue, according to the Stoics, is a consistent disposition, something choice-worthy for its own sake, and something that makes the whole of one's life consistent (Diog. Laert. 7.89). In general, virtue – or perhaps better "excellence" – is the perfection of something, and as such there can be a whole host of virtues, some intellectual and some non-intellectual. Thus, health and strength can be "virtues" of the body. As on many topics, the early Stoics offered different taxonomies of the virtues, with some referring to distinct logical, physical, and ethical virtues (ibid. 7.92). But the standard Stoic view emphasized four primary virtues of wisdom (*phronêsis*), courage (*andreia*), moderation (*sôphrosunê*), and justice (*dikaiosunê*), with other virtues subordinate to these four.[10] These were classified as good because, the Stoics claimed, they are consistently beneficial.

There are a number of passages where Marcus refers to the four principal virtues highlighted in the early Stoa. For example at 3.6 he writes "If you can discover in human life anything better than justice (*dikaiosunê*), truth (*alêtheia*), moderation (*sôphrosunê*), and courage (*andreia*)". At 7.63, he lists truth (*alêtheia*), justice (*dikaiosunê*), moderation (*sôphrosunê*), benevolence (*eumeneia*). At 8.1, he says, "nothing is good for a human (*anthrôpos*) except what makes him just (*dikaion*) and moderate (*sôphrona*), courageous (*andreion*) and free (*eleutherion*)".[11] In another passage he lists the four principal Stoic virtues, stressing that these are the only real goods:

> You could apprehend the character of what the majority of men fancy to be 'goods' like this. If a man were to conceive the existence of real goods, like wisdom (*phronêsis*), moderation (*sôphronsunê*), justice (*dikaiosunê*), courage (*andreia*), he could not with those in his mind still listen to the popular proverb about 'goods in every corner', for it will not fit.
>
> 5.12

As we can see, although in 5.12 Marcus list the four principal Stoic virtues, elsewhere his list sometimes includes variations. To give one further example:

> Does the light of the lamp shine and not lose its radiance until it be put out, and shall truth (*alêtheia*) and justice (*dikaiosunê*) and moderation (*sôphrosunê*) be put out in you before the end?
>
> 12.15

Here and in a number of the passages noted earlier Marcus prefers to list "truth" (*alêtheia*) in place of "wisdom" (*phronêsis*), although that can hardly be taken to be a significant deviation from the early Stoic view. It has been suggested that this substitution might reflect the influence of Plato, and that is certainly possible.[12] But ultimately this is mere terminological variation. Although early Stoics such as Chrysippus embraced a variety of virtues, others such as Aristo stressed the unity of virtue.[13] All the virtues were, for the Stoics ultimately different names expressing different aspects of the same thing, namely a soul in an excellent state. Thus, the virtues are inseparable, "for whoever has one has all, and whoever acts in accordance with one acts in accordance with all. They differ from one another by their own perspectives" (Stob. 2,63,8-11, *SVF* 2.280, LS 61D).

It has been suggested that when Marcus lists truth (*alêtheia*) and justice (*dikaiosunê*) and moderation (*sôphrosunê*), together, as we have just seen him do in 12.15, this is not a minor deviation from the standard list of Stoic virtues but instead a conscious development of his own list of virtues, inspired by Epictetus's list of three *topoi*, or areas of study.[14] In the *Discourses* Epictetus had proposed that there are three areas (*topoi*) in which people ought to be trained:

> The first has to do with desires and aversions, that he may never fail to get what he desires, nor fall into what he avoids; the second with cases of choice and of refusal, and, in general, with duty, that he may act in an orderly fashion, upon good reasons, and not carelessly; the third with the avoidance of error and rashness in judgement, and, in general, about cases of assent.
>
> *Diss. 3.2.1-2*

Hadot (1998: 234–6) argued that these three areas of study can help to explain Marcus's references to truth, justice, and moderation, and in support of this claim he focuses on one extended passage, 9.1. There Marcus warns against acts of injustice, of lying, and the pursuit of pleasure. In each case Marcus describes these as impious acts against universal Nature. Hadot takes these as expressions of Epictetus's three areas: desire, duty, and judgement. Thus, he argues that injustice correlates with duty, lying with judgement, and the pursuit of pleasure with desire. The three things that Marcus reminds himself to avoid are the three areas in which Epictetus thinks one ought to be trained, in order to cultivate the three virtues that Marcus mentions elsewhere, justice (*dikaiosunê*), truth (*alêtheia*), and moderation (*sôphrosunê*).

While those connections can certainly be made, and while Epictetus was no doubt an important influence on Marcus, this account seems to look for a degree of systematicity in the *Meditations* that may not be there. Although it is true that on occasion Marcus lists together the three virtues of justice, truth, and moderation, as we have already seen elsewhere, he produces a number of other lists too. At 3.6, he lists those three along with a fourth, courage (*andreia*). At 7.63, he swaps courage for benevolence (*eumeneia*). At 8.1, he swaps truth for freedom (*eleutheria*), and, at 5.12, he lists the four principal Stoic virtues without any alteration. While Hadot may be correct to discern an echo of Epictetus's three *topoi* in 9.1, the further claim that "Marcus makes the virtues correspond to each of the disciplines" (Hadot 1998: 232) does not seem warranted by the texts. Indeed, in all the passages just noted we get lists of four virtues, not three. All this seems to count against the claim that Marcus was engaged in a conscious development of a new system of Stoic virtues.[15]

The pre-eminence of justice

Putting that issue to one side, the one feature that stands out in Marcus's many references to the virtues is the pre-eminence of justice, which is mentioned far more often than any of the others.[16] This is not merely an unconscious preference to talk about this particular virtue, motivated perhaps by practical issues arising from his role as emperor. At 11.10, he is quite explicit about its pre-eminence, suggesting that justice is foundational for all the other virtues: "it is from justice that all the other virtues spring". It is unclear whether he means that justice is the origin of all other virtues, in the sense of being their *source*, or their origin in the sense that the other virtues exist *for the sake of* justice. Either way, Marcus is clear that justice is the most important of the virtues.

Why does Marcus give this pre-eminence to justice? One suggestion has been that this betrays the influence of Plato, who in the *Republic* accorded a special status to justice as the virtue that co-ordinates the relationship between the three other virtues that correspond to the three parts of the soul and city.[17] Justice, for Plato, involves each part of a thing fulfilling its function ("doing its own business") and not encroaching into a territory not its own (*Resp.* 433b). This leads Plato to state, like Marcus, that justice is the foundation of the other virtues (ibid.).

However, there is no evidence to suggest that Marcus adopted that Platonic model of justice, and the reason why Marcus prioritizes justice is fairly plain throughout the *Meditations*. Fundamentally, it is because it is the virtue that connects most closely with our nature as rational and social beings, and so brings us into accord with Nature as a whole. Throughout the *Meditations* he insists that this is our defining characteristic: see for example 4.24 ("a creature that is sociable by nature"), 7.55 ("rational beings exist for the sake of one another"), 9.1 ("universal Nature has created rational creatures for the sake of one another"), and 9.42 ("a human being is formed by nature to benefit others"). Indeed, as we saw earlier, Marcus presents our social and political instinct as the highest point of development in a human being, and he makes this point within an explicitly Stoic account of the scale of nature.[18]

This is closely connected to his arguments regarding the benefits of acting justly. These benefits come automatically from being part of a larger organic whole, which might be taken as a reference to either the community of all humankind or to Nature as a whole. He writes:

> No one wearies of receiving benefits, and to benefit another is to act according to Nature. Do not weary then of the benefits you receive by the doing of them.
>
> 7.74

At first glance the claim that acting to benefit others is in accordance with Nature might not seem immediately obvious. Here, we should perhaps take this reference to the *telos* formula to imply human nature and, in particular, our nature as social animals. To act for the benefit of others is to act in accordance with our social nature. By acting in this way we shall also benefit personally, by avoiding internal dissonance with our own nature. As he puts it:

> Withdraw into yourself: the governing self (*hêgemonikon*) is by its nature content with its own just actions and the tranquillity it thus secures.
>
> 7.28

The mind gains tranquillity or calm (*galênê*), Marcus writes, by acting justly, precisely because just actions are in accord with our nature as social beings. The anti-social person will never enjoy the contentment and smooth flow of life towards which the Stoics strived because of their fundamental internal disharmony with their own human nature. By contrast, as he puts it elsewhere, "a human being finds his delight in doing what is proper to a human being; and what is proper to him is to show goodwill to his own kind" (8.26).

Thus, the agent directly benefits from acting justly in two ways: (i) by being part of the whole, they benefit whenever the whole benefits, and (ii) by acting consistently with their own human nature, they avoid internal conflict and take pleasure in fulfilling their proper function. In this way the just agent is living in accord with Nature in all three of the ways outlined earlier. They achieve (i) internal consistency and tranquillity, (ii) consistency with human nature, and (iii) consistency with the larger whole of which they are a part. Marcus's focus on the virtue of justice, then, enables him to draw out the connections between the Stoic account of the virtues and the Stoic *telos* of living consistently with Nature in his own distinctive way. Yet, the orthodoxy of his position should never be in doubt, as is clear if we compare what we have seen him say with the following statement from Arius's summary of Stoic ethics (§ 6):

> As man is a rational mortal animal, political by nature, they [the Stoics] also say that every virtue which is associated with man and the happy life is consistent with and in agreement with Nature.
>
> *Stob. 2, 75, 7-10*

Spontaneous ethical action

In all this, there is one passage that stands out among Marcus's various reflections on ethical action. It is worth quoting at length:

> It is the way of one person, when he has done someone a good turn, to count as a matter of course on being repaid in kind. Another is not as quick to do so, but all the same, in his own mind, he regards the beneficiary as being in his debt, and he is conscious of what he has done. A third is, in a sense, not even conscious (*oude oiden*) of what he has done; he is rather like a vine which has produced its grapes, and seeks for no further reward once it has borne its proper fruit, as with a horse when it has run its race, or a dog when it has followed its trail, or a bee when it has made its honey. And so such a person, when he has done a good deed, does not shout about it, but passes straight on to the next one, as the vine yields new clusters of grapes when the season comes around.
>
> 5.6

Marcus distinguishes between three different types of people: (i) the person who expects a favour in return whenever they act well towards someone; (ii) the person who does not explicitly expect a favour but still thinks that the beneficiary of their action is in some sense in their debt; and (iii) the person who benefits others with absolutely no thought at all of receiving anything in return. The third type of person is, of course, the most admirable and the one to be emulated.

Thus, Marcus champions almost unconscious ethical action over ethical acts where the agent is fully aware of what they have done and, even if only implicitly, expect some kind of reward or praise for their action. The analogies he draws with vegetative processes and animal behaviour underline that he thinks this kind of spontaneous ethical action is entirely natural. We might call this "almost unconscious" because Marcus carefully qualifies his claim by writing "in a sense" and "in a way" (*tropon tina*). He does not want to be taken too literally here; it is the broader point that matters. Indeed, the passage continues with an exchange with an imaginary interlocutor who objects that surely a social being will be aware that their actions are appropriate to their nature. Marcus accepts this but objects that it takes his main point too literally. Moreover, once one goes down that path, one easily falls back into one of the other two types that Marcus wants to reject. As soon as an agent becomes conscious that they are acting appropriately as a social being, the implicit desire for reward or recognition is likely to creep back in. The way to avoid this, Marcus suggests, is to focus on natural spontaneity in ethical action.

Indeed, the naturalness of this sort of spontaneous ethical action is stressed elsewhere in the *Meditations* too:

> For when you have done good, what more, oh man, do you wish? Is it not enough that what you did was in agreement with your nature and do you seek a recompense for this? As if the eye asked a return for seeing or the feet for walking; for just as these were made for this which they effect according to their proper constitution, and so get what is theirs, even thus man is made by Nature to be benevolent, and whenever he contributes to the common stock by benevolence or otherwise, he has done what he was constituted for, and gets what is his own.
>
> 9.42

> When you have done good and another has been its object, why do you require a third thing besides, like the foolish – to be thought to have done good or to get a return?
>
> 7.73

At first glance this might appear to be at odds with standard Stoic thinking about ethical action, which is often said to stress the role of intentions. It is the intention standing behind an act that matters most, and it is tempting to assume that this is a conscious intention. Moreover, if intentions are the sorts of things that belong only to rational animals, then it looks as if Marcus's appeal to the vine that unconsciously produces grapes is somewhat out of step. Seneca, for instance, stresses the importance of (conscious) intentions in ethical action:

> So what is a benefit? It is a well-intentioned action that confers joy and in so doing derives joy, inclined towards and willingly prepared for doing what it does. And so it matters not what is done or what is given, but with what attitude, since the benefit consists not in what is done or given but rather the intention of the giver or agent.
>
> Ben. 1.6.1

For Seneca, then, such acts are willingly prepared with a deliberate attitude and intention, nothing like the unconscious act of the vine producing grapes. But here Seneca is addressing someone at an early stage in the process of learning how to develop the appropriate attitude, someone who will need to deliberate carefully. Marcus, by contrast, is describing someone at a far more advanced stage of ethical development who has attained a virtuous character from which virtuous actions flow automatically, without need for further deliberation. (There might, of course be deliberation about means – about *how* to do what one is doing – but not about ends – not about *what* to do.) The genuinely virtuous person does not need to stop and think before, say, offering assistance to someone in need; they just do it. Although the process of training required to develop the virtues might require quite a lot of thought, the goal is to reach a point where virtuous actions themselves are, in a sense, thoughtless. They are simply a natural expression of a person's virtuous character.

Indeed, elsewhere Seneca comes closer to Marcus's view, praising the person who forgets what they have given to others, even while they are giving it (*Ben.* 2.6.2). The best person (*optimus*), he comments, never seeks anything in return for what he gives to others, forgetting what he has given (*Ben.* 2.17.7). The good man (*vir bonus*) does not act well, he adds, because he has deliberated about how best to act, but rather cannot help but act in the way that he does (*Ben.* 6.21.2), just as the vine cannot help but produce grapes. On this, then, Marcus is in line with his Roman Stoic predecessor.

Notes

1 See the account in Diog. Laert. 7.88 (*SVF* 3.4, LS 63C).
2 There are numerous other passages throughout the *Meditations* that allude to the same idea. See for example 5.3, 5.9, 7.74, 9.1. On this topic see also Ackeren (2011: II, 613–26); Gourinat (2012b: 421–2).
3 See Diog. Laert. 7.87-9 (LS 63C) and Stob. 2,75,11–76,23 = Ar. Did. 6a (part LS 63B). The latter is reprinted with a translation and notes in Pomeroy (1999).
4 See Stob. 2,75,11-12 (*SVF* 1.179, LS 63B).
5 See for example Xenophon, *Oec.* 1.11 and, using *homologoumenôs* in a different sense, Plato, *Symp.* 186b.
6 It is worth noting that the word *katêgorêma* was a technical term in Stoicism; see for example Diog. Laert. 7.64, with discussion in Gaskin (1997).
7 For further discussion, which also opts for "consistency", see Rist (1977). The claim that later Stoics were ultimately engaged in glossing and expanding the foundational ideas of Zeno is explored in Sedley (1989).
8 On some problems with the text of Arius, see Brennan (2014).
9 See the doxographical account in Diog. Laert. 7.101-5 and the discussion in Cicero, *Fin.* 3.16-24. For further discussion see Inwood (1985), Schofield (2003), Jedan (2009), and Sellars (2018c: 103–8).
10 For definitions of the four principal virtues, see Stob. 2,59,4-11 (*SVF* 3.262, LS 61H). I translate *sôphrosunê* as "moderation". It is also often translated as "temperance" or "self-control". In the context of early Stoic ethics, Long and Sedley (1987: 490) translate it as "moderation"; Pomeroy (1999: 157) translates it as "self-restraint". In *Tusc.* 3.16, Cicero translates it as *temperantia* (hence "temperance" in English), but also suggests *moderatio*, *modestia*, and *frugalitas*, signalling that in some respects he prefers the last of these options.
11 As well as 3.6, 7.63, 8.1, and 5.12 and 12.15 quoted below, note also 2.5, 4.18, 9.1, 11.1, and 12.27.
12 Hadot (1998: 234) notes that this substitution in the traditional list of virtues has precedence in Plato's *Republic*, 487a. One might add that at 7.35 Marcus quotes a passage from the *Republic* just a few lines earlier, 486a, which adds weight to the thought that Marcus may well have picked this up from Plato.
13 For Aristo see Plutarch, *De virt. mor.* 440f (*SVF* 1.375, LS 61B). Although Aristo is often presented as heterodox, Plutarch notes that his position did not differ much from Zeno's. See the same passage (441a, *SVF* 3.255) for Chrysippus as well. For further discussion see Schofield (1984).
14 See Hadot (1998: 232–6), with comment in Gourinat (2012b: 429), who endorses Hadot's interpretation. This is but one expression of Hadot's wider claim that "the *Meditations* as a whole are thus organized in accordance with a threefold structure […] developed, and perhaps invented, by Epictetus" (1998: 232).
15 The passage in Epictetus as it continues relates the three *topoi* to managing emotions, duties, and attaining certainty. It states (*Diss.* 3.2.5) that the third is only for those already making progress.

This suggests that the three *topoi* might be taken as three stages in a philosophical education: first learn to manage emotions, then understand ethical duties, and finally gain certainty in judgements. Epictetus goes on to criticize philosophers who skip the first and second and go straight to the third (*Diss.* 3.2.6), again suggesting that they ought to be understood as a progressive series of stages in an education.

16 For examples of Marcus mentioning justice (*dikaiosunê*) see 3.5, 3.16, 8.7, 8.23, 9.23, 10.6, 10.11, 11.10, 11.21, 12.3, 12.24.
17 See Hadot (1998: 233), with Plato, *Resp.* 427d–441e. Hadot suggests that the three other virtues straightforwardly correspond to the three parts of the soul and city, although Plato (e.g. 432a) gives a more complex account of moderation (*sôphrosunê*).
18 See 6.14, with discussion in Chapter 6 above.

9
THE COSMIC CITY

Marcus's focus on the virtue of justice and on actions intended to benefit others highlights the social aspect of his thought.[1] Although his ethical project might be described as one primarily concerned with self-cultivation, the "self" that is being cultivated is that of a social animal who is a member of a series of wider communities.

Circles of concern

This idea was standard Stoic doctrine and most famously outlined by a late Stoic writer who may have been contemporary with Marcus: Hierocles.[2] We have fragments for two works by Hierocles, *Elements of Ethics* (*Êthikê stoicheiôsis*) and *On Appropriate Acts* (*Peri tôn kathêkontôn*), which may have been parts of a single larger work.[3] In *Elements of Ethics*, Hierocles outlines the Stoic theory of *oikeiôsis*, which posits a natural instinct for self-care and self-preservation in all animals, including humans.[4] This is, he says, the starting point for ethics, and other accounts of Stoic ethics also place it at the beginning.[5] He describes it thus:

> An animal, when it has received the first perception of itself, immediately becomes its own and familiar to itself and to its constitution [...] in accord with its own ability, each animal does what contributes to its own preservation, avoiding every attack even from afar and contriving to remain unharmed by dangers, while it leaps toward whatever brings safety and provides for itself from far and wide whatever tends towards its survival.
> *El. Eth.* 6.51-9

In the same work he also stresses the social nature of humans: "we are an animal, but a sociable one and in need of others [...] there is no human being who is not part of a city (*polis*)" (*El. Eth.* 11.15-17). These two ideas are combined and developed further in *On Appropriate Acts*, where he presents an image of a series of concentric circles of care or concern, starting with the individual in the centre, expanding to include immediate family, local community, wider nation, and ultimately all humankind.[6] Thus, humans are born with a natural instinct for self-care, but that instinct can – and indeed should – expand to include others as an individual develops into a rational adult. In fact, Hierocles does not use the imagery of expansion but instead contraction: the task is to bring people from the outer circles closer into the centre, treating strangers as extended relatives and extended relatives as siblings. He is fully conscious of the limits of this procedure, however, commenting that "a greater distance in respect to blood will subtract something of goodwill, but, nevertheless, we must make an effort about assimilating them" (Stob. 4,672,16-18).

Stoic cosmopolitanism

The widest circle of care mentioned by Hierocles embraces all humankind. This is often connected with the idea of cosmopolitanism, and Marcus, along with the other Roman Stoics, is usually taken to be a proponent of cosmopolitanism.[7] The idea itself was by his time already well established. A number of ancient sources attribute cosmopolitan ideas to Socrates,[8] although some commentators have sceptically suggested that this might be a later projection back onto him. It is most closely associated with Diogenes of Sinope, who is the first person reported to have described himself as a *kosmopolitês*, a citizen of the cosmos (Diog. Laert. 6.63). Diogenes and the early Cynics were an important influence on the early Stoics (see Goulet-Cazé 2003) and Diogenes would later become an idealized role model for Epictetus (see esp. *Diss*. 3.22, 4.1). For Diogenes, his citizenship of the cosmos went hand in hand with a rejection of citizenship of any actual city.

When we turn to the Roman Stoics we find a slightly different, more moderate, account. The most famous expression is in Seneca:

> Let us take hold of the fact that there are two communities (*duas res publicas*) – the one, which is great and truly common (*magnam et vere publicam*), embracing gods and men, in which we look neither to this corner nor to that, but measure the boundaries of our citizenship by the sun; the other, the one to which we have been assigned by the accident of our birth.
>
> *De otio 4.1, LS 67K*[9]

Note how this differs from Diogenes' Cynic cosmopolitanism. Seneca is not rejecting his citizenship of his actual city; he is affirming two allegiances. In this way, Seneca affirms his commitment to the Stoic ideal of a single cosmopolitan community of all humankind without rejecting his status as a Roman citizen and his position within Roman politics.

Marcus's cosmic city

With these preliminaries in place, we can now turn to see what Marcus has to say. To begin, we should note that Marcus does not use the word *kosmopolitês*, but he does refer to "the great city of the cosmos (*polis tou kosmou*)" (10.15) and to being "a citizen of this great city" (12.36). He also follows Seneca's image of there being two cities of which he is a citizen: "As Antoninus, my city and fatherland is Rome; as a human being, it is the cosmos, so what brings benefits to these is the sole good for me" (6.44). At 3.11, he refers to human beings as "citizens of that highest of cities of which all other cities are, as it were, mere households". At 2.16, he says that the goal (*telos*) for all rational creatures is "to conform to the reason and law of the most venerable of cities and constitutions", i.e. the cosmos. So, *qua* Roman he is a citizen of

Rome, but *qua* rational being, he is a citizen of the cosmos. Marcus's comments also suggest a clear hierarchy between these two cities of which he is a citizen. If his commitments were to come into conflict, his first loyalty would be to the natural law of Nature, not the manmade laws of Rome.

His few comments about traditional politics are somewhat dismissive. In 9.29, he counsels himself not to hope for Plato's ideal republic, to do what he can but without expecting to change the minds of others, and not to be impressed by leaders like Alexander the Great, who were not governed by reason.[10] Despite his own pre-eminent role in Roman politics, Marcus's attitude in the *Meditations* pays far more attention to the philosophical ideal of a community of all humankind than it does to the politics of the local community of which he was part.

Central to this prioritization of the cosmic city over the political state was the Stoic claim that Nature is governed by a rational law. Zeno of Citium had written a *Republic*, in which he outlined an ideal image of all humans living together under a single common law (*nomos*).[11] A century and a half later, Diogenes of Babylon is reported to have argued that Rome was not a real city, because it was not governed by a common rational law (see Cicero, *Acad.* 2.137). He is reported to have said, "among the foolish there exists no city nor any law",[12] and one might note that this view continues the attitude of his namesake from Sinope rather than pre-empting the later, more moderate view of Seneca and Marcus. Drawing on this Stoic natural law tradition, Marcus puts it like this:

> If mind is common to us all, then also the reason, whereby we are reasoning beings, is common. If this be so, then also the reason which enjoins what is to be done or left undone is common. If this be so, law also is common; if this be so, we are citizens; if this be so, we are partakers in one constitution; if this be so, the cosmos is a kind of state (*polis*).
>
> 4.4

This cosmic city is a shared fellowship among the wise wherever they may be geographically. As he puts it elsewhere, "Among rational creatures, political communities could be found […] among beings which are higher still, there existed a sort of union in separation" (9.9). The ideal sage, then, will recognize other sages as fellow citizens of the cosmic city, no matter how near or far they may be in physical space, simply by virtue of the fact that they live according to a shared law, the law of Nature. While Marcus hints at this idea, it is worth stressing that the vast majority of his comments regarding the cosmic city do not point towards an exclusive community of a handful of sages; on the contrary, his principal motivation is to see *all* humans – no matter what their level of rational and ethical progress – as his fellow citizens and members of a single community. In so doing, he is following the theory of *oikeiôsis* that extends care to others regardless of whether they are wise or foolish and, indeed, acknowledges that the foolish will also extend care to others in this way, presumably because such actions arise out of a natural instinct and so are independent of rational knowledge.[13]

Putting whole before part

Marcus's image of all humans as equal citizens in a single cosmic city draws, as we have seen, on earlier Stoic thinking. However, he develops his own thoughts on this topic further, insisting on an even stronger connection between individuals and between each individual and the whole. One might say that the problem with cosmopolitanism as it is usually conceived is that it continues to see individuals as distinct, isolated agents. There may be a single, universal city, but there remains a plurality of citizens within it, each with their own needs and concerns. Marcus's aim is move beyond this individualistic model and replace it with something more integrated and organic. In this section and the next, we shall see how he attempts to do this.

The first way in which Marcus tries to move to a more integrated model is to insist that one ought to put the interests of the community before those of the individual. The first stage in the process is to align one's own interests with the interests of the cosmic city. At 5.22, he writes "what is not injurious to the city does not injure the citizens either". This statement is made as part of a consolatory argument aimed at reducing the impact of perceived injuries. He continues: "On the occasion of every impression that you have been injured apply this canon: 'if the city is not injured by this neither am I injured'".

This thought is developed at greater length in 10.6, where he states that "I am part of the whole (*to holon*)". As we saw in a previous chapter, this is a technical term in Stoic physics used to describe the totality of Nature.[14] To this he adds that "I am allied (*oikeiôs*) in some way to parts that are of the same kind with me", which is to say other rational human agents. His use of *oikeiôs* here alludes to the Stoic theory of *oikeiôsis* mentioned earlier. If he can remember these two things, he writes, then "I shall, in so far as I am a part (*meros*), not be disaffected to anything assigned to the whole". Nothing that benefits the whole, he continues, injures the part. But everything that happens within the whole benefits it in some way, and nothing external can damage the whole because, by definition, there is nothing external to it.[15] Thus, Marcus concludes, if he can hold on to the thought that he is part of the whole, fully aligning his own interests with the interests of the whole, then no event will ever feel like an injury.

This is his conclusion drawn from the first of his two opening statements. He also draws a conclusion from his second statement: by remembering that he is allied to other parts of the whole that share a similar nature, he will, he writes, "do no unsocial (*akoinônêtos*) act". Instead, he will focus on what is the common benefit for all humankind and direct his energies towards that goal rather than his own interests, narrowly conceived. It seems clear that Marcus is drawing a parallel between the two cases, the first concerned with his place in Nature, the second concerned with his place within the community of humankind. He seems to take the first to be the more self-evident – that we are parts of Nature and dependent on it – and wants carry that thought over to the case of community, where thinking of individuals as isolated and autonomous agents is perhaps more firmly engrained, at least in his own case. Marcus concludes by making explicit that the goal behind this is to achieve a smooth flow of life, one of Zeno's formulations of the goal of Stoic philosophy (Diog. Laert. 7.88). A citizen's life will be smooth, Marcus writes, if they act for the benefit of their fellow citizens and welcome whatever the city decrees. It is worth stressing, though, that this is not a political leader arguing for obedience and quietism. The city he has in mind here, as the immediate context makes clear, is the cosmic city, governed by the reason permeating Nature.

The same theme appears again in 10.33. Here Marcus connects it with a reflection on human nature. It is, he says in a number of places, the nature of a social animal to act sociably and to benefit others.[16] Any human being that acts in a manner inappropriate to their constitution will inevitably suffer distress, he writes. All entities act according to their own nature, and so should humans too. Among the examples he picks – fire moves upwards, stones fall downwards – most striking is the cylinder that naturally rolls down a slope. It is tempting to take this as an allusion to Chrysippus's famous cylinder analogy, still current in philosophical discussions and recounted by Marcus's rough contemporary Aulus Gellius.[17] Although that is usually associated with debates about compatibilism, it involves drawing an analogy between the cylinder acting according to its internal nature and humans doing the same, just as Marcus does here. Marcus concludes his thought by making explicit the claim that humans are by nature social animals, describing them as natural citizens (*politês phusei*). This is part of a reflection on the relationship between the citizen of the cosmos and the cosmic city. As in 10.6, this is presented as something that must be remembered:

> Remember that nothing harms the natural citizen which does not harm the city and nothing harms the city which does not harm the law. Now none of what are called strokes of bad luck harms the law: wherefore, not harming the law, it harms neither city nor citizen.
>
> *10.33[8]*

Here Marcus gives an explicit argument for the consolatory claim he is making. The citizen is only harmed if the city is harmed; the city is only harmed if the law is harmed; but the law – the divine reason permeating Nature – can never be harmed; therefore, neither the city nor the citizen can be harmed. This loosely parallels the argument we saw earlier in 10.6, where similarly the structure of the argument was that the part is only harmed if the whole is harmed; but the whole is never harmed (either by itself or something external to it); therefore, the part is never harmed.[18] As we saw there, the aim seemed to be to transfer that argument over to the context of human communities; here we see him do it explicitly.

In these three passages – 5.22, 10.6, 10.33 – there are a number of things happening at once. At first glance they are primarily concerned with offering consolation for perceived injuries. The way in which that consolation is offered is by aligning the interests of the individual with a larger entity, the cosmic city and the whole. In the present context these are more or less the same thing. Although in the first of these passages, 5.22, Marcus seems to admit the possibility that the city might be injured ("if the city is injured you must not be angry"), by the time he gets to Book 10 he argues more forcibly that the cosmic city simply cannot be harmed in any way. Here he can be seen to follow earlier Stoic advice, such as Epictetus's suggestion that one ought to align one's will with the will of Nature (*Ench.* 8), and Marcus further echoes that advice elsewhere (e.g. 4.23). For Marcus's arguments in the passages here really to work, though, he must convince himself that his own interests are completely aligned with the interests of the larger whole. To see how he tries to do that we need to consider some further passages.

Parts versus limbs

Marcus uses a variety of images to characterize the person who fails to act for the benefit of the community of humankind and, indeed, for the benefit of Nature as a whole. The soul of such a person, he writes in 2.16, does violence to itself, becoming an abscess (*apostêma*) or tumour (*phuma*) on the cosmos. This happens whenever someone turns away from other human beings or acts antisocially towards them. This presentation of antisocial or vicious behaviour as unnatural or in some way diseased was already well established.[19] The goal of any rational animal (*logikon zôion*), he continues, is to follow the law of the greatest city and state (*polis kai politeia*), namely Nature. Acting with regard to the wellbeing of others is a central feature of his conception of a life in harmony with Nature.

We find similar imagery in 4.29. The way to avoid becoming a foreigner (*xenos*) in the cosmic city is to comprehend properly what it is and how it operates, which is to say to understand the reason (*logos*) that governs this cosmic community (*politeia*). The person who fails to do this, who remains a foreigner, is an abscess (*apostêma*) on the cosmos, an unnatural growth separated off from the larger whole. Although the central point concerns the relationship between the individual and Nature as a whole, once again Marcus concludes his thought by stressing the social aspect involved. The person cut off from the whole is cut off from the cosmic city (*polis*) and from other rational souls, his fellow citizens.

This is one type of imagery Marcus uses to describe the antisocial person: an unnatural growth or abscess on the face of Nature. Elsewhere, he characterizes such a person in different terms. The antisocial person is a part of Nature that has become broken off or severed from the whole. In 11.8, he draws an analogy with a branch broken off from its tree. The antisocial person is similarly broken off from society as a whole. The difference though, Marcus insists, is that while a branch is only ever broken off by some external force, the antisocial person cuts themselves off in an act that is ultimately a self-inflicted wound. Any antisocial act against another person is not only an act against that particular person; it is also an act that servers oneself from the whole community (*politeuma*). Like the branch, however, Marcus wants to insist that it is possible to graft a dismembered part back onto the whole, although inevitably the more often this is done, the weaker the bond will be.

If a broken branch is not striking enough to grab one's attention, at 8.34, Marcus opts for a more visceral image:

> If you have ever seen a dismembered hand or foot or a head cut off, lying somewhere apart from the rest of the trunk, you have an image of what a man makes of himself [...] when he] cuts himself off or when he does some unneighbourly act.
>
> *8.34[1]*

As naturally social animals, Marcus insists that we all come into the world as parts of a community, so any act that separates us off from other people is quite unnatural. Although the image of a severed foot or head might seem to count against the possibility of being grafted back on to the body, Marcus in fact explicitly states that, in the case of humans cut off from society, it is indeed possible to re-join the whole, "to come back again once more and to grow together and to recover his portion as a part (*meros*)" (8.34[5]).[20]

In these passages, then, Marcus strikes a more positive tone about the possibility of the antisocial person being able to re-join the community of humankind. But what both the abscess and the dismembered part passages share is that they describe unnatural states. The antisocial person is deeply unnatural, Marcus insists, and antisocial behaviour is out of the question for anyone attempting to live up to the Stoic idea of a life in harmony with Nature.

In many of the passages just considered Marcus refers to a part (*meros*) separated from the whole (*to holon*), the community (*politeia*), or the cosmos (*kosmos*). In one of the most interesting passages where he addresses this issue, 7.13, he reflects on whether this is in fact the best term to use. Continuing with the imagery of the dismembered foot, Marcus wonders whether we ought to think of individuals not as a part (*meros*) of something larger but instead as a limb (*melos*).[21] It is a much stronger claim, he says, to say that someone is a limb, rather than a mere part, and involves only the change of a single letter. The person who sees themselves as a part may act for the benefit of the whole, all the while retaining their own identity as an individual, a part of, but still distinct from, society as a whole. By contrast, if someone sees themselves as a limb of society, as an integrated part of a larger organism, then they will act for the good of the whole knowing that it is also for the good of themselves. While a part might still experience a conflict between its interests and the interests of the whole, a limb will experience no such thing, for its wellbeing depends on the wellbeing of the whole. A mere part (*meros*), Marcus writes, may act sociably out of sense of duty, but someone who sees themselves as an integrated limb (*melos*) will do so in full knowledge that they are benefitting themselves.

This, then, is how Marcus develops his thought that one ought to align one's interests with those of the whole. It is not mere alignment that he is proposing; instead, it is a thoroughgoing identification based on conceiving oneself as a fully integrated limb of a larger organism. As a limb, one has no narrow self-interests, for one only ever benefits or suffers along with the organism as a whole. The foot will only ever flourish if the body as a whole is in good health. The same applies with people, Marcus suggests; the individual's wellbeing depends upon the wellbeing of the community of which they are a part, and Marcus primarily has the cosmic city embracing all humankind in mind.

This way of conceiving a social community is a striking feature of the *Meditations*, but what Marcus says is not without precedent. The analogy with limbs of the body can also be found in Epictetus (*Diss*. 2.5.24), who argued that while it might be in the nature of a foot considered in isolation to remain clean, when considered as a limb of a larger organism it will often be appropriate for it to get muddy from time to time. Indeed, on some occasions it may be necessary for the foot to be amputated for the sake of the organism. The foot, if it were conscious, might protest at such a move, but only because it failed to comprehend that if the organism were to die, it would die too anyway. Epictetus is quite explicit about the analogy:

> If you regard yourself as a thing detached, it is natural for you to live to old age, to be rich, to enjoy health. But if you regard yourself as a man and as part of some whole, on account of that whole it is fitting for you now to be sick, and now to make a voyage and run risks, and now to be in want, and on occasion to die before your time.
>
> *Diss. 2.5.25*

Just as a foot, understood properly as an organ with a particular function, would no longer be a foot if separated from the body, so too a human is no longer a proper human, conceived as a social animal, when separated from other people. It is worth noting that here Epictetus refers to both the cosmic city embracing gods and humans, and local political communities, as Seneca had done before him (compare *De otio* 4.1 with *Diss*. 2.5.26). The well-functioning limb will be a proper-functioning member of both the cosmic city and their local community, Epictetus seems to suggest.

Epictetus was not obviously innovating here either. The image of the foot willingly embracing mud because it understands it role as a limb of the body had already been articulated by Chrysippus. Indeed, Epictetus quotes Chrysippus on this topic in the next chapter of the *Discourses*:

> As long as the consequences are not clear to me, I cleave ever to what is better adapted to secure those things that are in accordance with Nature; for God himself has created me with the faculty of choosing things. But if I really knew that it was ordained for me to be ill at this present moment, I would even seek illness; for the foot also, if it had a mind, would seek to be covered with mud.
>
> *Chrysippus, in Diss. 2.6.9-10, SVF 2.191*

This passage is interesting for the hint it gives about how it is that people fall into antisocial behaviour, according to the Stoics. Humans are born as naturally social animals but all too often lose sight of this and have to undertake significant philosophical work to reconceive themselves as part of a larger community. It is, Chrysippus suggests, a lack of proper understanding that leads people to focus on their own interests. That impulse to self-interest is an inevitable consequence of our natural instinct for self-preservation, the Stoics would claim, but it can expand out of control. As people develop, they will hopefully attain a fuller understanding and so grow out of that selfish way of thinking. But it is worth noting that on their account: (i) the instinct for self-preservation is perfectly natural, as is (ii) a period of limited understanding before one achieves fully developed rationality. This offers the beginnings of an explanation for why antisocial behaviour arises among animals that are by nature social.

In the light of this, we can see that Marcus's reflections on parts and limbs had good precedent within the Stoic tradition, and he could have encountered it in his reading of either Epictetus or Chrysippus. What looks like a colourful analogy chosen for rhetorical effect in fact has a firm foundation in Stoic thinking about the place of humans in Nature.[22]

Summary

These reflections on the cosmic city bring together many of the themes we have seen in the *Meditations*. This city is co-extensive with Nature, governed by divine reason. Acting for the benefit of this city involves acting consistently with both human nature and Nature as a whole. If we do, we shall automatically benefit ourselves, in so far as we are integrated parts of the whole. To live in a way that is cut off from this global community of humankind is against Nature, for we are by nature social beings. Our primitive sociability connects us with people closest to us, but a more developed sociability – acknowledging what we share in common with *all* others – involves embracing the idea of a single global community of all humankind.

Notes

1 The most relevant passages where he engages with ideas connected to politics are 2.16, 3.11, 4.4, 4.23, 4.29, 5.22, 6.44, 9.9, 9.29, 10.6, 10.15, 10.33, 11.8, 12.36.
2 Hierocles' precise dates are unknown. The only evidence is a remark in Aulus Gellius, *NA* 9.5.8, that refers to Gellius's teacher Calvenus Taurus quoting him. Taurus was active in the middle of the second century AD (*fl.* 145), so Hierocles must have been active before or around the same time (see further Holford-Strevens 2003: 90–7; *DPhA* VI, 713–22). Bastianini and Long (1992: 281) date him to the middle of the second century AD, while Ramelli (2009: xxvi) pushes him slightly earlier to the first half of the second century AD. Either way, it is conceivable that he was alive and active around the time Marcus first encountered Stoicism in his youth. It is equally conceivable that he could have read works by Hierocles, but there is no evidence for this, and if he had been an important influence one might have expected Marcus to name him.

3 Hierocles' *Elements of Ethics* survives incomplete on papyrus (*PBerol* 9780) and was first published in von Arnim (1906), later re-edited in Bastianini and Long (1992), and printed with a facing English translation in Ramelli (2009). The fragments of *On Appropriate Acts* are preserved by Stobaeus and are gathered together and translated in Ramelli (2009). On the relationship between the two works, there has been some debate: see Ramelli (2009: xxvii–xxx) for discussion and further references; at xlix, she notes that while they are likely to be two distinct works, "there is a clear thematic continuity" between them. Note also *DPhA* III, 686–8.

4 On the theory of *oikeiôsis*, see the texts in *SVF* 3.178-89, with extended discussion in Engberg Pedersen (1990).

5 See *El. Eth.* 1.35-7 and compare with Diog. Laert. 7.85 (*SVF* 3.178) and Cicero, *Fin.* 3.16 (*SVF* 3.182). Diogenes Laertius (ibid.) cites from Chrysippus, confirming that the theory goes back to the early Stoa; see also Plutarch, *St. rep.* 1038b (*SVF* 3.179); Aulus Gellius, *NA* 12.5.7 (*SVF* 3.181). For some doubts as to whether this really was the foundation for Stoic ethics, see Schofield (2003: 237–8).

6 The key passage, which I shall not quote at length, is in Stob. 4,671,3–673,18, reprinted and translated in Ramelli (2009: 90–1), and also printed as LS 57G.

7 On cosmopolitanism in Marcus, and the Roman Stoics more widely, see for example Stanton (1968), Gill (2000), Gueye (2006), Laurand (2012), Reydams-Schils (2012a), and Gueye (2013).

8 See for example Epictetus, *Diss.* 1.9.1, Musonius Rufus 9 (Hense 1905: 42,1-2), Cicero, *Tusc.* 5.108, Plutarch, *De exil.* 600f.

9 See also *Helv.* 9.7, *Ep.* 28.4. Note also Epictetus, *Diss.* 2.5.26 where, echoing Seneca, he mentions the cosmic city (*polis*) embracing gods and men and smaller cities on earth that are copies of the cosmic city.

10 See further Reydams-Schils (2005: 86–9 and 2012a: 439–42).

11 See Plutarch, *De Alex. fort.* 329a-b (LS 67A), with discussion in Schofield (1991), Sellars (2007), and Vogt (2008).

12 Obbink (1999: 193); see also Obbink and Vander Waerdt (1991: 376).

13 See Cicero, *Fin.* 3.59, with Ramelli (2009: xlix).

14 See Chapter 4 above.

15 Compare with Cicero, *Nat. D.* 2.35, recounting the Stoic view: "there can be nothing that can frustrate nature as a whole, since she embraces and contains within herself all modes of being" (LCL trans.).

16 See for example 4.24, 7.55, 9.1, 9.42.

17 See Aulus Gellius, *NA* 7.2.11 (*SVF* 2.1000); see also Cicero, *Fat.* 43 (*SVF* 2.974). It is worth noting that Gellius refers to Cicero's *De fato* a little later at 7.2.15, and so Cicero may have been his source here.

18 The structure is: if p then q; not q; therefore not p (i.e. *modus tollens*). This is the second of the Stoic indemonstrable syllogisms (see Diog. Laert. 7.80).

19 See further Gill (2013: 101).

20 It is worth noting that this passage, 8.34, comes before 11.8 in which he uses the analogy with a branch broken off its tree. In both passages he makes the point about humans being able to be rejoined; perhaps the shift from dismembered limb in 8.34 to broken branch in 11.8 was because the latter enabled him more effectively to make the point about the possibility of being grafted back on to the whole.

21 On the distinction between parts and limbs see Aristotle, *Hist. an.* 1.1, 486a5-14, although it seems unlikely that Marcus had this in mind. A mere part, Aristotle says, can be divided into further parts that resemble the original (flesh can be divided into two pieces of flesh), whereas a limb is a part that cannot be so divided (a foot cannot be divided into two feet) and contains other undividable parts within it (such as toes). Farquharson (1944: II, 725) notes that, despite his comment in 7.13, Marcus generally falls back into talking about parts, not limbs. But, following Aristotle, one might respond by saying that a limb is a type of part rather than a distinct category, so there is no error in falling back into the admittedly less precise language of parts.

22 Note also Cicero, *Fin.* 3.64 where he reports that the Stoics see the universe as "a city or state of which both men and gods are members, and each one of us is a part of this universe; from which it is a natural consequence that we should prefer the common advantage to our own". The same thought is developed in *Off.* 3.21-2, where Cicero characterizes people as limbs (*membra*) of human society, and 3.32, where he refers to the body (*corpore*) of humanity and the dangers posed by sick limbs to the whole.

CONCLUSION

I have tried to defend Marcus's status as a philosopher, and in particular a Stoic philosopher, in a number of different ways. The first way was biographical, looking at his education in Stoic philosophy and the predominance of Stoics among his teachers. The second way was literary, looking at the sort of text the *Meditations* is and the way in which that sort of text might have a specific function within a conception of philosophy as an art of living. The third way was philosophical, examining the ideas in the *Meditations* and the way in which they engage with Stoic doctrines in both the early Stoa and his Roman Stoic predecessors. As we have seen, Marcus engages with topics in all three parts of Stoic philosophy – logic, physics, and ethics – and we have also seen Marcus deploy explicit arguments, making use of standard Stoic syllogistic forms. I have tried to show that the claims that have often been made that Marcus was a confused eclectic, merely interested in moral exhortation, or not a serious philosopher because he resorted to rhetoric rather than argument, do not stand up to close scrutiny.

APPENDIX

Editions of the *Meditations*

There are two complete sources for the text of the *Meditations*. The first is a manuscript in the Vatican Library (Vaticanus Graecus 1950), dated to the fourteenth century, containing not just the *Meditations* but a number of other ancient philosophical texts, including Xenophon's *Memorabilia of Socrates*, the *Paraphrasis Christiana* of Epictetus's *Enchridion*, and a collection of quotations from Epicurus now known as the *Vatican Sayings*.[1] This was acquired by the Vatican Library in 1683. The second is the first printed edition of the *Meditations*, based on a now lost manuscript once in the Palatine Library, in Heidelberg. This edition was initiated by Conrad Gesner and was accompanied by a translation into Latin by Wilhelm Xylander and published either towards the end of 1558 or early in 1559. It was reprinted in 1568 and 1590. A number of other manuscripts exist that preserve extracts from the *Meditations*,[2] but the Vatican manuscript and the *editio princeps* are the only two complete witnesses for the text.

A new edition prepared by Amadeus Sally in 1626 is noteworthy for being the first to number individual sections within each book. It was reprinted in 1635 and followed not long after by two important editions, by Meric Casaubon (1634) and Thomas Gataker (1652). Both contained important notes on the text and Gataker's constitute one of the most detailed commentaries ever produced. These two editions also number sections within books, dividing them up in slightly different ways. It was, however, Gataker's that proved to be the most popular and is the basis for the subdivisions used today. Indeed, the reason for this is easy to see: while Casaubon's edition was never reprinted, Gataker's was reprinted in 1697 and 1707, and was the basis for subsequent editions in 1704, 1728, and 1744.

The century or so from the mid-1700s to the mid-1800s saw a variety of new editions, none especially noteworthy. De Joly's, 1774, attempted to re-organize the text, grouping sections under thematic headings, an experiment that did not catch on. Other editions were prepared by Morus (1775), Schultz (1802), and Koraes (1816), among others.

The late nineteenth century saw a Teubner edition by Stich, 1882 (reprinted 1903), and in the same year a text, translation, and detailed commentary on Book 4 only, by Hastings Crossley. In an introductory note, he reported that he was working on a complete translation and commentary, but only this portion made it into print. The early twentieth century saw editions in newly formed series of ancient texts such as Leopold for the Oxford Classical Texts

(1908), Schenkl for Teubner (1913), Haines for the Loeb Classical Library (1916), and Trannoy for Budé (1925). The last two of these have been reprinted often.

In 1944, A. S. L. Farquharson's major edition was published posthumously, containing text, translation, and two separate commentaries on the text. While a number of other editions have be published since, often with facing translations into vernaculars, such as Theiler (1951), Cortassa (1984), R. Nickel (1990), the most significant recent edition is Dalfen's critical edition for Teubner, first published in 1979, with a second edition in 1987. Although this has been criticized for bracketing many passages as interpolations,[3] it has become the standard modern edition of the *Meditations*.

Since Dalfen, there has also appeared the first volume of a new edition by Hadot and Luna, containing just Book 1, prefaced by an extensive introduction. Although Hadot's work on the rest of the text was cut short by his death, further volumes are expected to complete this new Budé edition.

Fuller accounts of the history of the text can be found in Schenkl (1913: vi–xvi, xxvii–xxxi), Farquharson (1944: xxii–lv), Dalfen (1987: vi–xxvii), and Hadot and Luna (1998: cxci–cciv). For a bibliography of editions and translations printed up to 1908, see Wickham Legg (1910).

Notes

1 For a full description of Vaticanus Graecus 1950 and its contents, see Canart (1970–73: I, 762–6). The contents are also listed in Schenkl (1913: xi) and Farquharson (1944: I, xxix–xxx). See also Boter (1999: 14–15) (also 204), who notes that the version of the *Enchiridion* contained therein is a hybrid, part the original *Enchiridion* and part the *Paraphrasis Christiana*. On the Epicurean *Sententiae Vaticanae*, first noticed and printed in 1888, see Bailey (1926: 375).
2 See the descriptions in Farquharson (1944: I, xxx–xxxii) and Dalfen (1987: viii–xix).
3 See for example the review in Sandbach (1981).

BIBLIOGRAPHY

Editions of ancient texts are listed under their editors or translators.

Ackeren, Marcel van (2011), *Die Philosophie Marc Aurels*, 2 vols (Berlin: De Gruyter).
Africa, T. W. (1961), 'The Opium Addiction of Marcus Aurelius', *Journal of the History of Ideas* 22, 97–102.
Amato, Eugenio (2010), *Favorinos d'Arles, Oeuvres III: Fragments* (Paris: Les Belles Lettres).
Annas Julia (1992), *Hellenistic Philosophy of Mind* (Berkeley: University of California Press).
Annas, Julia (2004), 'Marcus Aurelius: Ethics and Its Background', *Rhizai* 2, 103–19.
Arnim, H. von (1903–24), *Stoicorum Veterum Fragmenta*, 4 vols (Leipzig: Teubner).
Arnim, H. von (1906), *Hierokles, Ethische Elementarlehre (Papyrus 9780)*, Berliner Klassikertexte 4 (Berlin: Weidmann).
Arnold, E. Vernon (1911), *Roman Stoicism* (Cambridge: Cambridge University Press).
Arrighetti, Graziano (1973), *Epicuro: Opere* (Turin: Giulio Einaudi editore).
Ashley Cooper, Anthony (2011), *Standard Edition II, 6: Askêmata* (Stuttgart: Frommann-Folzboog).
Asmis, Elizabeth (1989), 'The Stoicism of Marcus Aurelius', in Wolfgang Haase, ed., *Aufstieg und Niedergang der römischen Welt II: 36.3* (Berlin: De Gruyter), 2228–52.
Asmis, Elizabeth (2001), 'Choice in Epictetus' Philosophy', in A. Collins and M. Mitchell, eds, *Antiquity and Humanity: Essays on Ancient Religion and Philosophy* (Tübingen: Mohr Siebeck), 385–412.
Babut, Daniel (1969), *Plutarque et le Stoïcisme* (Paris: Presses Universitaires de France).
Bailey, Cyril (1926), *Epicurus: The Extant Remains* (Oxford: Clarendon Press).
Barigazzi, Adelmo (1966), *Favorino di Arelate: Opere* (Florence: Felice Le Monnier).
Barigazzi, Adelmo (1991), *Galeno: Sull'ottima maniera d'insegnare, Esortazione alla medicina*, CMG 5.1.1 (Berlin: Akademie-Verlag).
Barnes, Jonathan (1997), *Logic and the Imperial Stoa* (Leiden: Brill).
Barnes, T. D. (1978), *The Sources of the Historia Augusta* (Brussels: Latomus).
Bastianini, Guido, and Long, A. A. (1992), 'Hierocles, *Elementa moralia*', *Corpus dei Papiri Filosofici Greci e Latini*, Parte I, Vol. 1** (Florence: Leo S. Olschki), 268–451.
Bénatouïl, Thomas (2009), *Les Stoïciens III: Musonius, Épictète, Marc Aurèle* (Paris: Les Belles Lettres).
Bergson, H. (1911), *La Perception du Changement: Conférences faites a l'Université d'Oxford, les 26 et 27 mai 1911* (Oxford: Clarendon Press).
Bergson, H. (1934), *La Pensée et le mouvant* (Paris: Félix Alcan).
Bergson, H. (1946), *The Creative Mind*, trans. M. L. Andison (New York: Philosophical Library).
Berryman, Sylvia (2010), 'The Puppet and the Sage: Images of the Self in Marcus Aurelius', *Oxford Studies in Ancient Philosophy* 38, 187–209.

Birley, Anthony (1997), *Hadrian: The Restless Emperor* (London: Routledge).
Birley, Anthony (2000), *Marcus Aurelius: A Biography*, Revised Edition (London: Routledge); first published 1966, revised 1987.
Bobzien, Susanne (1998), *Determinism and Freedom in Stoic Philosophy* (Oxford: Clarendon Press).
Bobzien, Susanne (2003), 'Logic', in Brad Inwood, ed., *The Cambridge Companion to The Stoics* (Cambridge: Cambridge University Press), 85–123.
Bonhöffer, Adolf (1894), *Die Ethik des Stoikers Epictet* (Stuttgart: Ferdinand Enke).
Boter, Gerard (1999), *The Encheiridion of Epictetus and Its Three Christian Adaptations* (Leiden: Brill).
Boudon-Millot, Véronique (2007), *Galien I: Introduction générale, Sur l'ordre de ses propres livres, Sur ses propres livres, Que l'excellent médecin est aussi philosophe* (Paris: Les Belles Lettres).
Boudon-Millot, Véronique, et al. (2010), *Galien IV: Ne pas se chagriner* (Paris: Les Belles Lettres).
Boys-Stones, George (2018), *L. Annaeus Cornutus: Greek Theology, Fragments, and Testimonia* (Atlanta: SBL Press).
Brennan, Tad (2014), 'Arius, Stobaeus, and the Scholiast', *Classical Quarterly* 64, 270–79.
Brunschwig, J. (2003), 'Stoic Metaphysics', in B. Inwood, ed., *The Cambridge Companion to The Stoics* (Cambridge: Cambridge University Press), 206–32.
Brunt, P. A. (1974), 'Marcus Aurelius in His *Meditations*', *Journal of Roman Studies* 64, 1–20 (repr. in Brunt 2013).
Brunt, P. A. (2013), *Studies in Stoicism* (Oxford: Oxford University Press).
Butler, H. E., and Owen, A. S. (1914), *Apulei Apologia sive Pro Se De Magia Liber* (Oxford: Clarendon Press).
Canart, Paulus (1970–73), *Codices Vaticani Graeci, Codices 1745–1962*, 2 vols (Vatican: Bibliotheca Vaticana).
Casaubon, Meric (1634), *Marcus Aurelius Antoninus The Roman Emperor, His Meditations Concerning Himselfe …* (London: M. Flesher, for Richard Mynne).
Casaubon, Meric (1643), *Marci Antonini Imperatoris De Seipso et Ad Seipsum Libri XII.* (London: Typis M. Flesher, sumptibus R. Mynne).
Cassanmagnago, Cesare (2008), *Marco Aurelio, Pensieri* (Milan: Bompiani).
Ceporina, Matteo (2012), 'The *Meditations*', in Marcel van Ackeren, ed., *A Companion to Marcus Aurelius* (Chichester: Wiley-Blackwell), 45–61.
Chadwick, Henry (1953), *Origen: Contra Celsum* (Cambridge: Cambridge University Press).
Champlin, Edward (1974), 'The Chronology of Fronto', *Journal of Roman Studies* 64, 136–59.
Champlin, Edward (1980), *Fronto and Antonine Rome* (Cambridge, MA: Harvard University Press).
Collier, Jeremy (1708), *The Emperor Marcus Antoninus His Conversation with Himself*, The Second Edition Corrected (London: Richard Sare).
Collis, Karen (2016), 'How Shaftesbury Read Marcus Aurelius: Two 'Curious and Interesting Volumes' with His Manuscript Annotations', *Journal of the Warburg and Courtauld Institutes* 79, 263–93.
Cooper, John M. (2004), 'Moral Theory and Moral Improvement: Marcus Aurelius', in his *Knowledge, Nature, and the Good: Essays in Ancient Philosophy* (Princeton: Princeton University Press), 335–68.
Cooper, John M. (2012), *Pursuits of Wisdom: Six Ways of Life in Ancient Philosophy from Socrates to Plotinus* (Princeton: Princeton University Press).
Cortassa, Guido (1984), *Marco Aurelio, Scritti: Lettere a Frontone, Pensieri, Documenti* (Turin: Unione tipografico-editrice Torinese).
Cortassa, Guido (1989), *Il filosofo, i libri, la memoria: Poeti e filosofi nei Pensieri di Marco Aurelio* (Turin: Tirrenia Stampatori).
Crivelli, Paolo (2007), 'Epictetus and Logic', in Theodore Scaltsas and Andrew S. Mason, eds, *The Philosophy of Epictetus* (Oxford: Oxford University Press), 20–31.
Crossley, Hastings (1882), *The Fourth Book of the Meditations of Marcus Aurelius Antoninus: A Revised Text with Translation and Commentary* (London: Macmillan).
Dalfen, J. (1987), *Marci Aurelii Antonini Ad Se Ipsum Libri XII* (Leipzig: Teubner).
Daly, Lloyd William, and Suchier, Walther (1939), *Altercatio Hadriani Augusti et Epicteti Philosophi* (Urbana: University of Illinois Press).

De Boer, Wilko (1937), *Galeni De Propriorum Animi Cuiuslibet Affectuum Dignotione et Curatione, De Animi Cuiuslibet Peccatorum Dignotione et Curatione, De Atra Bile*, CMG 5.4.1.1 (Leipzig & Berlin: Teubner).
De Lacy, Phillip (1978–84), *Galen, On the Doctrines of Hippocrates and Plato / Galeni De Placitis Hippocratis et Platonis*, 3 vols, CMG 5.4.1.2 (Berlin: Akademie Verlag).
Diels, H. (1879), *Doxographi Graeci* (Berlin: De Gruyter [Editio Quarta 1965]).
Diels, H., and Kranz, W. (1964), *Die Fragmente der Vorsokratiker*, 3 vols (Zürich & Berlin: Weidmann).
Dobbin, Robert (1991), '*Proairesis* in Epictetus', *Ancient Philosophy* 11, 111–35.
Dobbin, Robert (1998), *Epictetus, Discourses Book 1* (Oxford: Clarendon Press).
Donini, Pierluigi (2008), 'Psychology', in R. J. Hankinson, *The Cambridge Companion to Galen* (Cambridge: Cambridge University Press), 184–209.
Edelstein, L. (1966), *The Meaning of Stoicism* (Cambridge, MA: Harvard University Press).
Edelstein, L., and Kidd, I. G. (1972), *Posidonius I: The Fragments* (Cambridge: Cambridge University Press).
Eijk, Philip van der (2014), 'Aetiology of Disease and Archaeology of Medicine in Greek and Latin Medical Texts', in Christiane Reitz and Anke Walter, eds, *Von Ursachen sprechen: Eine aitiologische Spurensuche* (Hildesheim: Olms), 461–90.
Engberg Pedersen, Troels (1990), *The Stoic Theory of Oikeiosis* (Aarhus: Aarhus University Press).
Engberg Pedersen, Troels (1998), 'Marcus Aurelius on Emotions', in Juha Sihvola and Troels Engberg Pedersen, eds, *The Emotions in Hellenistic Philosophy* (Dordrecht: Kluwer), 305–37.
Farquharson, A. S. L. (1944), *The Meditations of the Emperor Marcus Antoninus*, Edited with Translation and Commentary, 2 vols (Oxford: Clarendon Press).
Farquharson, A. S. L. (1989), *The Meditations of Marcus Aurelius Antoninus*, and *A Selection from the Letters of Marcus and Fronto*, translated by R. B. Rutherford (Oxford: Oxford University Press).
Fleury, Pascal (2012), 'Marcus Aurelius' Letters', in Marcel van Ackeren, ed., *A Companion to Marcus Aurelius* (Chichester: Wiley-Blackwell), 62–76.
Fortenbaugh, William W., et al. (1992), *Theophrastus of Eresus: Sources for His Life, Writings, Thought, and Influence*, 2 vols (Leiden: Brill).
Fortenbaugh, William W. (2011), *Theophrastus of Eresus Commentary Volume 6.1: Sources on Ethics* (Leiden: Brill).
Gaskin, Richard (1997), 'The Stoics on Cases, Predicates, and the Unity of the Proposition', in Richard Sorabji, ed., *Aristotle and After*, BICS Suppl. 68 (London: Institute of Classical Studies), 91–108.
Gataker, Thomas (1652), *Marci Antonini Imperatoris de rebus suis, sive de eis qae ad se pertinere censebat, Libri XII* (Cambridge: Thomas Buck).
Geytenbeek, A. C. van (1963), *Musonius Rufus and Greek Diatribe* (Assen: Van Gorcum).
Giavatto, Angelo (2008), *Interlocutore di se stesso: La dialettica di Marco Aurelio* (Hildesheim: Olms).
Giavatto, Angelo (2012a), 'The Style of the *Meditations*', in Marcel van Ackeren, ed., *A Companion to Marcus Aurelius* (Chichester: Wiley-Blackwell), 333–45.
Giavatto, Angelo (2012b), 'Logic and the *Meditations*', in Marcel van Ackeren, ed., *A Companion to Marcus Aurelius* (Chichester: Wiley-Blackwell), 408–19.
Giavatto, Angelo (2012c), 'A Mind on Solid Ground: Perception and Ethics in the *Meditations*', in Marcel van Ackeren and Jan Opsomer, eds, *Selbstbetrachtungen und Selbstdarstellungen: Der Philosoph und Kaiser Marc Aurel im interdisziplinären Licht* (Wiesbaden: Reichert Verlag), 133–46.
Gill, Christopher (2000), 'Stoic Writers of the Imperial Era', in Christopher Rowe and Malcolm Schofield, eds, *The Cambridge History of Greek and Roman Political Thought* (Cambridge: Cambridge University Press), 597–615.
Gill, Christopher (2006), *The Structured Self in Hellenistic and Roman Thought* (Oxford: Oxford University Press).
Gill, Christopher (2007), 'Marcus Aurelius' *Meditations*: How Stoic and How Platonic?', in Mauro Bonazzi and Christoph Helmig, eds, *Platonic Stoicism – Stoic Platonism: The Dialogue between Platonism and Stoicism in Antiquity* (Leuven: Leuven University Press), 189–207.
Gill, Christopher (2010), *Naturalistic Psychology in Galen and Stoicism* (Oxford: Oxford University Press).

Gill, Christopher (2012), 'Marcus and Previous Stoic Literature', in Marcel van Ackeren, ed., *A Companion to Marcus Aurelius* (Chichester: Wiley-Blackwell), 382–95.
Gill, Christopher (2013), *Marcus Aurelius: Meditations Books 1–6* (Oxford: Oxford University Press).
Goldschmidt, V. (1953), *Le système stoïcien et l'idée de temps* (Paris: Vrin [4th edn 1979]).
Goldschmidt, V. (1972), '*Huparchein* et *huphistanai* dans la philosophie stoïcienne', *Revue des Études Grecques* 85, 331–44.
Gould, Josiah B. (1970), *The Philosophy of Chrysippus* (Leiden: Brill).
Goulet-Cazé, Marie-Odile, (1986), *L'Ascèse cynique: Un commentaire de Diogène Laërce VI 70–71* (Paris: Vrin).
Goulet-Cazé, Marie-Odile (2003), *les Kynica du stoïcisme*, Hermes Einzelschriften 89 (Wiesbaden: Franz Steiner Verlag).
Gourinat, Jean-Baptiste (2000), *La Dialectique des Stoïciens* (Paris: Vrin).
Gourinat, Jean-Baptiste (2012a), 'The Form and Structure of the *Meditations*', in Marcel van Ackeren, ed., *A Companion to Marcus Aurelius* (Chichester: Wiley-Blackwell), 317–32.
Gourinat, Jean-Baptiste (2012b), 'Ethics', in Marcel van Ackeren, ed., *A Companion to Marcus Aurelius* (Chichester: Wiley-Blackwell), 420–36.
Gourinat, Jean-Baptiste (2012c), 'Was Marcus Aurelius a Philosopher?', in Marcel van Ackeren and Jan Opsomer, eds, *Selbstbetrachtungen und Selbstdarstellungen: Der Philosoph und Kaiser Marc Aurel im interdisziplinären Licht* (Wiesbaden: Reichert Verlag), 65–85.
Graver, Margaret (2007), *Stoicism and Emotion* (Chicago: University of Chicago Press).
Graver, Margaret, and Long, A. A. (2015), *Seneca: Letters on Ethics to Lucilius* (Chicago: University of Chicago Press).
Griffin, Miriam (2018), *Politics and Philosophy at Rome: Collected Papers* (Oxford: Oxford University Press).
Grube, G. M. A. (1983), *The Meditations of Marcus Aurelius Antoninus* (Indianapolis: Hackett).
Gueye, Cheikh Mbacke (2006), *Late Stoic Cosmopolitanism: Foundations and Relevance* (Heidelberg: Universitätsverlag Winter).
Gueye, Cheikh Mbacke (2013), 'Politics in the *Meditations* of Marcus Aurelius', *Horyzonty Polityki* 4/6, 79–93.
Hadot, Ilsetraut (1969), *Seneca und die griechisch-römische Tradition der Seelenleitung* (Berlin: De Gruyter).
Hadot, Ilsetraut (1996), *Simplicius, Commentaire sur le Manuel d'Épictète* (Leiden: Brill).
Hadot, Pierre (1972), 'La physique comme exercice spirituel ou pessimisme et optimisme chez Marc Aurèle', *Revue de Théologie et de Philosophie* (Troisième série) 22, 225–39 (repr. in Hadot 1993).
Hadot, Pierre (1977), 'Exercices spirituels', *Annuaire de la Ve Section de l'École pratique des hautes etudes* 84, 25–70 (repr. in Hadot 1993).
Hadot, Pierre (1978), 'Une clé des *Pensées* de Marc Aurèle: les trois *topoi* philosophiques selon Épictète', *Les Études philosophiques* 1, 65–83 (repr. in Hadot 1993).
Hadot, Pierre (1984), 'Marc Aurèle était-il opiomane?', in E. Lucchesi and H. D. Saffrey, eds, *Antiquité païenne et chrétienne* (Geneva: Cramer), 33–41.
Hadot, Pierre (1991), 'Philosophie, Discours Philosophique, et Divisions de la Philosophie chez les Stoïciens', *Revue Internationale de Philosophie* 45, 205–19.
Hadot, Pierre (1992), *La Citadelle intérieure: Introduction aux Pensées de Marc Aurèle* (Paris: Fayard).
Hadot, Pierre (1993), *Exercices spirituels et philosophie antique* (Paris: Études Augustiniennes).
Hadot, Pierre (1995), *Philosophy as a Way of Life* (Oxford: Blackwell).
Hadot, Pierre (1998), *The Inner Citadel: The Meditations of Marcus Aurelius*, trans. Michael Chase (Cambridge, MA: Harvard University Press).
Hadot, Pierre, and Luna, Concetta (1998), *Marc Aurèle: Écrits pour lui-même I: Introduction générale, Livre I* (Paris: Les Belles Lettres).
Hahm, David E. (1977), *The Origins of Stoic Cosmology* (Columbus: Ohio State University Press).
Haines, C. R. (1916), *The Communings with Himself of Marcus Aurelius Antoninus*, LCL (London: Heinemann).
Haines, C. R. (1919–20), *The Correspondence of Marcus Cornelius Fronto*, 2 vols, LCL (London: Heinemann).

Hammond, Martin (2006), *Marcus Aurelius, Meditations* (London: Penguin).
Hankinson, R. J. (2008), *The Cambridge Companion to Galen* (Cambridge: Cambridge University Press).
Hard, Robin (2011), *Marcus Aurelius, Meditations*, With an Introduction and Notes by Christopher Gill (Oxford: Oxford University Press).
Hard, Robin (2014), *Epictetus: Discourses, Fragments, Handbook* (Oxford: Oxford University Press).
Harriman, Benjamin (forth.a), 'Disjunctions and Natural Philosophy in Marcus Aurelius', *The Classical Quarterly*.
Harriman, Benjamin (forth.b), 'Musonius Rufus, Cleanthes, and the Stoic Community at Rome', *Elenchos*.
Hays, Gregory (2003), *Marcus Aurelius, Meditations* (London: Weidenfeld & Nicolson).
Henry, W. Benjamin (2009), *Philodemus, On Death* (Atlanta: Society of Biblical Literature).
Hense, O. (1905), *C. Musonii Rufi Reliquiae* (Leipzig: Teubner).
Holford-Strevens, Leofranc (2003), *Aulus Gellius: An Antonine Scholar and his Achievement* (Oxford: Oxford University Press).
Hout, Michael P. J. van den (1988), *M. Cornelii Frontonis Epistulae* (Leipzig: Teubner).
Hout, Michael P. J. van den (1999), *A Commentary on the Letters of M. Cornelius Fronto* (Leiden: Brill).
Hülser, Karlheinz (1987), *Die Fragmente zur Dialektik der Stoiker*, 4 vols (Stuttgart: frommann-holzboog).
Hutcheson, Francis, and Moor, James [1742] (2008), *The Meditations of the Emperor Marcus Aurelius Antoninus* (Indianapolis: Liberty Fund).
Ierodiakonou, Katerina (1993), 'The Stoic Division of Philosophy', *Phronesis* 38, 57–74.
Inwood, Brad (1985), *Ethics and Human Action in Early Stoicism* (Oxford: Clarendon Press).
Inwood, Brad (2007), *Seneca: Selected Philosophical Letters* (Oxford: Oxford University Press).
Inwood, Brad (2009), 'Why Physics?', in Ricardo Salles, ed., *God and Cosmos in Stoicism* (Oxford: Oxford University Press), 201–23.
Jackson, John (1906a), *The Meditations of Marcus Aurelius Antoninus*, With an Introduction by Charles Bigg (Oxford: Clarendon Press).
Jackson, John (1906b), *The Thoughts of Marcus Aurelius Antoninus* (London: Oxford University Press).
Jagu, A. (1946), *Épictète et Platon: Essai sur les relations du Stoïcisme et du Platonisme à propos de la Morale des Entretiens* (Paris: Vrin).
Jedan, Christoph (2009), *Stoic Virtues: Chrysippus and the Religious Character of Stoic Ethics* (London: Continuum).
Kahn, Charles H. (1979), *The Art and Thought of Heraclitus* (Cambridge: Cambridge University Press).
Kasulke, Christoph Tobias (2005), *Fronto, Marc Aurel und kein Konflikt zwischen Rhetorik und Philosophie im 2. Jh. n. Chr.* (Berlin: De Gruyter).
Kidd, I. G. (1988), *Posidonius II: The Commentary*, 2 vols (Cambridge: Cambridge University Press).
Kühn, C. G. (1821–33), *Claudii Galeni Opera Omnia*, 20 vols in 22 parts (Leipzig: Knobloch).
Laks, A., and Most, G. W. (2016), *Early Greek Philosophy*, 9 vols, LCL (Cambridge, MA: Harvard University Press).
Lana, Italo (1992), 'La scuola dei Sestii', in Pierre Grimal, ed., *La langue latine, langue de la philosophie* (Rome: École Française de Rome), 109–24.
Lapidge, Michael (1973), '*Archai* and *Stoicheia*: A Problem in Stoic Cosmology', *Phronesis* 18, 240–78.
Laurand, Valéry (2012), 'Marc Aurèle et la politique', *Cahiers philosophiques* 128, 30–41.
Liddell, H. G., and Scott, R. (1940), *A Greek-English Lexicon*, rev. H. S. Jones (Oxford: Clarendon Press).
Long, A. A. (1971), 'Language and Thought in Stoicism', in A. A. Long, ed., *Problems in Stoicism* (London: Athlone), 75–113.
Long, A. A. (1975–76), 'Heraclitus and Stoicism', *Philosophia* 5, 133–56 (repr. in Long 1996).
Long, A. A. (1978), 'Dialectic and the Stoic Sage', in John M. Rist, ed. *The Stoics* (Berkeley: University of California Press), 101–24 (repr. in Long 1996).
Long, A. A. (1982), 'Soul and Body in Stoicism', *Phronesis* 27, 34–57 (repr. in Long 1996).
Long, A. A. (1996), *Stoic Studies* (Cambridge: Cambridge University Press).
Long, A. A. (2002), *Epictetus: A Stoic and Socratic Guide to Life* (Oxford: Clarendon Press).

Long, A. A. (2012), 'The Self in the *Meditations*', in Marcel van Ackeren, ed., *A Companion to Marcus Aurelius* (Chichester: Wiley-Blackwell), 465–80.
Long, A. A., and Sedley, D. N. (1987), *The Hellenistic Philosophers*, 2 vols (Cambridge: Cambridge University Press).
Long, George (1890), *The Thoughts of the Emperor Marcus Aurelius Antoninus* (London: George Bell).
Lutz, C. E. (1947), 'Musonius Rufus, "The Roman Socrates"', *Yale Classical Studies* 10, 3–147.
Mai, Angelo (1815), *M. Cornelii Frontonis Opera Inedita cum Epistulis item Ineditis*, 2 vols (Milan: Regiis Typis).
Mai, Angelo (1823), *M. Cornelii Frontonis et M. Aurelii Imperatoris Epistulae* (Rome: In Collegio Urbano apud Burliaeum).
Mattern, Susan P. (2013), *The Prince of Medicine: Galen in the Roman Empire* (Oxford: Oxford University Press).
Mattock, J. N. (1972), 'A Translation of the Arabic Epitome of Galen's Book *Peri êthôn*', in S. M. Stern, A. Hourani, and V. Brown, eds, *Islamic Philosophy and the Classical Tradition* (Oxford: Cassirer), 235–60.
Maurer, Christian (2016), 'Stoicism and the Scottish Enlightenment', in John Sellars, ed., *The Routledge Handbook of the Stoic Tradition* (Abingdon: Routledge), 254–69.
McLynn, Frank (2009), *Marcus Aurelius: Warrior, Philosopher, Emperor* (London: The Bodley Head).
Mill, John Stuart (1859), *On Liberty* (London: John W. Parker).
More, Henry (1668), *Enchiridion Ethicum, Praecipua Moralis Philosophiae Rudimenta* (London: J. Flesher, for W. Morden).
More, Henry (1690), *An Account of Virtue: or, Dr. Henry More's Abridgement of Morals, Put into English* (London: B. Tooke).
Morford, Mark (2002), *The Roman Philosophers: From the Time of Cato the Censor to the Death of Marcus Aurelius* (London: Routledge).
Newman, R. J. (1989), '*Cotidie meditare*: Theory and Practice of the *meditatio* in Imperial Stoicism', in Wolfgang Haase, ed., *Aufstieg und Niedergang der römischen Welt II 36.3* (Berlin: De Gruyter), 1473–1517.
Nickel, Diethard (2001), *Galen, Über die Ausformung der Keimlinge / Galeni De Foetuum Formatione*, CMG 5.3.3 (Berlin: Akademie Verlag).
Nickel, Rainer (2010), *Mark Aurel, Selbstbetrachtungen* (Mannheim: Artemis & Winkler).
Nutton, Vivian (1979), *Galen, On Prognosis / Galeni De Praecognitione*, CMG 5.8.1 (Berlin: Akademie Verlag).
Obbink, Dirk (1999), 'The Stoic Sage in the Cosmic City', in Katerina Ierodiakonou, ed., *Topics in Stoic Philosophy* (Oxford: Clarendon Press), 178–95.
Obbink, D., and Vander Waerdt, P. A. (1991), 'Diogenes of Babylon: The Stoic Sage in the City of Fools', *Greek, Roman, and Byzantine Studies* 32, 355–96.
Oldfather, W. A. (1925–28), *Epictetus: The Discourses as Reported by Arrian, The Manuel, and Fragments*, 2 vols, LCL (Cambridge, MA: Harvard University Press).
Petit, Caroline (2009), *Galien III: Le Médecin. Introduction* (Paris: Les Belles Lettres).
Petit, Caroline (2019), *Galen's Treatise Peri Alupias (De indolentia) in Context: A Tale of Resilience* (Leiden: Brill).
Pomeroy, A. J. (1999), *Arius Didymus, Epitome of Stoic Ethics* (Atlanta: Society of Biblical Literature).
Rabbow, Paul (1954), *Seelenführung: Methodik der Exerzitien in der Antike* (Munich: Kösel Verlag).
Rabe, Hugo (1906), *Scholia in Lucianum* (Leipzig: Teubner).
Ramelli, Ilaria (2009), *Hierocles the Stoic: Elements of Ethics, Fragments, and Excerpts*, trans. David Konstan (Atlanta: Society of Biblical Literature).
Renan, E. (1904), *Marcus Aurelius* (London: Walter Scott Publishing).
Rendall, Gerald, H. (1895), 'On the Text of M. Aur. Antoninus *Ta eis heauton*', *The Journal of Philology* 23, 116–60.
Rendall, Gerald H. (1898), *Marcus Aurelius Antoninus to Himself* (London: Macmillan).
Reydams-Schils, Gretchen (2005), *The Roman Stoics: Self, Responsibility, and Affection* (Chicago: The University of Chicago Press).

Reydams-Schils, Gretchen (2012a), 'Social Ethics and Politics', in Marcel van Ackeren, ed., *A Companion to Marcus Aurelius* (Chichester: Wiley-Blackwell), 437–52.
Reydams-Schils, Gretchen (2012b), 'Marcus Aurelius' Social Ethics', in Marcel van Ackeren and Jan Opsomer, eds, *Selbstbetrachtungen und Selbstdarstellungen: Der Philosoph und Kaiser Marc Aurel im interdisziplinären Licht* (Wiesbaden: Reichert Verlag), 111–32.
Richlin, Amy (2006), *Marcus Aurelius in Love: Marcus Aurelius & Marcus Cornelius Fronto* (Chicago: The University of Chicago Press).
Richlin, Amy (2012), 'The Sanctification of Marcus Aurelius', in Marcel van Ackeren, ed., *A Companion to Marcus Aurelius* (Chichester: Wiley-Blackwell), 497–514.
Rigo, Georges (2010), *Marcus Aurelius Antoninus, Index verborum in opus quod inscribitur Ta eis heauton*. (Hildesheim: Olms-Weidmann).
Rist, J. M. (1977), 'Zeno and Stoic Consistency', *Phronesis* 22, 161–74.
Rist, J. M. (1982), 'Are You a Stoic? The Case of Marcus Aurelius', in Ben F. Meyer and E. P. Sanders, eds, *Jewish and Christian Self-Definition: Volume 3. Self-Definition in the Graeco-Roman World* (London: SCM Press), 23–45.
Robertson, Donald (2019), *How to Think Like a Roman Emperor: The Stoic Philosophy of Marcus Aurelius* (New York: St. Martin's Press).
Roskam, Geert (2012), 'Siren's Song or Goose's Cackle? Marcus Aurelius' *Meditations* and Ariston of Chios', in Marcel van Ackeren and Jan Opsomer, eds, *Selbstbetrachtungen und Selbstdarstellungen: Der Philosoph und Kaiser Marc Aurel im interdisziplinären Licht* (Wiesbaden: Reichert Verlag), 87–109.
Rutherford, R. B. (1989), *The Meditations of Marcus Aurelius: A Study.* (Oxford: Clarendon Press).
Sally, Amadeus (1626), *Marci Antonini Imperatoris & Philosophi, de vita sua Libri XII* (Lyon: Francisci de la Bottiere).
Sandbach, F. H. (1981), 'The Teubner Marcus Aurelius', *The Classical Review* 31, 188–89.
Sandbach, F. H. (1985), *Aristotle and the Stoics*, Cambridge Philological Society Suppl. Vol. 10 (Cambridge: Cambridge: Philological Society).
Schenkeveld, D. M. (1999), 'Language', in K. Algra et al., eds, *The Cambridge History of Hellenistic Philosophy* (Cambridge: Cambridge University Press), 177–225.
Schenkl, Henricus (1913), *Marci Antonini Imperatoris in Semet Ipsum Libri XII* (Leipzig: Teubner).
Schenkl, Henricus (1916), *Epicteti Dissertationes ab Arriano Digestae*, Editio Maior (Leipzig: Teubner).
Schofield, Malcolm (1984), 'Ariston of Chios and the Unity of Virtue', *Ancient Philosophy* 4, 83–96.
Schofield, Malcolm (1988), 'The Retrenchable Present', in Jonathan Barnes and Mario Mignucci, eds, *Matter and Metaphysics* (Naples: Bibliopolis), 329–70.
Schofield, Malcolm (1991), *The Stoic Idea of the City* (Cambridge: Cambridge University Press).
Schofield, Malcolm (2003), 'Stoic Ethics', in Brad Inwood, ed., *The Cambridge Companion to The Stoics* (Cambridge: Cambridge University Press), 233–56.
Sedley, David (1989), 'Philosophical Allegiance in the Greco-Roman World', in M. Griffin and J. Barnes, eds, *Philosophia Togata: Essays on Philosophy and Roman Society* (Oxford: Clarendon Press), 97–119.
Sedley, David (2003), 'Philodemus and the Decentralisation of Philosophy', *Cronache Ercolanesi* 33, 31–41.
Sedley, David (2012), 'Marcus Aurelius on Physics', in Marcel van Ackeren, ed., *A Companion to Marcus Aurelius* (Chichester: Wiley-Blackwell), 396–407.
Sellars, John (2003), *The Art of Living: The Stoics on the Nature and Function of Philosophy* (Aldershot: Ashgate).
Sellars, John (2007), 'Stoic Cosmopolitanism and Zeno's *Republic*', *History of Political Thought* 28, 1–29.
Sellars, John (2012a), 'The *Meditations* and the Ancient Art of Living', in Marcel van Ackeren, ed., *A Companion to Marcus Aurelius* (Chichester: Wiley-Blackwell), 453–64.
Sellars, John (2012b), 'Marcus Aurelius in Contemporary Philosophy', in Marcel van Ackeren, ed., *A Companion to Marcus Aurelius* (Chichester: Wiley-Blackwell), 532–44.
Sellars, John (2014), 'Seneca's Philosophical Predecessors and Contemporaries', in Gregor Damschen and Andreas Heil, eds, *Brill's Companion to Seneca: Philosopher and Dramatist* (Leiden: Brill), 97–112.
Sellars, John (2016), 'Shaftesbury, Stoicism, and Philosophy as a Way of Life', *Sophia* 55, 395–408.
Sellars, John (2017), 'Henry More as Reader of Marcus Aurelius', *British Journal for the History of Philosophy* 25, 916–31.

Sellars, John (2018a), 'A Disputed Fragment of Epictetus in Marcus Aurelius', *Mnemosyne* 71, 331–5.
Sellars, John (2018b), 'Roman Stoic Mindfulness: An Ancient Technology of the Self', in Matthew Dennis and Sander Werkhoven, eds, *Ethics and Self-Cultivation: Historical and Contemporary Perspectives* (Abingdon: Routledge), 15–29.
Sellars, John (2018c), *Hellenistic Philosophy* (Oxford: Oxford University Press).
Sellars, John (2019), 'Socratic Themes in the *Meditations* of Marcus Aurelius', in C. Moore, ed., *Brill's Companion to the Reception of Socrates* (Leiden: Brill), 293–310.
Singer, P. N. (1997), *Galen, Selected Works* (Oxford: Oxford University Press).
Singer, P. N. (2013), *Galen, Psychological Writings* (Cambridge: Cambridge University Press).
Sorabji, Richard (1983), *Time, Creation, and the Continuum* (London: Duckworth).
Sorabji, Richard (2000), *Emotion and Peace of Mind: From Stoic Agitation to Christian Temptation* (Oxford: Oxford University Press).
Sorabji, Richard (2007), 'Epictetus on *proairesis* and Self', in Theodore Scaltsas and Andrew S. Mason, eds, *The Philosophy of Epictetus* (Oxford: Oxford University Press), 87–98.
Souilhé, J. (1975), *Épictète, Entretiens Livre I* (Paris: Les Belles Lettres).
Staniforth, Maxwell (1964), *Marcus Aurelius, Meditations* (Harmondsworth: Penguin).
Stanton, G. R. (1968), 'The Cosmopolitan Ideas of Epictetus and Marcus Aurelius', *Phronesis* 13, 183–95.
Stephens, William O. (2012), *Marcus Aurelius: A Guide for the Perplexed* (London: Continuum).
Theiler, W. (1951), *Kaiser Marc Aurel, Wege Zu Sich Selbst* (Zürich: Artemis).
Thom, J. C. (1995), *The Pythagorean Golden Verses* (Leiden: Brill).
Thom, J. C. (2001), 'Cleanthes, Chrysippus and the Pythagorean *Golden Verses*', *Acta Classica* 44, 197–219.
Thom, J. C. (2005), *Cleanthes' Hymn to Zeus: Text, Translation, and Commentary* (Tübingen: Mohr Siebeck).
Tieleman, Teun (1996), *Galen and Chrysippus on the Soul: Argument and Refutation in the De Pacitis Books II-III* (Leiden: Brill).
Trannoy, A. I. (1925), *Marc-Aurèle, Pensées* (Paris: Les Belles Lettres [repr. 1953]).
Usener, Hermann (1887), *Epicurea* (Leipzig: Teubner).
Vogt, Katja Maria (2008), *Law, Reason, and the Cosmic City: Political Philosophy in the Early Stoa* (New York: Oxford University Press).
Wachsmuth, C., and Hense, O. (1884–1912), *Ioannis Stobaei Anthologium*, 5 vols (Berlin: Weidmann).
Wickham Legg, J. (1910), 'A Bibliography of the *Thoughts* of Marcus Aurelius Antoninus', *Transactions of the Bibliographical Society* 10, 15–81.
Xylander, W. (1559), *M. Antonini Imperatoris Romani et Philosophi De seipso seu vita sua Libri XII …* (Zürich: Andreas Gesner filius).

INDEX OF PASSAGES

Abbreviations generally follow those in the *Oxford Classical Dictionary*; for Galen see the list in Singer (2013), which includes translations of *Aff. Pecc. Dig.*, *Ind.*, *Mor.*, and *QAM*. Where specific editions of texts have been used, these are noted. For Marcus Aurelius, passages mentioned in the text are listed, but those that appear in long lists of further examples in the notes are not included here.

Aetius (Diels 1879)
    1.3.25: 61
    1.7.33: 61, 103n32
    1.28.4: 68
    1.28.5: 78n3
    2.1.7: 66n12
    4.12.1-5: 41
    4.21.1-4: 88n12
    4.21.2: 88n15
Alexander of Aphrodisias
  in Top.
    1,8-14: 41
  Mixt.
    225,1-2: 61
Apuleius
  Apol.
    19: 9, 17n12
    38: 9
    85: 9
Arethas of Caesarea
  Scholia in Lucianum (Rabe 1906)
    207, 6-7: 34n9
Aristotle
  Hist. an.
    486a5-14: 125n21
  [*Mund.*]
    391b9-12: 79n22
  Phys.
    222a10-19: 103n29
Arius Didymus (Pomeroy 1999)
    6: 113

    6a: 108, 115n3
    10: 53n24, 88n26
    10b: 88n32
    11m: 53n24
Augustine
  Conf.
    11.26.33: 103n26
  De civ. D.
    5.8: 68–9
Aulus Gellius
  Noctes Atticae (*NA*)
    7.2.3: 68
    7.2.11: 125n17
    7.2.12: 35n39
    7.2.15: 125n17
    9.5.8: 124n2
    12.5.7: 125n5
    19.1.1-21: 53n28
    19.1.14: 18n45

Calcidius
  in Tim.
    144: 68
    220: 88n15
Carm. Aur. (Thom 1995)
    9: 35n37
    14: 35n37
    35: 35n37
    40-44: 30
    54: 35n39
    55-6: 35n39

Cicero
  Acad.
    1.40: 48
    2.23: 35n18
    2.137: 119
  Div.
    1.125-6: 68
  Fat.
    43: 125n17
  Fin.
    1.42: 35n18
    1.72: 35n18
    3.4: 35n18
    3.16-24: 115n9
    3.16: 125n5
    3.22: 103n42
    3.59: 125n13
    3.64: 126n22
    4.19: 35n18
    5.16: 35n18
    5.18: 35n18
  Off.
    3.21-2: 126n22
    3.32: 126n22
  Nat. D
    2.21-2: 66n5
    2.35: 125n15
    2.40-1: 18n39
  Tusc.
    2.12: 35n18
    3.1-21: 26
    3.16: 115n10
    3.24-5: 34n12, 88n26
    3.29: 36n44
    3.52: 31, 36n44
    4.14: 34n12
    5.108: 125n8
Cleanthes
  Hymn to Zeus (Thom 2005)
    23-5: 35n39
Clement of Alexandria
  Strom.
    5.105.2: 66n19

Dio Cassius
    69.21.2: 8
    71.1.2: 8
    72.35.1: 16n9
Diogenes Laertius
    6.63: 118
    6.70: 35n34
    7.39: 51n3
    7.41: 40, 51n3
    7.43: 40
    7.43-4: 40
    7.46-7: 40
    7.46: 52n17
    7.49-51: 48
    7.49: 41, 49, 51, 52n20
    7.64: 115n6
    7.80: 52n19, 125n18
    7.81: 79n27
    7.82: 51n5
    7.85: 125n5
    7.87-9: 66n4, 115n3
    7.87: 58, 108
    7.88: 108, 115n1, 120
    7.89: 108, 110
    7.92: 110
    7.101-5: 103n40, 115n9
    7.103-4: 79n13
    7.110-11: 34n12
    7.116: 88n27
    7.134: 66n8
    7.135: 61, 103n32
    7.138: 61
    7.139: 59
    7.141: 102n11
    7.148-9: 78n3
    7.157: 88n11, 103n30
    7.159: 52n21
    7.160: 11
    7.161: 17n32
    7.163: 17n32
    7.166-7: 30
    7.168: 12
    7.174: 18n40, 66n23
    7.178: 66n24
    7.187: 51n5
    7.201: 53n24

Epictetus
  Diss.
    Praef. 2: 13
    1.2.33: 84, 88n5
    1.6.13: 52n14
    1.7.1: 40
    1.7.32: 40
    1.9.1: 125n8
    1.11.33: 53n22
    1.15.1-5: 88n31
    1.15.2: 22, 25
    1.17.1-12: 40
    1.17.13-18: 17n27
    1.20.7: 21
    1.20.10: 21
    1.20.15: 52n14
    1.22.10: 103n41
    1.26.18: 53n29
    1.27: 35n33
    1.27.1: 46
    1.27.21: 46
    1.28: 46
    1.28.11-12: 52n14

Index of passages

  1.29.1-3: 48–9
  1.30: 35n33
  2.5.24: 123
  2.5.25: 123
  2.5.26: 123, 125n9
  2.6.9-10: 124
  2.17.34-40: 17n27
  2.17.34: 40, 51n5
  2.18.23-5: 46
  2.18.24: 50
  2.19: 36n53
  2.19.20-5: 26
  2.23.44: 40
  3.2.1-2: 18n50, 34n2, 111
  3.2.5: 115n15
  3.2.6: 116n15
  3.8.5: 43, 49
  3.12.15: 50
  3.16.15: 21
  3.21: 36n53
  3.21.1-4: 27
  3.22: 35n34, 118
  3.22.104: 21
  3.22.105: 82
  3.26.23: 12
  4.1: 118
  4.12: 21–3
  4.12.1: 22
  4.12.4: 21
  4.12.5: 22
  4.12.6: 22
  4.12.7-8: 22
  4.12.11-12: 23
  4.12.13: 22
  4.12.14: 22
  4.12.15: 22
  4.12.16: 23
  4.12.19: 23
Ench.
  1.1: 47, 78, 103n41
  1.5: 45
  5: 47, 63
  8: 121
  9: 88n5
  17: 97
  46: 27
  52: 52n12
  53.1: 18n37, 69
Epicurus
 Ep. Men.
  124: 98
  125: 98
 Rat. Sent.
  19: 98
Eusebius
 Praep. evang.
  15.20.2: 18n40
  15.20.6: 103n30

Fronto (Hout 1988)
 Ad M. Caes.
  2.3: 9
  4.13: 11
  51: 8
 De eloqu.
  1.3: 17n25
  2.11: 10, 11
  2.13: 10, 39
  2.14: 10
 De orat.
  3: 12
 Fer. Als.
  3.6: 10

Galen (Kühn 1821–33)
 Aff. Pecc. Dig. (De Boer 1937)
  1.1.4: 14
  1.3.10: 14
  1.4.4: 14
  1.5.1: 14, 28
  1.5.6: 14
  1.6.10: 14
  1.8.3: 13
  1.8.8: 19n58
  1.9.20: 15
 De moribus (*Mor.*)
  31 Kr.: 28
 Foet. Form. (Nickel 2001)
  6.31: 14
 Ind. (Boudon–Millot et al. 2010)
  46: 15
  49-50: 13
  54: 15
  56: 15
  65: 15
 Introductio sive medicus (Petit 2009)
  8 (15,16-23): 52n8
 Lib. Prop. (Boudon–Millot 2007)
  3.1: 18n52
  14.21: 18n56
  18.1-2: 18n56
 Opt. Doct. (Barigazzi 1991)
  1.2: 18n56
 PHP (De Lacy 1978–84)
  2.5.16: 88n25
  3.1.25: 88n14
  3.5.28: 88n25
  5.2.22-3: 26
 Praen. (Nutton 1979)
  9.5-8: 13
  11.1-8: 13
 Quod animi mores (*QAM*)
  3: 14

Hierocles
 El. Eth. (Ramelli 2009)
  1.31-3: 52–3n21

1.35-7: 125n5
6.51-9: 117
11.15-17: 117
Hippolytus
   Haer.
      1.21: 69
Historia Augusta (HA)
   1.16.10: 7
   3.10.4: 16n7
   4.1.1: 7
   4.2.1: 7
   4.2.4: 9
   4.2.6: 7
   4.2.7: 8
   4.3.1-2: 8
   4.3.2: 8
   4.3.3: 8
   4.3.4: 8

Iamblichus
   Vita Pythagorae
      196: 36n44

Lucan
   De bello civile
      2.7-15: 79n18
Lucian
   Demon.
      31: 16n7
   Ind.
      13: 13
Lucretius
   De rerum natura
      1.174-9: 67n31

Marcus Aurelius
   1.7: 8, 12
   1.8: 8
   1.9: 8, 107
   1.13: 9
   1.15: 9
   1.17: 9, 39, 40
   2.1: 31
   2.2: 83, 88n17
   2.3: 72, 73, 77, 78n11
   2.7: 23, 47
   2.8: 26
   2.10: 86, 89n33
   2.11: 72, 75, 77, 86
   2.12: 86
   2.13: 86
   2.14: 94, 98
   2.15: 48
   2.16: 118, 121
   2.17: 62, 63, 90, 101–2
   3.3: 66n9
   3.4: 21, 27, 45, 107
   3.6: 47, 70, 110, 111

3.7: 98
3.9: 51
3.10: 100
3.11: 33, 49, 51, 58, 118
3.13: 23
3.14: 34n9
3.16: 83, 88n30
4.2: 24
4.3: 20–21, 23, 34nn10–11, 48, 50, 53n30, 74, 77, 86, 94
4.4: 40, 119
4.7: 50
4.14: 97
4.19: 100
4.21: 60, 96, 97
4.22: 47
4.23: 121
4.24: 112
4.27: 74, 77, 79n27
4.29: 122
4.36: 14
4.37: 101
4.39: 84
4.40: 14, 49, 63, 64
4.41: 12
4.42: 63
4.43: 62, 63, 66n17
4.44: 63
4.45: 64
4.46: 12, 14, 63, 64, 66n27
4.48: 14
5.1: 24, 31
5.2: 44
5.6: 113
5.8: 11, 70, 71, 72, 77, 78, 78n6
5.12: 110, 111
5.13: 60, 61
5.16: 27–8, 42
5.22: 120, 121
5.24: 81
5.26: 50, 83, 85
6.3: 75
6.4: 74–5
6.5: 75
6.8: 66n13, 84
6.10: 75, 77
6.13: 32–3, 42, 45, 51, 58
6.14: 87, 89n38, 116n18
6.15: 62, 91
6.16: 24, 47, 85
6.24: 75
6.25: 75
6.28: 96
6.35: 24
6.36: 32, 91
6.42: 10, 12, 63, 66n27
6.44: 118
6.47: 12, 36n52, 63

6.49: 98
7.9: 59
7.11: 107
7.13: 122–3, 125n21
7.17: 44
7.19: 10, 36n52, 65
7.23: 97
7.28: 86, 112
7.29: 60, 100
7.32: 96
7.33: 97, 103n35
7.35: 115n12
7.46: 78n5
7.47-8: 32, 46
7.55: 112
7.56: 101, 107
7.63: 110, 111
7.64: 23, 97, 103n35
7.67: 24, 39, 41
7.68: 24
7.69: 101
7.73: 114
7.74: 110, 112
7.75: 75, 77
8.1: 39, 40, 110, 111
8.3: 12, 36n52, 61, 63, 66n7
8.7: 47
8.11: 60
8.13: 39, 43, 49, 57, 60
8.26: 113
8.29: 43
8.34: 122, 125n20
8.35: 70
8.36: 44, 96, 100
8.40: 43
8.47: 47
8.48: 86
8.49: 42–3, 49
8.50: 57
8.52: 57
8.58: 98–9
9.1: 72, 77, 111, 112
9.2: 96
9.3: 11, 96
9.7: 47
9.9: 119
9.11: 77
9.25: 60
9.28: 75, 77, 78n5
9.29: 119
9.30: 36n46
9.35: 65
9.39: 76
9.41: 98, 103n35
9.42: 112, 114
10.5: 71, 77, 78
10.6: 76, 77, 120, 121

10.7: 76–7, 97
10.9: 57
10.11: 57, 99, 100, 101
10.13: 31
10.15: 58, 107, 118
10.17-19: 103n22
10.17: 46, 95
10.18: 65, 95
10.19: 95
10.24: 84, 85
10.28: 69
10.31: 94
10.33: 120, 121
11.1: 66n9, 66n12
11.5: 24
11.8: 122, 125n20
11.10: 112
11.16: 11
11.18: 85
11.19: 85
11.20: 85
11.36: 82
11.37-9: 12
12.1: 57, 58, 66n13, 73, 77, 107
12.3: 83, 100
12.5: 73, 77
12.8: 48, 51
12.13: 57
12.14: 71, 72, 76, 77, 78n5
12.15: 110, 111
12.18: 60
12.19: 88n30
12.21: 65
12.22: 50, 51
12.23: 11, 65
12.24: 32, 73, 77
12.25: 51
12.26: 48
12.29: 60
12.30: 62, 67n28
12.33: 84
12.34: 99
12.36: 97, 118
Musonius Rufus (Hense 1905)
   1 (4,5-5,2): 18n37
   6 (22,6-27,15): 28–9, 35nn26–32
   9 (42,1-2): 125n8
   9 (47,7-9): 66n25
   18a (96,8-10): 66n25
   44 (128,7-11): 40

Origen
   C. Cels.
      6.2: 13

Philo
   Aet. mundi
      76-7: 66n9

Leg. alleg.
    2.22-3: 88n9
Philostratus
  Vitas Sophistarum (VS)
    2.11.1: 8
Photius
  Bibl.
    cod. 58 (17b11-20): 18n45
Plato
  Apology (Ap.)
    25a-b: 24
    28e: 25
    38a: 25, 53n29
    39c: 25
  Cratylus
    402a: 66n18
  Euthydemus
    278e-281e: 103n40
  Gorgias (Grg.)
    463a-466a: 25
    512d-e: 78n5
    514e: 26
    527d: 26
  Republic (Resp.)
    427d-441e: 116n17
    432a: 116n17
    433b: 112
    486a: 115n12
    487a: 115n12
  Symposium (Symp.)
    186b: 115n5
Plotinus
  Enn.
    3.7.1: 102n8
    3.7.11: 103n26
Plutarch
  Comm. not.
    1081c-1082a: 102n13
    1081e: 102n14
    1082a: 93
  De Alex. fort.
    329a-b: 125n11
  De exil.
    600f: 125n8
  De virt. mor.
    440f: 115n13
    441a: 115n13
  Quaest. Plat.
    1007d-e: 67n33
  St. rep.
    1038b: 125n5
    1055f: 53n24
Seneca
  Ben.
    1.6.1: 114
    2.6.2: 115
    2.17.7: 115
    6.21.2: 115
    7.1.3-4: 30
    7.2.1: 30
  De otio
    4.1: 118, 123
  Ep.
    2.2-4: 27
    2.5: 99
    8.8: 99
    12.7: 66n25
    16.4-6: 79n17, 79n25
    28.4: 125n9
    33.4: 16
    36.3: 17n30
    44.3: 12
    58.23: 66n25
    65.2: 61
    71.13-14: 102n3
    71.15: 90
    71.31: 35n20
    78.29: 36n45
    91.3-4: 36n45
    94.1-18: 17n30
    95.7-9: 35n18
    107.11: 18n37, 69
    115.8: 17n30
  Helv.
    9.7: 125n9
  Ira
    2.10.5: 66n25
    3.36.1-3: 29–30
  Nat. Quaest.
    2.45.2: 69
  Tranq.
    15.2: 66n25
  Vit. Beat.
    26.1: 36n45
Sextus Empiricus
  Math.
    8.224: 52n19
    9.71-4: 103n30
    9.104: 59
    9.110: 59
    9.332: 66n12
  Pyrrhoniae hypotyposes
    3.25: 26
Simplicius
  in Cael.
    294,4-7: 66n21
  in Ench. (Hadot 1996)
    Praef. 18-20: 35n33
    6,15-20: 46
  in Phys.
    23,33-24,11: 66n20
    480,27-30: 66n21
Stobaeus (Wachsmuth and Hense
    1884–1912)
    1,25,3-27,4: 78n4

1,105,17-106,4: 102n14
1,106,5-23: 102n12
1,171,2: 66n9
2,13,5-7: 73
2,59,4-11: 115n10
2,63,8-11: 111
2,75,7-10: 113
2,75,11-76,23: 66n4, 115n3
2,75,11-12: 115n4
2,76,1-8: 108
2,76,2-3: 108
2,76,9-15: 103n42
2,76,18-19: 109
2,88,6: 88n29
2,88,8-89,3: 53n24, 88n26
2,90,19-91,1: 88n32
2,111,18-113,11: 53n24
3,648-51: 35n26
4,671,3-673,18: 125n6
4,672,16-18: 118

Themistius
   Orationes (*Or.*)
      6.81c: 34n9

Xenophon
   Oeconomicus (*Oec.*)
      1.11: 115n5

SUBJECT INDEX

Academy, sceptical 46, 48, 53n27
Alexander of Aphrodisias 41
Alexander the Great 119
Antipater 101, 103n42
Antoninus Pius 7, 16n7
Apollonius of Chalcedon 8, 16n7
Archedemus 102n14, 108
archery, analogy with 101
Aristo of Chios 11, 17nn32–5, 18n36, 111, 115n13
Aristotle 103n29, 125n21
Arius Didymus 25, 108–9, 115n8
Arrian 12–13, 18n46
art of living 22, 24–7
assent 48, 49, 84
atomism 72, 73–7, 96–7, 98
attention 21–3
Augustine 68–9, 103n26

Bergson, Henri 95, 103n27

Casaubon, Meric 16n2, 20, 34nn4–5, 36n48, 67n27, 79n24, 103n22, 128
Cato the Younger 90–1, 102n2
Catulus, Cinna 8, 9
change 62–65, 76–7, 90–1, 99, 100, 101–2
Chrysippus 10–11, 13, 17n26, 25, 26, 30, 31, 40, 79n21, 101, 103n30, 111, 123–4; his cylinder analogy 121; on impressions 41, 43, 44; on emotions 85; on fate 68–9; on location of *hêgemonikon* 82; on time 91–3; on the Stoic *telos* 108–9
Cicero 25, 26, 31, 53n27
Cleanthes 11–12, 18nn37, 39, 30, 63, 66n23, 66n25; on fate 69; on the Stoic *telos* 108–9
conflagration (*ekpurôsis*), periodic 61, 62, 66n9

Cooper, Anthony Ashley 1
Cornutus 17n28, 73
cosmic city 74, 76, 117–24, 125n9, 126n22
cosmopolitanism 118, 125n7

death, reflections on 72, 75, 77, 95, 96–100, 101–2
Demetrius the Cynic 30
development, stages of philosophical 65, 70, 71
digestion, analogy with 27–8
Diocles of Magnesia 41
Diogenes of Babylon 108, 119
Diogenes of Sinope 29, 61, 63, 118
dyeing the soul 21, 27–8, 42

emotions 31, 34n12, 85–6, 88nn27–9, 96
Epictetus 10, 11, 12–13, 21–4, 26, 27, 40, 73, 79n19, 97, 101, 121, 123, 128, 129n1; his three *topoi* 18n50, 34n2, 111, 115n15; on impressions 46, 50; on judgements 47, 48–9; on *prohairesis* 81–2, 88n5; on things 'up to us' (*ep' hêmin*) 45, 47–8, 78, 82, 83, 86, 100
Epicurus, Epicureanism 73, 74, 76, 78, 103n34, 128, 129n1; on death 97–9
epistemology, Stoic 48–9, 53n27
eternity (*aiôn*) 91, 93, 94–5, 102n6, 103n20

fate (*heimarmenê*) 68–72, 78n1, 78n5
Favorinus 18n56
fire, primordial 61, 62, 76
freedom 22
Fronto, Cornelius 9–10, 11, 12, 17n15, 18nn42–3

Galen 13–15, 18nn51–57, 19nn58–62, 26, 28
Gataker, Thomas 36n48, 65n1, 67n29, 79n24, 80n30, 103n22, 128
Goldschmidt, Victor 91–2, 93, 94–5, 95–6

Hadot, Pierre 28, 34n2, 79n28, 95–6, 111, 115n12, 115n14, 116n17
Hadrian 7–8, 16n6
Hecato 108
hêgemonikon (ruling part of the soul) 21, 45, 47, 51, 52n21, 75, 82–5, 86–7
Heraclitus 12, 61, 62–4, 66nn18–27, 67n30, 72
Hierocles 117–18, 124n2, 125n3
Hutcheson, Francis 1

Ignatius of Loyola 28
impressions (*phantasiai*) 21, 40, 41–7, 48, 52n17, 58, 84; first impressions 42–3, 49, 50, 52n20
impulse (*hormê*) 47, 83–4
indifferents (*adiaphora*) 11, 18n36, 50, 51, 65, 72, 79n13, 100, 101, 110
intention in ethical action 114–15

Jackson, John 34n6
judgement (*hupolêpsis*) 21, 43–4, 45, 47–51, 53n22; value judgement 48–9, 50, 53n22, 58, 63, 85
Julius Capitolinus 16n5
justice, virtue of 110, 111–13, 116n16

Lipsius, Justus 78n8
logic 39–41
Lucan 73

Mai, Angelo 9, 17n16
Maximus, Claudius 8, 8–9, 17n12
medicine, analogy with 25–6
Mill, John Stuart 1
Moor, James 1
More, Henry 1
Musonius Rufus 28–9, 40, 63, 66n25

Nature 59–65, 68, 74, 76–7, 81, 90
Nature, living consistently with 11, 58, 66n4, 79n19, 107–10, 112–13, 115n7, 119

oikieôsis, theory of 117–18, 119, 120, 125n4

Palatine manuscript 34n8, 128
parts and limbs 121–4, 125nn20–1
Persius 17n28
Philodemus 98
Philopator 18n55
physical description 33, 45–6, 51, 58, 60, 64
physics 57–9, 64
Plato 13, 25–6, 109, 112, 115n12, 116n17, 119
Platonism 64, 78n11, 83
Plotinus 91, 102n8, 103n26
Plutarch 8, 16n11, 92–3
pneuma (breath) 61, 82, 83
Posidonius 25, 78n3, 102n14, 108
posthumous reputation 90, 100

present moment, focus on 22, 60, 73, 95–6, 98, 99, 100–1
principles (*archai*), two Stoic 59–62, 66n8
prohairesis (choice, will) 13, 48, 81–2, 84, 87n3, 88n4
providence (*pronoia*) 68–70, 72–3, 77, 78n1, 78n10; providence versus atoms 73–7
Pythagoras, Pythagoreanism 12, 14, 30, 33, 36n44, 36n52, 63
Pythagorean *Golden Verses* 30

ready to hand (*procheiros*) 21–3, 29–30, 32, 34n11, 35n33, 48
repetition 14, 28, 31
retreat inwards 21, 81, 86–7
rhetoric 9–10, 11, 40
Rusticus, Junius 8, 12, 16n9, 18n46
Rutherford, R. B. 10

scale of Nature, Stoic 62, 66n16, 82, 83–4, 87
Seneca 12, 18nn42–3, 25, 27, 29–30, 63, 66n25, 69, 70–1, 73, 90–1, 98, 99, 102n2; on cause and matter 61–2; on cosmopolitanism 118; on ethical action 114–15
Severus, Claudius 8, 9, 17n14
Sextius, Quintus 29–30
Sextus Empiricus 25, 26
Sextus of Chaeronea 8, 107
Shaftesbury, Third Earl of 1
Simplicius 46
social animals, humans as 72, 79n19, 87, 112, 114, 117, 122, 124
Socrates 24, 25–6, 34n13, 50, 61, 63, 118
soul 81–5
spermatikos logos 96–7, 103n32
Sphaerus 63
spiritual exercises 28–33
spontaneous ethical action 113–15
syllogisms 39, 40, 79n21; in the *Meditations* 42, 52n19, 75–6, 79n27, 125n18

Theophrastus 66n20, 86, 89n33
time, Stoic theory of 91–3
training (*askêsis*) 14–15, 19n61, 28–29, 30

Vaticanus Graecus 1950 16n3, 65n1, 128, 129n1
view from above 32, 46
virtues, the Stoic 110–11, 115n10

Xenophon 109, 128
Xylander, Wilhelm 16nn2–3, 34n8, 36n48, 65n1, 67n29, 79n24, 80n30, 128

Zeno of Citium 12, 17n25, 19n65, 48, 60, 63, 69, 102n15, 120; his *Republic* 119; on the Stoic *telos* 108–9

Printed in Great Britain
by Amazon